INTRODUCTION TO
DEMOGRAPHIC ANALYSIS

Principles and Methods

INTRODUCTION TO
DEMOGRAPHIC ANALYSIS

Principles and Methods

Guillaume J. Wunsch
University of Louvain (U.C.L.)
Louvain-La-Neuve, Belgium

and

Marc G. Termote
University of Quebec
Montreal, Quebec, Canada

PLENUM PRESS · NEW YORK AND LONDON

Library of Congress Cataloging in Publication Data

Wunsch, Guillaume.
  Introduction to demographic analysis.

  Includes bibliographies and index.
  1. Demography. I. Termote, Marc, joint author. II. Title.
HB881.W86   301.32   77-12814
ISBN 0-306-31041-4

© 1978 Plenum Press, New York
A Division of Plenum Publishing Corporation
227 West 17th Street, New York, N.Y. 10011

Printed in the United States of America

PREFACE

This book is the result of several years of experience in teaching principles and methods of demographic analysis at the Department of Demography of the University of Louvain. Chapters 1 and 2 deal with the basic principles and methods involved in the two approaches demographers usually take, i.e., cohort and period analysis. Chapters 3–6 are devoted to applying these principles and methods to the particular phenomena with which the demographer is especially concerned: mortality, nuptiality, natality, and spatial mobility.

In order to maintain coherence, examples have been placed at the end of each major section instead of being dispersed throughout the text. This should enable the reader to grasp both the theory and the example as a whole, rather than envisaging the theory as a particular reply to a specific problem. Finally, each chapter ends with a list of references, to which is added a selection of major books and articles in population analysis drawn mainly from the American, British, and French demographic literature.

The authors wish to thank wholeheartedly the various demographers who, at one stage of this book or another, have helped them by suggesting useful modifications or by pointing out paragraphs that had to be revised or clarified. Our students, notably A. Canedo, were also helpful in this respect; they were always quick to notice proofs that did not prove, as well as factual inaccuracies in the text and examples. Among our fellow demographers, we would especially like to thank C. Blayo, V. C. Chidambaram, C. Dionne, J. Duchêne, P. Festy, D. Sly, C. Wattelar, and S. Wijewickrema for their helpful criticisms and comments. A word of praise should also be said for those unfortunate secretaries, Mrs. A. Bonbled-Davaux and Mrs. M. J. Forthomme, upon whom fell the disagreeable task of typing the manuscript. Finally, we would like to thank the Presses Universitaires de France, which have kindly granted us the permission to include in the appendix various tables drawn from work published by the I.N.E.D. in Paris.

Guillaume J. Wunsch
Marc G. Termote

CONTENTS

2
BASIC PRINCIPLES OF PERIOD ANALYSIS

6
THE ANALYSIS OF MIGRATION

INTRODUCTION

Demography is the study of population, its increase through births and immigration, and its decrease through deaths and emigration.

In a broader context, demography is also the study of the various determinants of population change and of the impact of population on the world around us. The determinants of population change are diverse; some are of biological or genetic origin (as in the case of the maximum span of life), but many others are socioeconomic in nature (such as the environmental causes of death or the social norms affecting fertility). The impact of population factors can be observed in many fields. An aging population, for example, may have detrimental effects on the labor force composition. A major variation in the number of annual births will have an impact on the educational system in the years to come. And population growth itself may eventually encroach on the carrying capacity of the world, and, at the very least, be a major determinant of the quantity and type of agricultural products that will have to be produced. Population factors may therefore be studied from a variety of viewpoints, and population sociology or the economics of population, for example, have become flourishing fields of inquiry.

This book has not been designed, however, to encompass the many ramifications of population investigation. Its more limited ambition is to present the methods by which a formal analysis of population trends and composition may be conducted. This book is therefore only concerned with "demographic analysis," that is, that aspect of demography devoted to the mathematical procedures that measure population change and its underlying factors. One should not forget, however, that demography cannot be restricted to these techniques alone. On the one hand, statistical analysis is a powerful tool, which the demographer should not eschew. On the other hand, as with all social sciences, demographic factors interplay with those from many other fields; the core demographic events (births, deaths, and

1

migrations) cannot therefore be properly explained without having recourse to other disciplines.

One of the main concerns of the demographer has always been to disentangle the various factors conducive to population change. Take the yearly number of births for instance. This depends on the "risk" of child-bearing on the one hand, and on the number of women or couples exposed to this "risk" on the other. The risk of giving birth during a particular year varies, however, with the age of the female and marginally with that of the male, with their marital status (in many countries only a low proportion of births are illegitimate), with their duration of marriage, the number of children already born, etc. The corresponding population exposed to child-bearing will therefore be distributed accordingly by age, marital status, duration of marriage, etc. Measuring the risk of childbearing is not, how-ever, as simple as it seems: the risk relating to, e.g., a group of women during a specific year is not independent of their past fertility, and is influenced by circumstances particular to the year of observation. For example, during a war births are usually postponed, and made up when the war is over. The demographer often wants to reach a *"pure"* measure of fertility, excluding any accidental behavior of this sort. Even if he is able to do away with these particular circumstances temporarily influencing reproductive behavior, the demographer is still confronted with the fact that this would-be measure of fundamental reproductive behavior is not that "pure": women die, or emigrate, and are therefore excluded from observation. What would have been the "pure" risk of childbearing if these women had not died or emigrated? Is it the same as the risk for the population escaping death or emigration during the period of observation? Under what conditions would both risks be the same?

As one can see, demographic analysis cannot be restricted to a collec-tion of simple techniques applied to simple problems in order to yield unequivocal results. In most cases the problems are not that easy to define and methods may be used only when certain conditions are met. The situation becomes even more complicated when the available data are not adequate enough to apply the techniques that have been constructed. The basic purpose of this book is, therefore, first to define the right questions for a specific problem and then to construct methods of answering these questions, to stress the assumptions under which these methods have been set up, and to determine the possible biases when assumptions are not met. A corollary to this approach has been to point out the similarities among techniques applied in the main fields covered by demography. The same type of measures are used in the study of mortality, first marriage, or the effectiveness of contraception, for example; methods currently used in fertility can easily be extended to nuptiality, etc. The arsenal of demographic techniques can therefore be restricted to a small core of methodology, once the *basic principles* applicable to all have been clarified. These basic principles are developed in the first two chapters of this book, which therefore constitute essential reading material before tackling the other chapters where the principles are applied to the various components of population change. In fact, after having read the first two chapters, the reader may pass on to any of the subsequent chapters without necessarily following the order of the book, since the latter chapters are mostly self-contained, apart from references to the first two chapters.

The two preliminary chapters are concerned with the double viewpoint a demographer usually adopts when analyzing population data. One approach is to determine, for example, how many children are born on the average to a woman during her lifetime, or how many changes of residence one has made during one's life. The purpose here is to relate demographic events to the span of life, and this is called *cohort analysis*. The other approach is to examine how a population changes from year to year; for example, to what extent has the population of the United States increased over the past 10 years, and what are the components of this change? Demographic events are studied in this case on a yearly basis, and this approach is called *period analysis*. The two points of view are not contradictory, but are in fact complementary. Looking at a cross section of a population, as in period analysis, one apprehends the contribution to population change of individuals observed at a particular stage of their life; part of the change may be due to transitory behavior and is an effect of the period in question (e.g., the postponement of births during a war), and part possibly is derived from a modification in fundamental behavior (such as a decrease in the number of children ever born). The latter can be ascertained by cohort analysis, and this type of analysis is therefore a necessary complement to the period approach. However, to understand how a population changes and how its composition varies, the cohort measures have to be translated into period measures.

A further simple example will show the necessary relations between both approaches. Suppose a demographer wants to predict the future course of a population. He will start by projecting the probable trend in the average number of children born per woman (cohort approach), but then he will have to translate these figures into yearly numbers of births (period approach).

This will imply evaluating changes in the average age at childbearing (cohort approach), but also the effect of possible future economic or social circumstances, such as a temporary economic depression (period approach). The same procedure could also be adopted for projecting future mortality and migration. Both cohort and period analyses are therefore required in population studies. Cohort analysis studies the fundamental changes in behavior, but needs a recording of demographic events extending over a lifespan and refers to past experience. Period analysis shows how a population changes from year to year, and therefore has less extensive data requirements; on the other hand, period analysis cannot easily discriminate between transient and fundamental changes in behavior.

Chapter 1 introduces some fundamental concepts in *cohort analysis*: how a cohort is defined, how cohorts and events can be represented on a two-dimensional graph (called the *Lexis diagram*), and how time intervenes in demographic measures. Basic principles of analysis in the absence of disturbances (i.e., in a "pure" state) are then dealt with. A fundamental distinction is drawn between *renewable* and *nonrenewable* events. The distribution of these two types of events can be characterized by their *intensity* and *tempo*, once they have been transformed into one of the three basic measures of demographic analysis: *reduced events, exposure rates*, and *probabilities of attrition*. Chapter 1 ends with a section dealing with the evaluation of these indexes in the presence of disturbances. For this purpose another major distinction is made, this time between phenomena that *exclude* or do *not exclude* people from observation; methods that can be used for the latter cannot always be applied to the former.

Basic principles of *period analysis* are covered in Chapter 2. The double purpose of period analysis is stressed: *standardization*, or the respective impact of structures and frequencies on change and *translation*, or the estimation through period measures of the intensity and tempo of the phenomenon being measured. It is shown that, though the former purpose is always valid, the latter approach is not without problems and may lead to biased results.

The subsequent chapters deal with the application of these basic principles to the components of population change: mortality, natality, and spatial mobility. However, since in many countries most births are legitimate, i.e., born to married women (the definition of what constitutes a married woman depending on local laws and custom), a special chapter devoted to marriage and marriage dissolution has been included in the text. Though not strictly a demographic phenomenon (i.e., not one of the components of population growth), nuptiality has, in many cases, such an important impact on natality that its exclusion could not be warranted even if this viewpoint is open to question.

Most of the methods outlined in this book rely on an adequate collection of data, either by a series of censuses or through vital registration. Unconventional methods, developed for historical demography or the demography of developing countries lacking current population statistics (and even more statistics of population change), are not dealt with in this book, partly to avoid an oversized volume but mostly because many of these unconventional methods are responses to a specific situation and do not refer to broader principles of analysis, which constitute the main aim of this book. It should be noted, however, that even in countries presently developed, data collection is not perfectly accurate and many important items are not or cannot be collected at all, except possibly through special surveys. The chapter on migration covers some of these problems, as migration data are notoriously unsatisfactory even in highly developed countries; indirect methods of migration estimation are intimately linked moreover with various basic principles of demographic analysis, and can therefore be considered to lie within the scope of this book.

Finally, the recourse to mathematics has been restricted to a minimum and though some of the sections, especially in the first two chapters, may seem rather abstract, the developments can be followed with minimum mathematical prerequisites. In fact, most of the material in this book requires only the elementary operations of arithmetic. If some formal rigor has consequently been sacrificed, we hope it is compensated for by the relative ease in following the proofs. We have shunned, however, the perilous task of presenting demographic *models* without the help of higher mathematics, and have preferred therefore to exclude most mathematical models from the text. We believe this voluntary omission is not particularly regrettable in an introductory textbook; various references to further reading in this field can be found in the bibliography at the end of each chapter.

BASIC PRINCIPLES OF COHORT ANALYSIS

1

1.1. FUNDAMENTAL CONCEPTS

1.1.1. Event-Origin; Cohort

Consider a demographic process (natality or mortality, for example) relating to a group of N persons having experienced a particular event, hereafter called *event-origin*, during the same period of time, for example, during the same calendar year. This group of persons having experienced a particular event-origin (e.g., birth or marriage) during the same period will be called a *cohort*. For example, when birth is the event-origin considered, the related cohort will be specified by the name *birth-cohort*[1]; birth-cohort 1936 will thus refer to all persons born during the year 1936 in the area considered (e.g., in the USA).

1.1.2. Bounds

Process A can be characterized by the number and distribution over time of *events* of a certain type E: births in the study of natality, deaths in the study of mortality, etc. If time is measured by the duration elapsed since event-origin then we will use the following notation:

e_1: number of events of type E at duration 1 since event-origin

e_2: number of events of type E at duration 2 since event-origin

$\vdots$

e_i: number of events of type E at duration i since event-origin

---

[1]In the French demographic literature, one often finds the terms "promotion" for a cohort of marriages and "génération" for a cohort of births. There are no equivalents in English.

These events will be distributed between the time of occurrence of event-origin (time 0) and the time of extinction of all members of the cohort (time ω); 0 and ω are thus the maximum lower and upper bounds of the interval of variation of process A. In the case of a birth cohort, these bounds coincide with the beginning and end of life.

In many instances, however, the process under study is observed between certain bounds α and β, such that $0 \leq \alpha$ and $\beta \leq \omega$; for example, births occurring in a female birth-cohort will take place between the ages of puberty and menopause, roughly between ages $\alpha = 15$ and $\beta = 50$. In this book, in most instances, the bounds will be taken as $\alpha \geq 0$ and $\beta \leq \omega$ without further specification, the exact bounds depending on the phenomenon studied. Observations of segments of cohorts' existences will be referred to as *segmented observations*.

1.1.3. Time References

Time has been measured until now by the duration elapsed since event-origin; however, one can also locate events according to the calendar period during which they occur: year, month, day, for example; one speaks of the number of births or deaths during the year 1936 or, with increased precision, during the month of November, 1936.

All demographic events can thus be located in time in two ways: by calendar period (e.g., year or month) and by *duration* elapsed since the event-origin of the cohort under study. For example, one may observe children born to mothers aged 20 (i.e., 20 years elapsed since birth, the event-origin of the cohort of mothers) during calendar year 1950, for female cohorts born in 1929 and 1930.

1.1.4. Lexis Diagram

The *Lexis diagram* is a useful tool enabling one to locate events on a two-dimensional diagram[2] with reference to duration elapsed since event-origin, to the cohort, and to the calendar period (see Fig. 1.1). The units of time (u) on both horizontal and vertical axes are the same (calendar years, for example).

Calendar periods are located on the horizontal axis (abscissa), and durations elapsed since event-origin on the vertical axis (ordinate); the coordinate system is right-angled: vertical and horizontal axes intersect at 90° (see example Section 1.1.7.1).

[2]One could extend the method to three or more dimensions in order to take into account multiple event-origins (see Section 1.2.9), Wunsch (1968, pp. 408–409).

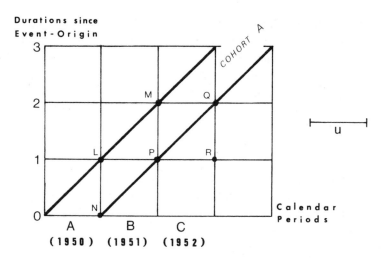

FIGURE 1.1

On the horizontal axis, let A, B, C, ... represent particular calendar periods (e.g., years 1950, 1951, 1952, ...); on the vertical axis, the labels 1, 2, 3, ... represent the *exact durations u, 2u, 3u,* ... elapsed since event-origin at time 0. Draw parallels to the abscissa at exact durations 1, 2, 3, ..., and draw parallels to the ordinate at the end of periods A, B, C, ... (i.e., on the 31st of December of 1950, 1951, 1952, ...). This coordinate system is called a *Lexis diagram*, after the German statistician and demographer W. Lexis, who first introduced it.[3]

The cohort A of persons having experienced event-origin during period A (year 1950) can be delimited by its *lifelines*. Persons having experienced event-origin (time 0) at the beginning of period A (1st of January, 1950) will reach exact duration 1 at the beginning of period B (point L, 1st of January, 1951), exact duration 2 at the beginning of period C (point M, 1st of January, 1952), and so on. The lifeline of these persons will be represented by the straight line drawn through points O, L, M, ... Similarly, all persons having experienced event-origin at the end of period A (December 31, 1950) will be characterized by the lifeline passing through points N, P, Q, ... on the diagram; this lifeline for all practical purposes coincides with the lifeline of persons born at the beginning of period B.[4]

---

[3]The original diagram is slightly different from the one presented here, which conforms to modern practice, e.g., see Pressat (1969, pp. 76–79) and Henry (1972, pp. 172–173).

[4]Strictly speaking, this is only true for persons born on the 31st of December at midnight. However, such a high degree of precision is usually not required when one works with calendar years.

All lifelines relating to cohort A are comprised between the boundaries O, L, M, . . . and N, P, Q, . . . , i.e., between the lifelines of persons born, respectively, at the beginning and the end of period A; the sloped corridor thus delineated will include all events relating to cohort A during a certain period of time (or calendar year) at a particular duration elapsed since event-origin.

1.1.5. Durations

Various types of durations since event-origin can be usefully distinguished. The meaning of *exact duration* has already been introduced: it is the duration since event-origin expressed in time units and a fraction of these; for example, a child three and one-half years old will have an exact age of 3.5. One can also round off the duration to the number of complete units of time elapsed since event-origin: in order to distinguish this measure from the former, it will be called here *completed duration*. In the above example, the child will have a completed duration of 3, i.e., his age at last birthday is 3 or, in other words, his age is comprised between exact ages 3 and 4. Looking at Fig. 1.1, one sees that events occurring during period C at completed duration 1 are located in the *square* MPQR and relate to *two cohorts*: cohort A and cohort B. If only events relating to cohort A at completed duration 1 are considered, they will be located in parallelogram LMPQ and will relate to *two periods* of time: period B (triangle LMP) and period C (triangle PMQ) (see example, Section 1.1.7.2).

One sometimes also encounters *durations in period difference* obtained by subtracting the period of occurrence of event-origin from the period of occurrence of the event under study. For example, in cohort A (Fig. 1.1), events occurring at duration in period difference one (B minus A or 1951 minus 1950 equals one unit of time or one year) are located in *parallelogram* LNPM and relate to *two completed durations*: completed duration 0 (triangle LNP) completed duration 1 (triangle LPM).

1.1.6. Related Problems

With the help of the Lexis diagram, it is now possible to envisage the following problems: First, knowing the completed durations and the period of observation, determine the period of occurrence of event-origin.

Consider the Lexis diagram of Fig. 1.2. For a given period of observation, deaths of children aged 2 in completed years relate to two birth-

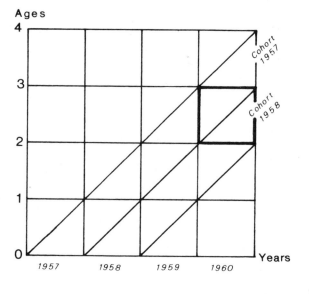

FIGURE 1.2

cohorts. On December 31, 1960, one of the two cohorts only is aged 2 in completed years, cohort $1960 - 2 = 1958$. Part of the deaths considered are thus ascribed to the 1958 birth-cohort; the other part can then be assigned to the previous cohort, i.e., birth-cohort 1957.[5]

One can thus obtain the period of occurrence of event-origin in all cases by subtracting from the period of observation the completed duration attained at the end of this period (on the 31st of December, if periods are expressed in calendar years).

Another problem one may consider is to compute the number of cohorts observed during n years[6] between exact ages x and $x + a$. As noted above, events occurring during one calendar year between exact ages x and $x + 1$ must necessarily be assigned to two cohorts; this result may now be extended: when events are observed during n years between exact ages x and $x + a$, the number of cohorts concerned is $n + a$. During each of the n years, one cohort attains exact age x; to these n cohorts must then be added the a cohorts reaching completed years x to $x + a - 1$ at the beginning of the period of n years (see Fig. 1.3 for an example based on completed years 20–24 and 9 years of observation). The total number of cohorts observed is

[5]This cohort is aged 3 in completed years on December 31, 1960; its year of birth is therefore $1960 - 3 = 1957$.
[6]Periods are expressed here in years; the extension to other units of time is obvious.

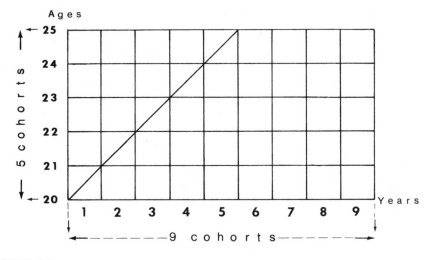

FIGURE 1.3

thus $n+(x+a)-x=n+a$. In Fig. 1.3, 9 cohorts reach exact age 20 during the total period of observation, and 5 cohorts attain completed ages 20–24 (20–25 in exact years) at the beginning of the first year of observation. The total number of cohorts concerned is in this case $9+5=14$.

1.1.7. Examples

1.1.7.1. Lexis Diagram. The number of survivors and deaths in a cohort[7] born in 1966 (for example) are given in Table 1.1. These data can be represented on a Lexis diagram as in Fig. 1.4.

1.1.7.2. Types of Ages. Consider deaths recorded between *exact* ages 1 and 2 in Fig. 1.4, i.e., at age 1 in *completed* years; ages at death in *period differences* are equal to 1 for deaths occurring in 1967 ($1967-1966=1$) and 2 for deaths occurring in 1968 ($1968-1966=2$).

The number of survivors at *completed* age 3 on December 31, 1969 (i.e., in cohort $1969-3=1966$) can be estimated by the average $\frac{1}{2}(9761+9755)=9758$ *if* deaths are uniformly distributed between exact ages 3 and 4.[8] This population number can also be obtained by subtracting $9761-\frac{6}{2}$, six deaths being recorded between exact ages 3 and 4.

---

[7]Source: Male life-table 1964–1966, England and Wales, *Statistical Review of England and Wales 1966* (Part II). London: H.M.S.O., 1966, p. 9.
[8]Supposing there is no migration.

TABLE 1.1

Age (years)	Males	Deaths
0	10,000	217
1	9,783	14
2	9,769	8
3	9,761	6
4	9,755	6
5	9,749	—

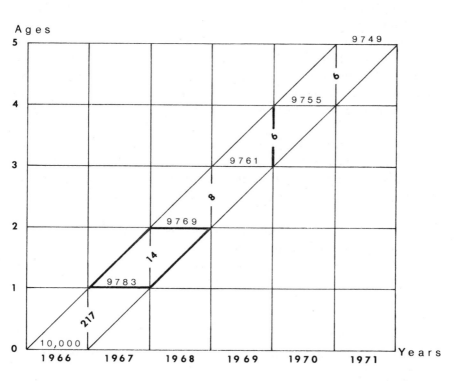

FIGURE 1.4

1.2. BASIC PRINCIPLES IN THE ABSENCE OF DISTURBANCES

1.2.1. Renewable Events

1.2.1.1. Introduction. With reference to the concepts introduced in Section 1.1, and with the help of the Lexis diagram, the basic principles of demographic analysis will now be introduced. As noted in Section. 1.1.2, consider a demographic phenomenon A (e.g., natality) characterized by certain events of type E (e.g., births), which are distributed over time in a cohort between bounds α and β (as before, $\alpha \geqslant 0$ and $\beta \leqslant \omega$). At each duration i elapsed since the event-origin of the cohort, one observes e_i events of type E, assumed first to be renewable events[9] (e.g., births of all orders).

The *intensity* of process A will be derived from the number of events of type E affecting the cohort; the *tempo* of the process will be characterized by the distribution of these events between bounds α and β.[10]

The essential assumption introduced at this stage is that between bounds α and β the cohort is subjected to no phenomenon other than the process under study; in other words the events recorded are in no way influenced by *disturbances* (mortality, for example). When this is the case, the study of process A affecting the cohort will be accomplished in a *pure state*.

1.2.1.2. Average Intensity and Average Duration. Two basic measures will now be defined: the *average intensity* of process A and the *average duration* of its tempo. These are two summary measures widely used by demographers; they are in fact two simple parameters of the distribution of events by time.

The total intensity of process A for the cohort at time β, i.e., the total number of events of type E observed between α and β is simply $\sum_{\alpha}^{\beta} e_i$; the average intensity, or *average number of events per head* (e.g., the average number of births per woman) can be written as

$$\bar{e} = \frac{1}{N} \sum_{\alpha}^{\beta} e_i$$

N being the number of persons having experienced event-origin at time α.

---

[9]Similar expressions are "repeatable" or "recurrent" events.

[10]Some authors speak of "quantity" and "schedule" instead. "Intensity" and "calendar" have become standard in French demographic literature; "calendar" is used here in the sense of a list of events arranged according to a particular system of reckoning time.

The distribution of events e_i, or the tempo of process A, will be summarized by the *weighted average of durations i*[11] (e.g., the mean age at childbearing) at which e_i events are recorded:

$$\bar{\imath} = \frac{\sum\limits_{\alpha}^{\beta} ie_i}{\sum\limits_{\alpha}^{\beta} e_i}$$

Other measures, incorporating higher moments of the distribution (variance, skewness, etc.), can also be used to summarize the distribution of events. Though useful as supplementary information on the type of distribution, these descriptive measures are not often found in the general demographic literature; some of these measures are, however, ill suited for certain types of distributions, as in the case of mortality.[12] In this introductory textbook, characteristics of the distribution will be mostly restricted to the basic simple measures of intensity and tempo defined above.

1.2.1.3. Reduced Events. The two indexes $\bar{e}$ and $\bar{\imath}$ introduced in the preceding sections can be computed otherwise; instead of computing the frequency of the absolute number of events e_i, one can start by computing their relative frequencies e_i/N at each duration i; e_i/N will be called hereafter the number of events at duration i reduced to the initial population of the cohort or, for short, *reduced events* at duration i.[13] Then

$$\bar{e} = \sum_{\alpha}^{\beta} (e_i/N) = (1/N) \sum_{\alpha}^{\beta} e_i$$

$$\bar{\imath} = \frac{\sum\limits_{\alpha}^{\beta} i(e_i/N)}{\sum\limits_{\alpha}^{\beta} (e_i/N)} = \frac{\sum\limits_{\alpha}^{\beta} ie_i}{\sum\limits_{\alpha}^{\beta} e_i}$$

One can also write

$$\bar{\imath} = \frac{\sum\limits_{\alpha}^{\beta} i(e_i/N)}{\bar{e}}$$

---

[11]The durations i are usually expressed in *exact* durations.

[12]Most descriptive statistics are ill suited for u-shaped distributions as one finds, for instance, in the case of deaths or probabilities of dying by age.

[13]One sometimes finds also the equivalent terms *diminished events*, or simply *frequency* or *rate*.

since $\sum_{\alpha}^{\beta}(e_i/N)=\bar{e}$. In other words, the average intensity of the studied process is simply obtained by adding reduced events between α and β[14]; the average duration is obtained by weighting durations i by the corresponding number of reduced events e_i/N.

1.2.2. Nonrenewable Events

1.2.2.1. Introduction. Consider now *nonrenewable* events (e.g., births or marriages classified by order, death, etc.). Events of type E can now be subdivided into different categories $E^{(1)}$, $E^{(2)}, \ldots, E^{(k)}, \ldots$ such that an event of order k (type $E^{(k)}$) cannot be experienced by a person without first experiencing the event of order $k-1$, i.e., of type $E^{(k-1)}$. For example, let $E^{(1)}$ correspond to birth order one, $E^{(2)}$ to birth order two, $E^{(k)}$ to birth order k (k being a positive whole number). In the cohort, one will now observe:

$e_i^{(1)}$:   the number of events of type $E^{(1)}$ at duration i

$e_i^{(2)}$:   the number of events of type $E^{(2)}$ at duration i

.
.
.

$e_i^{(k)}$:   the number of events of type $E^{(k)}$ at duration i

Furthermore, one has $e_i = \sum_k e_i^{(k)}$; for example, the number of births (all birth orders) occurring to women of completed age 25 (between exact ages 25 and 26) will be equal to the sum of births of all birth orders k at completed age 25.

1.2.2.2. Average Intensity. The average intensity of events of type $E^{(1)}$ in the cohort can be defined as

$$\bar{e}^{(1)} = (1/N)\sum_{\alpha}^{\beta} e_i^{(1)} = \sum_{\alpha}^{\beta}(e_i^{(1)}/N)$$

N being, as before, the number of persons having experienced event-origin at time α. Generally speaking, the average intensity of type $E^{(k)}$ events can be written as

$$\bar{e}^{(k)} = (1/N)\sum_{\alpha}^{\beta} e_i^{(k)} = \sum_{\alpha}^{\beta}(e_i^{(k)}/N) = \sum_{i}(e_i^{(k)}/N)$$

---

[14]When there is no possible confusion, this specification will be assumed hereafter, symbols α and β accordingly being dropped.

The average intensity of renewable events of type E (no order specified) will be

$$\bar{e} = (1/N) \sum_k \sum_i e_i^{(k)}$$

$$= (1/N)\left(\sum_i e_i^{(1)} + \sum_i e_i^{(2)} + \cdots + \sum_i e_i^{(k)} + \cdots \right)$$

$$= \bar{e}^{(1)} + \bar{e}^{(2)} + \cdots + \bar{e}^{(k)} + \cdots$$

$$= \sum_k \bar{e}^{(k)}$$

For example, for a cohort of N females, the average number of **births** per woman, at the end of the reproductive period, will be equal to the **sum** of the average number of first births, second births, etc.[15]

1.2.2.3. Average Duration. The average duration of type $E^{(k)}$ events will be obtained as before by the weighted average for order k:

$$\bar{\imath}^{(k)} = \frac{\sum\limits_i ie_i^{(k)}}{\sum\limits_i e_i^{(k)}} = \frac{1}{\bar{e}^{(k)}} \sum_i (ie_i^{(k)}/N)$$

The average duration of renewable events of type E will **correspond** to a weighted mean of the average durations[15] relating to the various $E^{(k)}$ weights being equal to the corresponding average intensities of **the various** nonrenewable events considered. To show this, take the simple **case where** E is subdivided into only two nonrenewable events of type $E^{(1)}$ and $E^{(2)}$ (e.g., first and second marriage). One will then have the following **relations:**

$$\bar{\imath} = \frac{\sum\limits_i (e_i^{(1)} + e_i^{(2)})i}{\sum\limits_i (e_i^{(1)} + e_i^{(2)})}$$

$$= \frac{\sum\limits_i ie_i^{(1)}}{\sum\limits_i (e_i^{(1)} + e_i^{(2)})} + \frac{\sum\limits_i ie_i^{(2)}}{\sum\limits_i (e_i^{(1)} + e_i^{(2)})}$$

Writing this as

$$\frac{\sum\limits_i ie_i^{(1)}}{\sum\limits_i (e_i^{(1)} + e_i^{(2)})} \cdot \frac{\sum\limits_i e_i^{(1)}}{\sum\limits_i e_i^{(1)}} + \frac{\sum\limits_i ie_i^{(2)}}{\sum\limits_i (e_i^{(1)} + e_i^{(2)})} \cdot \frac{\sum\limits_i e_i^{(2)}}{\sum\limits_i e_i^{(2)}}$$

[15]See example, Section 1.2.10.1.

one obtains

$$\bar{\imath} = \bar{\imath}^{(1)}(\bar{e}^{(1)}/\bar{e}) + \bar{\imath}^{(2)}(\bar{e}^{(2)}/\bar{e})$$

with

$$\bar{e}^{(1)} = \sum_i (e_i^{(1)}/N)$$

$$\bar{e}^{(2)} = \sum_i (e_i^{(2)}/N)$$

$$\bar{\imath}^{(1)} = \frac{\sum_i i e_i^{(1)}}{\sum_i e_i^{(1)}}$$

$$\bar{\imath}^{(2)} = \frac{\sum_i i e_i^{(2)}}{\sum_i e_i^{(2)}}$$

The generalized formula becomes

$$\bar{\imath} = (1/\bar{e})(\bar{\imath}^{(1)}\bar{e}^{(1)} + \bar{\imath}^{(2)}\bar{e}^{(2)} + \cdots + \bar{\imath}^{(k)}\bar{e}^{(k)} + \cdots)$$

with

$$\sum_k \bar{e}^{(k)} = \bar{e}$$

1.2.3. Other Characteristics

Some other characteristics of the distributions of nonrenewable events $e_i^{(k)}$ can also be derived. We consider first the proportion of persons experiencing *at least once* the renewable event of type E. In order to experience E, one has at least to experience $E^{(1)}$, the first nonrenewable event of E (ascribing an order to the renewable events E). The number of persons in the cohort experiencing $E^{(1)}$ is $\sum_i e_i^{(1)}$; the proportion experiencing at least once renewable event E is thus $(1/N)\sum_i e_i^{(1)}$ or $\bar{e}^{(1)}$, the average intensity of the first-order events.

For example, the proportion of persons in the cohort who have married at least once, renewable event E being marriage, is obviously equal to the average number of first marriages per head.

Another related problem consists in computing the proportion of persons in the cohort who will experience nonrenewable event $E^{(k+1)}$, knowing that they have already experienced event $E^{(k)}$ of immediately preceding order. The number of persons to whom event $E^{(k)}$ has occurred is equal to $\sum_i e_i^{(k)}$; the number experiencing $E^{(k+1)}$ will be $\sum_i e_i^{(k+1)}$. The

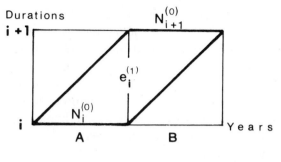

FIGURE 1.5

required proportion is thus $\sum_i e_i^{(k+1)}/\sum_i e_i^{(k)}$, which is equal to $\bar{e}^{(k+1)}/\bar{e}^{(k)}$, i.e., the corresponding ratio of average intensities of orders $k+1$ and k. For example, if the proportion (in a cohort of N females) of women having had at least two children is $\bar{e}^{(2)}$ (average intensity of birth order 2) and the proportion of women having at least three children (average intensity of birth order 3) is $\bar{e}^{(3)}$, the ratio $\bar{e}^{(3)}/\bar{e}^{(2)}$ represents the proportion of women having two children who have given birth to a third child.

1.2.4. Probability of Attrition

Here and below we will need to distinguish carefully between *exact* and *completed* durations. To do this we will use lightface letter symbols $(i, i+1)$ for exact duration and boldface letter symbols $(\mathbf{i}, \mathbf{i+1})$ for completed duration.[16]

The probability[17] of occurrence of a nonrenewable event during a specified interval of time is a widely used measure in demography. Still restricting analysis to a cohort in a *pure state* (as defined in Section 1.2.1.1), consider the number of persons in a cohort of N persons having experienced event-origin, for which nonrenewable event $E^{(1)}$ of order one (e.g., first marriage) has not yet occurred. At *exact* duration i, denote $N_i^{(0)}$ as this subpopulation of the cohort (see Fig. 1.5), e.g., the number of spinsters at exact age i if event $E^{(1)}$ is first marriage. If, between exact durations i and $i+1$, $e_i^{(1)}$ nonrenewable events are observed, the *probability of* attrition q_i due to event $E^{(1)}$ is equal to $q_i = e_i^{(1)}/N_i^{(0)}$ if the cohort is observed in a pure state.

This concept can be generalized first to compute probabilities of attrition by events of type $E^{(k)}$ at completed duration $\mathbf{i}$; the denominator of

---

[16]This distinction is carried over to subscripts; the reader should keep this in mind here and throughout.

[17]Other terms used as synonyms include chance, risk, rate. The French equivalent is "quotient."

the probability will consist in all persons at exact duration i having already experienced event of type $E^{(k-1)}$, but not yet event of type $E^{(k)}$. For example, in order to marry twice, one has first to be married once (and usually be divorced or widowed).

Another generalization of the above concept is to extend the probability to cover durations x to $x+n$. If there are no disturbances (i.e., if the observation is in a pure state), the extrapolation is immediate: writing $_ne_i^{(1)}$ as the number of events occurring between exact ages[18] i and $i+n$, the corresponding probability $_nq_i$ will be

$$_nq_i = \frac{_ne_i^{(1)}}{N_i^{(0)}}$$

As before, extension to events of type $E^{(k)}$ is immediate.

1.2.5. Attrition Table

For an event of order k, suppose that all probabilities of attrition have been computed between bounds α and β; for example, if $\alpha = 0$, $\beta = \omega$, and $n = 1$, the following probabilities have been computed by the formula given above: $q_0, q_1, q_2, \ldots, q_{\omega-1}$ with $q_x = 0$, for $x \geq \omega$ such that each q_i is equal to[19] e_i/N_i. The *attrition table*[20] corresponding to nonrenewable event $E^{(k)}$ can now be drawn up as follows: Between exact durations 0 and 1, the number of nonrenewable events is equal to N_0 (or N) times q_0, i.e., $N_0q_0 = e_0$. Therefore, $N_1 = N_0 - e_0$ and $N_1q_1 = e_1$. The process continues with $N_1 - e_1 = N_2$ and $N_2q_2 = e_2$, etc. The average intensity and tempo can then be derived from e_i as in Section 1.2.2.

Three distributions are thus obtained (see example, Section 1.2.10.1): (1) the distribution of "survivors" N_i, i.e., the number of persons at exact duration i not yet having experienced the nonrenewable event $E^{(k)}$ considered; (2) the distribution of probabilities q_i of experiencing event $E^{(k)}$ between exact durations i and $i+1$, and (3) the distribution of nonrenewable events e_i observed between exact durations i and $i+1$.

Another distribution can be derived: the distribution of probabilities p_i of *not* experiencing event $E^{(k)}$ between exact durations i and $i+1$. This

---

[18]For exact durations i to $i+1$, one could adopt the expression $_1e_i^{(1)}$; however, $e_i^{(1)}$ is usually preferred. Furthermore, q_i is usually written for $_1q_i$.

[19]In order to simplify expressions, we have dropped the reference to order k; it is, however, assumed in the following discussion that e_i is written for $e_i^{(k)}$ and N_i for $N_i^{(k-1)}$.

[20]"Probability table" or "decrement table" are synonyms.

probability is obviously equal to

$$p_i = N_{i+1}/N_i = 1 - q_i$$

As soon as one considers a nonrenewable event, it is often useful to draw up the corresponding attrition table. In addition to the average duration and intensity of the distribution, this table has the advantage of providing the probabilities of experiencing (or not experiencing) the process between exact durations i and $i + 1$. Furthermore, these probabilities can be extended to durations i and $i + n$ by noting as above that $_nq_i = {_ne_i}/N_i$; in this case, $_np_i = N_{i+n}/N_i = 1 - {_nq_i}$.

Other applications of the attrition table will be given later on, especially in the chapter devoted to the study of mortality (Chapter 3). In the case of mortality, the attrition table is commonly known as the *life table*.

1.2.6. Probabilities between Completed Durations

Instead of computing probabilities between two exact durations, one can also compute them between two *completed* durations (or two groups of completed durations). As shown in Fig. 1.6, N_i and N_{i+1} relate to the number of "survivors" at completed durations **i** and **i+1**, i.e., the number of persons not yet having experienced nonrenewable event $E^{(k)}$ at completed durations **i** and **i+1**. The number of events observed between completed durations **i** and **i+1** being e_{i+1} (on the average, they occur at *exact* duration $i + 1$), the

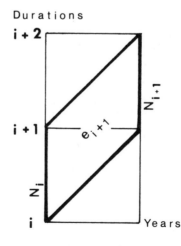

FIGURE 1.6

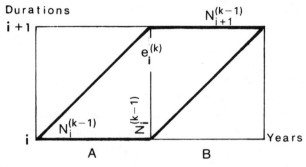

FIGURE 1.7

corresponding probability of attrition is

$$k_i = e_{i+1}/N_i$$

The probabilities of nonattrition are simply, as before, the complement to one of the probabilities of attrition. As in Section 1.2.4, these probabilities can be extended to cover intervals of time greater than one unit (e.g., from completed durations **i** to **i + n**). These measures are often used in population projections.

Note that, *on the average*, the number of persons N_i in Fig. 1.6 relates to an average *exact duration* of $i + 0.5$. Therefore, one has the approximate relation $k_i \cong q_{i+0.5}$ (the symbol $\cong$ meaning "approximately equal to") and one can therefore derive quite easily (e.g., by graphic interpolation) one set of probabilities from the other.

1.2.7. Exposure Rates

An exposure rate[21] is defined as the ratio of the number of *nonrenewable* events $e_i^{(k)}$ observed between durations i and $i+1$ (see Fig. 1.7) to the total time lived between durations i and $i + 1$ by the subcohort not yet having experienced event $E^{(k)}$. Consider Fig. 1.7, the time unit being expressed in years: the total number of person-years lived by the subcohort not yet having experienced event $E^{(k)}$ is equal to $N_{i+1}^{(k-1)} + \Delta$, where $N_{i+1}^{(k-1)}$ is the number of persons at exact duration $i + 1$ to whom event $E^{(k)}$ has not yet occurred (expressed in persons times 1 year), and Δ is the total number of person-years lived by the group $N_i^{(k-1)} - N_{i+1}^{(k-1)}$ between exact durations i

[21]The term *rate* is often used with various meanings; when in this textbook the meaning differs from the one presented in Section 1.2.7, the term "rate" will be put in quotation marks.

and $i+1$ *before* being subjected to event $E^{(k)}$. The denominator of the rate is therefore the total time the cohort has been exposed to a specific risk between durations i and $i+1$. This is referred to in the demographic literature as *exposure time* or *person-years* of exposure to risk, and the corresponding rate is sometimes called an *occurrence-time* rate.[22]

Noting that $N_i^{(k-1)} - N_{i+1}^{(k-1)}$ is equal to $e_i^{(k)}$, one has $\Delta = e_i^{(k)} \cdot \tau$, where τ is the average duration lived by group $N_i^{(k-1)} - N_{i+1}^{(k-1)}$ between i and $i+1$ before experiencing $E^{(k)}$. If the number of $e_i^{(k)}$ events is *evenly distributed* between exact durations i and $i+1$, $\tau = \frac{1}{2}$ and finally the total time (person-years) lived during this period by the subcohort is equal to $N_{i+1}^{(k-1)} + \frac{1}{2}e_i^{(k)}$. In this case the exposure rate t_i will therefore be

$$t_i = \frac{e_i^{(k)}}{N_{i+1}^{(k-1)} + \frac{1}{2}e_i^{(k)}}$$

The denominator of this rate is also equal, in this case, to $N_i^{(k-1)} - \frac{1}{2}e_i^{(k)}$ if events are assumed to be evenly distributed between i and $i+1$. Finally, one may therefore also write

$$t_i = \frac{e_i^{(k)}}{N_i^{(k-1)} - \frac{1}{2}e_i^{(k)}}$$

or

$$t_i = \frac{e_i^{(k)}}{\frac{1}{2}(N_i^{(k-1)} + N_{i+1}^{(k-1)})}$$

$$= \frac{e_i^{(k)}}{N_i^{(k-1)}}$$

where $N_i^{(k-1)}$ is the number of "survivors" (in person-years) to event $E^{(k)}$ at *completed* duration **i**.[23] Noting that $N_i^{(k-1)} = N_{i+0.5}^{(k-1)}$ at *exact* age $i+0.5$, one can also write, under the above assumption of even distribution of events $e_i^{(k)}$,

$$t_i = \frac{e_i^{(k)}}{N_{i+0.5}^{(k-1)}}$$

These relations are only approximately satisfied when the distribution of events $e_i^{(k)}$ between i and $i+1$ is not uniform, or in other words when the "survivorship" function $N_j^{(k-1)}$ is not linear between durations i and $i+1$.[24]

---

[22]See Sheps (1966) for a general discussion of this type of index.

[23]Looking at Fig. 1.7, one notes that $N_i^{(k-1)}$ is the number of "survivors" at the end of period A (e.g., on December 31, year A).

[24]Another way to express the exposure rate is to write $t_i = e_i^k / [\int_i^{i+1} N_j^{(k-1)} \, dj]$. If $N_j^{(k-1)}$ is a linear function between i and $i+1$, one obviously obtains $t_i = e_i^k / N_{i+0.5}^{(k-1)}$.

The concept of exposure rate can be extended to periods i to $i+n$. If events are uniformly distributed between i and $i+n$, the number of person-years will be equal to $n \cdot N_{i+n}^{(k-1)} + \Delta$, with Δ equal this time to $_n e_i^{(k)} \cdot (n/2)$ as $\tau = [(i+n)-i]/2$. Therefore, the rate can now be written as

$$_n t_i = \frac{_n e_i}{(n/2)(N_i^{(k-1)} + N_{i+n}^{(k-1)})}$$

Again, this formula is only approximate[25] if events are not evenly distributed between duration i and $i+1$.

Exposure rates can also be computed between *completed* durations **i** and **i+1** (or between groups of completed durations). The extension of the above formulas is immediate and requires no particular consideration.

1.2.8. Relations between Exposure Rates and Attrition Probabilities

Suppose that, for an event of specified order, the distribution of events is uniform between exact durations i and $i+1$, or in other words that the "survivorship" function is *linear* between i and $i+1$. Dropping references to the specified order, in order to simplify the symbols, one can write

$$q_i = \frac{e_i}{N_{i+0.5} + e_i/2}$$

since $N_i = N_{i+0.5} + e_i/2$, and multiplying by t_i with $t_i = e_i/N_{x+0.5}$ we have

$$q_i = \frac{e_i t_i}{N_{i+0.5} t_i + e_i t_i/2}$$

$$= \frac{t_i}{1 + t_i/2}$$

Finally, $q_i = 2t_i/(2 + t_i)$ and the probability q_i can therefore be easily derived from t_i. For a detailed example, see Section 1.2.10.2.

This formula can be extended to the case when exact durations considered are i to $i+n$; if events are again uniformly distributed, the corresponding formula for transforming rates into probabilities will be

$$_n q_i = \frac{2n \, _n t_i}{2 + n \, _n t_i} \qquad \text{with } _n t_i \leq \frac{2}{n}, \text{ since } _n q_i \leq 1$$

---

[25]More generally, writing $na_i = \tau_i$, one obtains (with $0 \leq a_i \leq 1$) $_n t_i = {}_n e_i/[n(N_i - {}_n e_i) + na_i \, _n e_i]$.

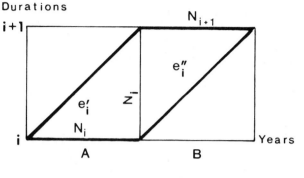

FIGURE 1.8

If events are not evenly distributed between the exact durations considered, the above formulas will give a biased estimate of the attrition probability.[26]

Consider, for example (Fig. 1.8), the case where, instead of observing $e_i/2$ events in cohort $A - i$ during years A or B at completed duration **i**, one observes, respectively, e_i' and e_i'' events. Write $e_i' = ke_i''$ ($k \neq 1$) and estimate probability q_i by the above formula. Denoting this estimate by $\hat{q}_i$, one has

$$\hat{q} = \frac{2t_i}{2 + t_i}$$

$$= \frac{e_i}{N_i + 0.5e_i} \qquad \text{for } t_i = e_i/N_i$$

Taking into account that $e_i = ke_i'' + e_i''$, one obtains $\hat{q}_i = e_i/[N_i - 0.5e_i''(k-1)]$. The true probability obviously is $q_i = e_i/N_i$ so that $q_i/\hat{q}_i = 1 - [0.5e_i''(k-1)]/N_i$.

The term $[0.5e_i''(k-1)]/N_i$ reflects the bias introduced by supposing a linear "survivorship" function between i and $i+1$; this bias tends, however, to be rather small in most circumstances. This will not necessarily be the case, however, when the interval of time i to $i+n$ increases, as the linear assumption will become less and less adequate.

Other assumptions concerning the trend of the "survivorship" function can naturally be considered. If, for example, the trend of N_j is assumed to be *exponential* between exact durations i and $i+1$, the corresponding

---

[26]More generally, with $na_i = \tau_i$, one obtains $_nq_i = 2n\,_nt_i/[2 + 2(1 - a_i)n\,_nt_i]$.

transformation formula will be[27] $q_i = 1 - \exp(-t_i)$ and, for duration i to $i + n$, $_nq_i = 1 - \exp(-n\ _nt_i)$.

Another approach has been to derive empirical relations between rates and probabilities based on observed data (Reed and Merrell, 1939); in most cases, however, the linear transformation formula is quite adequate and further refinement is not necessary and sometimes not even recommended (Péron, 1971).

Finally, one should note that the above formulas can also be used when probabilities and rates are computed between completed durations instead of exact durations. The similarity between the two transformations is obvious and needs no further comment.

1.2.9. Final Comments

Three basic types of measures have been introduced in the above sections: reduced events, exposure rates, and attrition probabilities. A simple example will show the relations and differences between these measures. Consider a female birth-cohort (Fig. 1.9) subjected to first marriage only (i.e., in a pure state). At a specified completed age $\mathbf{x}$, the number of first marriages will be denoted by $M_{\mathbf{x}}$, and the number of spinsters at exact ages x and $x + 1$ by N_x and N_{x+1}. Finally, since there are no deaths and migrations between bounds α and β (age $\mathbf{x}$ being comprised between α and β), the total population (spinsters and ever-marrieds) at age x (exact or completed) will be N, the initial population having experienced event-origin. The number of reduced first marriages $r_{\mathbf{x}}$ will be

$$r_{\mathbf{x}} = M_{\mathbf{x}}/N$$

The probability of first marriage between x and $x + 1$ is

$$q_x = M_{\mathbf{x}}/N_x$$

and the exposure rate is

$$t_{\mathbf{x}} = M_{\mathbf{x}}/N_{x+0.5}$$

supposing that marriages are evenly distributed between ages x and $x + 1$.

In a *pure state*, as considered here, one can draw the following relations:

$$q_x = t_{\mathbf{x}}(N_{x+0.5}/N_x), \qquad q_x = r_{\mathbf{x}}(N/N_x)$$

---

[27]Write $N_j = \exp(aj + b)$. Then $t_i = (N_i - N_{i+1})/\int_i^{i+1} N_j dj = -a$. As $q_i = (N_i - N_{i+1})/N_i = 1 - e^a$, one finally obtains $q_i = 1 - \exp(-t_i)$.

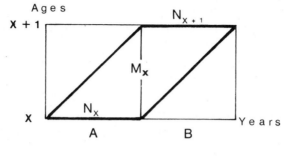

FIGURE 1.9

One sees that q_x and t_x are quite similar concepts, the "correction factor" $N_{x+0.5}/N_x$ relating to the population of spinsters at one-half year's differ-ence. On the contrary, r_x differs from q_x (and t_x) as the "correction factor" N/N_x relates the total population (spinsters and *ever-marrieds*) to the population of spinsters. In reality, marriage will never be observed in a pure state; the problem will then be to derive *estimates* of r_x, q_x, or t_x by eliminating as much as possible the extraneous interference of mortality and migration. This problem will be considered in the next section. However, before taking up this subject, two other points should be stressed:

First, in the theoretical framework presented here, attrition prob-abilities (and exposure rates) have been limited to nonrenewable events, while reduced events cover both nonrenewable and renewable events. One could also extend the concept of probability to include renewable events (no order specified); for example, A_x represents all marriages (including remar-riages) during the period, and A_x/N represents the "probability" (here also equal to the exposure rate and reduced marriages) for a person (married or not) to experience marriage (first marriage or remarriage) during the period of time. Due to conceptual difficulties involved, this extended concept of probability is not used in this book: attrition probabilities and exposure rates will be restricted to nonrenewable events of order $E^{(k)}$, the related popu-lation being the number of persons $N^{(k-1)}$ having experienced event $E^{(k-1)}$ but not yet event $E^{(k)}$.

Second, as seen in Section 1.1.1, experiencing event-origin is a neces-sary condition in order to become capable of experiencing the process under study. For example, to be born (event-origin: birth) is a necessary condition to die eventually (process observed: mortality); to marry (even-origin: marriage) is a prerequisite for divorcing or for being widowed (process observed: marriage dissolution). The type of event-origin obviously depends on the type of phenomenon studied; therefore, more precision will be given in the chapters devoted to the various demographic processes. However, one should note that a cohort is not necessarily characterized by a sole event-origin: it is often necessary to introduce *multiple* event-origins characterizing specific types of subcohorts, in view of defining a more *homogeneous* population exposed to risk. For example, if married persons only are exposed to widowhood (first event-origin: marriage), one must also take into account the age of spouses (second event-origin: birth of spouse). The study of widowhood will thus take place in a marriage-cohort partitioned into subcohorts characterized by the year of birth of spouse. Other examples will be given in the following chapters.

1.2.10. Examples

1.2.10.1. A Cohort without Disturbances. Consider the following births in a marriage-cohort of 10,000 couples without disturbances (Table 1.2) classified by order according to duration of marriage (in completed years) at birth (Wunsch, 1967). We assume that fertility, after duration 15, is negligible.

TABLE 1.2

Duration (in completed years)	All birth orders	Birth order 1	Birth order 2	Birth order 3	Birth order 4	Birth order 5+
0	3,517	3,485	31	1	0	0
1	2,676	2,078	564	32	2	0
2	2,098	813	1,138	132	14	1
3	1,739	460	825	395	51	8
4	1,513	307	614	419	149	24
5	1,313	208	456	375	201	73
6	1,167	151	359	316	207	134
7	1,024	111	262	282	200	169
8	883	73	193	221	194	202
9	752	57	138	181	155	221
10	687	42	117	153	138	237
11	563	30	87	111	108	227
12	464	22	64	89	90	199
13	415	17	48	74	77	199
14	350	11	36	59	62	182
15	298	11	28	49	49	161
Total	19,459	7,876	4,960	2,889	1,697	2,037

The *average number of births per marriage* can be obtained as follows, the number of marriages being equal to 10,000:

All birth orders $\qquad \bar{e} = \dfrac{19,459}{10,000} = 1.9459$

Birth order 1 $\qquad \bar{e}^{(1)} = \dfrac{7,876}{10,000} = 0.7876$

Birth order 2 $\qquad \bar{e}^{(2)} = \dfrac{4,960}{10,000} = 0.4960$

Birth order 3 $\qquad \bar{e}^{(3)} = \dfrac{2,889}{10,000} = 0.2889$

Birth order 4 $\qquad \bar{e}^{(4)} = \dfrac{1,697}{10,000} = 0.1697$

Birth order 5+ $\qquad \bar{e}^{(5+)} = \dfrac{2,037}{10,000} = 0.2037$

In all these examples, the numerator is equal to the total number of births of order j drawn from the previous table. As seen in Section 1.2.2.2, one may also write $\bar{e} = \bar{e}^{(1)} + \bar{e}^{(2)} + \bar{e}^{(3)} + \bar{e}^{(4)} + \bar{e}^{(5+)}$ or $1.95 = 0.79 + 0.50 + 0.29 + 0.17 + 0.20$.

The *average duration of marriage at birth* can be computed as seen in Section 1.2.2.3 by the relation $\bar{t}^{(k)} = \sum i e_i^{(k)} / \sum e_i^{(k)}$. With the above data, one obtains:

All birth orders $\qquad \bar{t} = \dfrac{95,834}{19,459} = 4.925$

Birth order 1 $\qquad \bar{t}^{(1)} = \dfrac{15,624}{7,876} = 1.983$

Birth order 2 $\qquad \bar{t}^{(2)} = \dfrac{23,748}{4,960} = 4.787$

Birth order 3 $\qquad \bar{t}^{(3)} = \dfrac{20,085}{2,889} = 6.952$

Birth order 4 $\qquad \bar{t}^{(4)} = \dfrac{14,473}{1,697} = 8.528$

Birth order 5+ $\qquad \bar{t}^{(5+)} = \dfrac{21,902}{2,037} = 10.752$

TABLE 1.3

Duration of marriage (years)	Childless couples	First births	Probabilities of first birth
0	10,000	3,485	0.3485
1	6,515	2,078	0.3190
2	4,437	813	0.1832
3	3,624	460	0.1269
4	3,164	307	0.0970
5	2,857	208	0.0728

As seen in Section 1.2.2.3, the average duration $\bar{t}$ for all birth orders can also be obtained by using the following relation: $\bar{t} = (1/\bar{e})[\bar{t}^{(1)}\bar{e}^{(1)} + \bar{t}^{(2)}e^{(2)}\bar{e}^{(2)} + \bar{t}^{(3)}\bar{e}^{(3)} + \bar{t}^{(4)}\bar{e}^{(4)} + \bar{t}^{(5+)}\bar{e}^{(5+)}]$ or $4.93 \cong (1/1.95) \times [1.98(0.79) + 4.79(0.50) + 6.95(0.29) + 8.53(0.17) + 10.75(0.20)]$. The *fertility table for birth order 1* (Table 1.3) can be set up as seen in Section 1.2.5.

1.2.10.2. Relations between Rates and Probabilities. The above probabilities of first birth can also be estimated by transforming duration-specific first birth rates into probabilities, by one of the methods developed in Section 1.2.8. From the data in Table 1.3, the following rates (Table 1.4) can be computed, assuming uniform distribution of births at each duration.

Having recourse to the two transformation formulas $q_i = 2t_i/(2 + t_i)$ and $q_i = 1 - \exp(-t_i)$, where t_i and q_i, respectively, denote the first birth rate and probability, one obtains the estimates in Table 1.5.

Due to the linear assumption when calculating person-years of exposure to risk, probabilities derived from the linear transform function are equal, in the present case, to the true probabilities of first birth.

TABLE 1.4

Duration (years)	Person-years	First births	First-birth rates
0	8,257	3485	0.4221
1	5,476	2078	0.3794
2	4,030	813	0.2017
3	3,394	460	0.1355
4	3,010	307	0.1020

TABLE 1.5

Duration (years)	True probability	Estimate by $2t_i/(2+t_i)$	Estimate by $1-\exp(-t_i)$
0	0.3485	0.3485	0.3443
1	0.3189	0.3189	0.3157
2	0.1832	0.1832	0.1827
3	0.1269	0.1269	0.1267
4	0.0970	0.0970	0.0970

1.3. BASIC PRINCIPLES IN THE PRESENCE OF DISTURBANCES

1.3.1. Types of Demographic Processes

In the preceding section, a theoretical framework has been set up concerning some basic principles of analysis in the absence of disturbances, i.e., in a pure state. In the real world, demographic processes are never observed in a pure state; for example, in the study of natality, analysis is disturbed by the interference of mortality and migration. The problem consists therefore in eliminating the extraneous influence of disturbances in view of bringing the problem back to an observation accomplished in a pure state; this has traditionally been one of the main purposes of demographic analysis even if not always explicitly stated.[28]

As one will see in the following sections, two types of demographic processes have to be distinguished at this stage: some of the processes considered (natality, nuptiality) do not exclude persons from observation; others do exclude them (mortality, emigration). One should consider apart, in this framework, the case of immigration, which adds people to the population observed (see Section 6.5.1); immigration cannot strictly be integrated into the basic framework of demographic analysis as it now stands,[29] as it consists of an exogenous process in relation to the population under observation.[30] For example, one cannot compute true "immigration

---

[28]This is not always the case. In population projections, for example, one is interested in projecting the actual numbers of births, deaths, and migrations, and not those one would observe in a pure state.

[29]The same can be said of interactions of male and female populations in the study of nuptiality (see Section 4.3). Demographic analysis still has trouble taking into account the interaction of populations, as in migration or nuptiality.

[30]Immigration into area A obviously consists of emigration from other areas; theoretically at least, one could thus study immigration indirectly through an analysis of emigration.

probabilities" as the set of immigrants is distinct from the population of arrival (theoretically, such a "probability" could even be greater than 1, which is impossible with a "well-behaved" probability as defined in Section 1.2.4). Immigration will, however, be introduced in the next chapter, which is devoted to period analysis (i.e., during a certain calendar period, as opposed to cohort analysis).

1.3.2. Absence of Population Exclusion

This section will be devoted to the study of demographic processes that do not exclude persons from observation, e.g., natality or nuptiality. It will be useful to distinguish, as before, between renewable and nonrenewable events.

1.3.2.1. Renewable Events. In order to simplify symbols, the process under study will be considered to be disturbed by the interference of one other process only, e.g., natality disturbed by mortality. The problem consists then in deriving the series of reduced events e_i/N (see Section 1.2.1.3) in a pure state from an observation disturbed by another process. As before, a cohort approach will be adopted.

Let ε_i represent the number of renewable events (e.g., births) *really observed* at completed duration $\mathbf{i}$ in cohort $(A - \mathbf{i})$ (see Fig. 1.10). P_i will represent the average population observed between i and $i+1$ not yet having experienced the disturbance (e.g., mortality), though it may or may not have already experienced the process *studied* (natality). The main assumption, called the *condition of independence*,[31] is that persons who have been subjected to the disturbance (who have died in this case) before reaching the upper bound β, would have experienced at each duration the process under study in the absence of disturbances, in the same way as the P_β persons who reach bound β.[32] If the reduced events in the subcohort that reaches β are denoted by ε_i'/P_β, the condition of independence implies then that, at each duration $\mathbf{i}$, one has

$$\varepsilon_i = P_\beta(\varepsilon_i'/P_\beta) + (P_i - P_\beta)(\varepsilon_i'/P_\beta)$$

from which one derives $\varepsilon_i'/P_\beta = \varepsilon_i/P_i$.

Since there is *no selection*, the observed frequencies ε_i/P_i in the cohort with disturbances are equal to the corresponding frequencies ε_i'/P_β in the cohort without disturbances, i.e., in the pure state. In this case, since

---

[31]L. Henry's terminology will be used in this section [see L. Henry (1966)].

[32]In other words, persons being subjected to the disturbance are *not a selected group* with respect to the process studied.

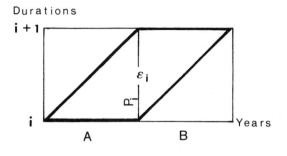

FIGURE 1.10

$e_i/N = \varepsilon_i'/P_\beta$ for the subcohort without disturbances,[33] one has finally $e_i/N = \varepsilon_i/P_i$, where e_i/N is the number of reduced events at duration i, which would have been observed had the cohort not been subjected to disturbances between bounds α and β. If, on the other hand, the persons who die constitute a selected group with regard to the process studied, there is no more equality between ε_i/P_i, e_i/N, and ε_i'/P_β.

If the condition of independence is satisfied, one simply uses the *observed reduced events*[34] ε_i/P_i in place of the reduced events without disturbances e_i/N, and applies the general principles of analysis developed in the pure state. In particular, the average intensity of the phenomenon will be

$$\bar{e} = \sum_i (e_i/N) = \sum_i (\varepsilon_i/P_i)$$

and the average duration

$$\bar{i} = \frac{\sum\limits_i i(e_i/N)}{\bar{e}} = \frac{\sum\limits_i i(\varepsilon_i/P_i)}{\bar{e}}$$

It is probable that in most cases the condition of independence is not perfectly satisfied, i.e., the subcohort surviving until bound β might be selected according to the process studied (in the above example, mortality might have selected especially fertile women). It is impossible, however, to

[33]One has

$$\frac{e_i}{N} = \frac{\varepsilon_i + (N - P_i)(\varepsilon_i'/P_\beta)}{N} = \frac{\varepsilon_i'}{P_\beta}$$

where e_i/N are the reduced events without disturbances.
[34]Note that if $\varepsilon_i/P_i = e_i/N$, one has $\varepsilon_i \neq e_i$ and $P_i \neq N$. Usually $\varepsilon_i < e_i$ and $P_i < N$, as the cohort is subjected to attrition.

test if the condition of independence is satisfied or not in actual practice; one should therefore keep in mind that measures of intensity and tempo derived from actual data constitute only an approximation to the corresponding measures in the (unknown) pure state.

1.3.2.2. Nonrenewable Events. When the event of type E can be subdivided into a succession of nonrenewable events of type $E^{(1)}$, $E^{(2)}, \ldots, E^{(k)}, \ldots$, one may also draw a parallel as in Section 1.3.2.1 between measures in a pure state and measures under disturbances, as long as a supplementary condition (called *condition of continuity*) is satisfied.

Consider, for example, the study of female first marriage[35] disturbed by the interference of mortality of spinsters (Fig. 1.11). Let n_x be the probability of first marriage between exact ages x and $x + 1$, in the absence of mortality of spinsters; q_x the probability of death for a spinster, between exact ages x and $x + 1$, in the absence of nuptiality; S_x and S_{x+1} the number of spinsters at exact ages x and $x + 1$; m'_x the number of first marriages actually recorded between ages x and $x + 1$; d'_x the number of deaths of spinsters actually recorded between ages x and $x + 1$; and P_x the total population (spinsters and ever-marrieds) at completed duration x.

If the condition of *independence* between nuptiality and mortality is satisfied (i.e., if there is no selection[36]), one can write

$$S_{x+1} = S_x(1 - n_x)(1 - q_x) \tag{1.1}$$

where $1 - n_x$ and $1 - q_x$ represent the probabilities of "surviving" to marriage and death, between exact ages x to $x + 1$.

Nuptiality has, however, prevented a certain number of deaths *of spinsters* from occurring; on the average the risk of nuptiality for the number $S_x q_x$ of females who would have died as spinsters in the absence of nuptiality is $n_x/2$, as deaths are distributed between x and $x + 1$.[37] Therefore $S_x q_x (n_x/2)$ females have in fact been married, and the actual number of deaths of spinsters is equal to

$$d'_x = S_x q_x - S_x q_x (n_x/2)$$
$$= S_x q_x (1 - n_x/2)$$

[35]The main theory was developed by Henry (1959, 1963). For the case where the disturbance is immigration see Wunsch (1970). A strict probabilistic approach is presented by Duchêne and Wijewickrema (1973).

[36]Dead spinsters, if they had lived, would have experienced marriage as those alive. A similar condition holds for mortality. This condition must hold between *all ages* from α to β, the bounds of the phenomenon considered.

[37]A more general approach would be to write this risk as $\lambda n_x (0 \leq \lambda \leq 1)$.

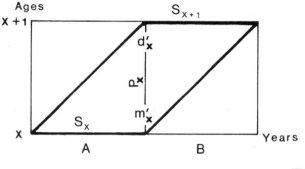

FIGURE 1.11

The actual number of first marriages is then

$$m'_x = (S_x - S_{x+1}) - S_x q_x (1 - n_x/2)$$

since S_x is reduced by marriages and deaths between x and $x+1$. Introducing Eq. (1.1), the above relation becomes

$$m'_x = S_x - S_x(1-n_x)(1-q_x) - S_x q_x(1-n_x/2)$$
$$= S_x n_x (1-q_x/2)$$

This expression could also have been derived by a line of arguments similar to the one that has given d'_x.

In summary, one can write[38]

$$m'_x = S_x n_x (1-q_x/2)$$
$$d'_x = S_x q_x (1-n_x/2)$$

$$(1.2)$$

Moreover, let $p_{0,x} = (1 - {}_x n_0)$ be the probability of remaining a spinster between ages 0 and x, and $s_{0,x} = (1 - {}_x q_0)$ the probability for a spinster to remain alive between ages 0 and x.

If N is the initial population of the cohort at birth, one may write

$$S_x = N p_{0,x} s_{0,x}$$
$$m'_x = N p_{0,x} s_{0,x} (1 - q_x/2) n_x$$
$$= N p_{0,x} (s_{0,x+0.5}) n_x$$

[38] A more general formulation would be, with λ as before comprised between 0 and 1, $m'_x = S_x n_x [1 - q_x(1 - \lambda)]$ and $d'_x = S_x q_x (1 - \lambda n_x)$.

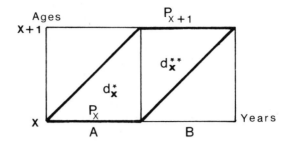

FIGURE 1.12

taking into account the approximate relation

$$s_{0,x+0.5} \cong s_{0,x}(1 - q_x/2)$$

Furthermore, with P_x as the total population (spinsters and ever-marrieds) at completed age x, one may write[39] (Fig. 1.12)

$$P_x = (P_x + P_{x+1})/2 = P_{x+0.5}$$

If $s'_{0,x+0.5}$ represents the probability of survival from ages 0 to $x + 0.5$ for the whole population (spinsters and ever-marrieds), then

$$\frac{m'_x}{P_x} = \frac{Np_{0,x}s_{0,x+0.5}n_x}{Ns'_{0,x+0.5}}$$

In the cohort without disturbances, one has $Np_{0,x}n_x = e_x$ or $e_x/N = p_{0,x}n_x$, where e_x/N are the number of reduced events without disturbances. Therefore

$$\frac{m'_x}{P_x} = \frac{e_x}{N}\left(\frac{s_{0,x+0.5}}{s'_{0,x+0.5}}\right) \tag{1.3}$$

Finally, $m'_x/P_x = e_x/N$ if $s_{0,x+0.5} = s'_{0,x+0.5}$, that is, if the disturbance identically strikes persons who have and have not experienced the phenomenon studied. In the above example, there should be no differences in mortality between spinsters and ever-marrieds; if this is the case the

---

[39] If there is no migration, let d^*_x and d^{**}_x represent the number of deaths (total population of spinsters and ever-marrieds) in the first and second triangles of the Lexis diagram (Fig. 1.12). If $P_{x+0.5} = \frac{1}{2}(P_x + P_{x+1})$, one must have $d^*_x = d^{**}_x$. If q^*_x and q^{**}_x are the probabilities of dying (total population) relating to the two triangles, and q'_x is the probability of dying (total population) between exact ages x and $x + 1$, one has $P_{x+1} = P_x(1 - q'_x) = P_x(1 - q^*_x)(1 - q^{**}_x)$ and $q'_x = q^*_x + q^{**}_x - q^*_x q^{**}_x$. Since $q^*_x = d^*_x/P_x$ and $q^{**}_x = d^*_x/(P_x - d^*_x)$ if, as assumed, $d^*_x = d^*_x$, then $q^*_x = q'_x/2$ and $q^{**}_x = q'_x/(2 - q'_x)$. Assuming a linear survivorship function implies that $q'_x/2$ corresponds to the probability of dying in the *first* triangle of the Lexis diagram; furthermore, with the same linear condition, $q^{**}_x > q^*_x$; this *implicit assumption* is not valid at young ages (e.g., less than 15 years of age).

observed reduced events m'_x/P_x will be equal to the number of reduced events in the absence of disturbances e_x/N. This assumption has been called the *condition of continuity* by the French demographer L. Henry.[40]

The above conclusion is quite general; it applies to all nonrenewable events characterizing demographic phenomena, which do no exclude persons from observation (natality, nuptiality). As long as the conditions of independence and continuity are satisfied,[41] one can easily compute, for example, the average intensity and duration of the process in a pure state using observed reduced events in place of the unknown ones in the absence of disturbances. The observed reduced events are always obtained by dividing the actual number of events by the average population of the cohort, having or having not experienced the phenomenon studied (see example, Section 1.3.5.3).

The above argument can be extended to the case of intervals greater than one year. For example, if marriages are observed between ages x to $x + n$, one may write

$$\frac{{}_n m'_x}{P_{x+n/2}} = \frac{{}_n e_x}{N} \frac{s_{0,x+n/2}}{s'_{0,x+n/2}}$$

The same conclusion holds once again if the condition of continuity is satisfied.

If the impact of discontinuity is important, one cannot have recourse to observed reduced events without introducing a bias into the evaluation of the intensity and tempo of the process under study. One may then correct the observed reduced events by multiplying them by the ratio $s'_{0,x+0.5}/s_{0,x+0.5}$ if the latter is known. Usually this is not the case, and one has to have recourse to *corrected attrition probabilities*, excluding disturbances,[42] as follows:

Referring to relations (1.2), one may write

$$n_x = \frac{m'_x}{S_x - \frac{1}{2}S_x q_x}$$

$$S_x q_x = \frac{d'_x}{1 - \frac{1}{2}n_x}$$

$$(1.4)$$

[40]With reference to mortality, there should be no *discontinuity* between the states of spinster and ever-married.

[41]The condition of continuity cannot always be assumed. For example, in the case of first marriages, there are slight differences in mortality between spinsters and ever-marrieds; the differences seem more pronounced when migration is also taken into account.

[42]Note that $n_x = m'_x/S_x$ is incorrect, since it does not eliminate the extraneous influence of mortality, which has prevented some marriages to occur due to the death of the spinster.

or

$$\tfrac{1}{2}S_xq_x = d'_x/(2-n_x)$$

Therefore, the probability of first marriage is equal to

$$n_x = \frac{m'_x}{S_x - d'_x/(2-n_x)}$$

from which one derives the quadratic equation

$$-S_xn_x^2 + (2S_x - d'_x + m'_x)n_x - 2m'_x = 0$$

which can be solved for n_x (with $0 \leq n_x \leq 1$):

$$n_x = \left[1+0.5\left(\frac{m'_x}{S_x}-\frac{d'_x}{S_x}\right)\right] - \left\{\left[1+0.5\left(\frac{m'_x}{S_x}-\frac{d'_x}{S_x}\right)\right]^2 - 2\frac{m'_x}{S_x}\right\}^{\frac{1}{2}}$$

At the price of an approximation, it is possible to obtain a much simpler expression for the corrected value of n_x, excluding disturbances. From relation (1.2), $d'_x = S_xq_x - \tfrac{1}{2}S_xq_xn_x$, or $\tfrac{1}{2}d'_x = \tfrac{1}{2}S_xq_x - \tfrac{1}{4}S_xq_xn_x$. Neglecting $\tfrac{1}{4}S_xq_xn_x$ and using $\tfrac{1}{2}d'_x = \tfrac{1}{2}S_xq_x$ in relation (1.4), one obtains the approximate value[43] for the corrected probability eliminating disturbances (see example, Section 1.3.5.1)

$$n_x \cong m'_x/(S_x - \tfrac{1}{2}d'_x) \tag{1.5}$$

In summary, when the conditions of independence and continuity are satisfied, the reduced events in the pure state are equal to the observed reduced events obtained by dividing, at each duration i, the actual number of events ε_i by the total population P_i of the cohort, P_i having or having not been subjected to the phenomenon *studied*.

When the condition of continuity is not satisfied, one can have recourse to the correction factors s'/s or, if the latter are unknown, to the corrected

---

[43]Another way of reasoning is to write $n_x = (m'_x + \Delta)/S_x$, where Δ is the number of marriages that would have been observed among the spinsters who died between x and $x+1$. In other words, $\Delta = m_x - m'_x$ (with $m_x = S_xn_x$). Therefore, $\Delta = S_xn_x - S_xn_x(1-\tfrac{1}{2}q_x) = S_xn_xq_x/2$ and $n_x = (m'_x + \tfrac{1}{2}S_xn_xq_x)/S_x$, from which one derives relation (1.4). Strictly, therefore, one may not write $\Delta = d'_x(\tfrac{1}{2}n_x) = (S_xq_x - \tfrac{1}{2}S_xq_xn_x)(\tfrac{1}{2}n_x)$; one introduces in this case an error term equal to $\tfrac{1}{4}S_xq_xn_x$, which is, however, small with respect to $\tfrac{1}{2}S_xq_xn_x$. The error is the same as the one introduced in relation (1.5): to obtain (1.5), one has assumed the approximation $\tfrac{1}{2}S_xq_x \cong \tfrac{1}{2}d'_x$, which is equal to the approximation introduced here, $\tfrac{1}{2}S_xn_xq_x \cong d'_x(\tfrac{1}{2}n_x)$.

attrition probabilities, which only assume that the condition of independence be satisfied. As long as discontinuity is not too strong, it is much easier to use reduced events: these can be very simply combined to obtain the average intensity and duration[44]; furthermore, they require less sophisticated data than attrition probabilities, since it is not necessary to distinguish between the subcohorts that have and have not already been subjected to the process considered.[45] This distinction is a prerequisite when computing attrition probabilities: Any error introduced in the evaluation of these subcohorts is reflected in the probabilities. This error is not necessarily smaller than the bias due to neglecting discontinuities in the computation of reduced events.

1.3.2.3. Use of Census-Type Data. In the preceding sections, it has been assumed that data were obtained through current population statistics and statistics of population movement. It is possible, however, to obtain very adequate data through the sole use of census-type data[46] if retrospective questions were included. This type of analysis requires, however, that the conditions of independence and continuity be satisfied or, in other words, that the population interviewed is not a particular selected subset of the initial cohort.

In the case, first, of *renewable events,* survivors of the cohort may be interviewed at bound β elapsed since event-origin in view of obtaining data on the number of demographic events and their timing during the period $\alpha - \beta$. From these data, one can derive an average intensity per head defined by

$$\hat{\hat{e}} = \sum_i \varepsilon'_i / P_\beta,$$

where $\sum_i \varepsilon'_i$ is the total number of renewable events recorded and P_β is the actual population number observed at bound β. If the condition of *independence* between observed phenomena and disturbances is satisfied, the reduced events ε'_i / P_β at each duration **i** in the subcohort attaining bound β will not differ from those (denoted ε_i / P_i) that would have been observed by combining, as in Section 1.3.2.1, data from statistics of current population and of population change. Therefore, $\varepsilon'_i / P_\beta = \varepsilon_i / P_i = e_i / N$, where the latter is the number of reduced events that would have been observed

---

[44]Using probabilities, one has usually to derive the whole attrition table in order to obtain average measures of intensity and tempo.

[45]In the above example, it is not necessary to distinguish spinsters from ever-marrieds in order to compute reduced first marriages.

[46]That is, data provided by a census or a survey.

without disturbances. One can then write

$$\hat{\bar{e}} = \bar{e} = \sum_i (e_i/N) = \sum_i (\varepsilon_i'/P_\beta)$$

$$\bar{\imath} = \sum_i \left[i \frac{(e_i/N)}{\bar{e}} \right] = \sum_i \left[i \frac{(\varepsilon_i'/P_\beta)}{\bar{e}} \right]$$

One can thus derive the average measures of intensity and tempo in a pure state from data collected from respondents to a census or survey, having survived disturbances (mortality, migration) until upper bound β.[47]

The same can be said in the case of *nonrenewable events*, as long as the supplementary condition of *continuity* is satisfied. If this is the case, it is simple to derive, for example, the proportion in a pure state of persons in a cohort at bound β, which have not been subjected to the process studied,[48] e.g., the proportion ultimately single.

Let N be the initial population of the cohort at event-origin and $p_{\alpha,\beta}$ the probability (in a pure state) of not experiencing the process studied (e.g., nuptiality) between bounds α and β. The population $Np_{\alpha,\beta}$ would not have experienced the process studied, had there been no disturbances. Actually, the population not being subjected to attrition, either by the process studied or by disturbances, is equal[49] to $Np_{\alpha,\beta}s_{\alpha,\beta}$, where $s_{\alpha,\beta}$ represents the probability of escaping disturbances between α and β. The *proportion* ϕ_β of persons escaping both processes actually observed (e.g., the proportion of surviving spinsters) is

$$\phi_\beta = \frac{Np_{\alpha,\beta}s_{\alpha,\beta}}{Ns_{\alpha,\beta}'}$$

where $s_{\alpha,\beta}'$ represents the probability of escaping disturbances for the whole population (e.g., spinsters and ever-marrieds). If continuity is fulfilled (i.e., if $s_{\alpha,\beta} = s_{\alpha,\beta}'$), $\phi_\beta = p_{\alpha,\beta}$ from which one immediately derives

$$\bar{e}^{(1)} = \sum_i (e_i^{(1)}/N) = 1 - p_{\alpha,\beta}$$

In the above equation $p_{\alpha,\beta}$ represents the proportion ultimately single in the pure state (if there is no discontinuity) and $\bar{e}^{(1)}$ represents the proportion ever married.

---

[47]One immediately notices that this method is impracticable for studying events that *exclude* persons from observation: these persons obviously cannot be interviewed at bound β.

[48]This measure is the complement to unity of the proportion of persons having experienced at least once the process studied, i.e., $\bar{e}^{(1)}$ (see Section 1.2.3).

[49]If the condition of independence is satisfied.

Generally speaking, the proportion of persons in a cohort, having experienced type $E^{(k)}$ event of order k in the surviving population interviewed at bound β, corresponds to the proportion [or average intensity $\sum_i (e_i^{(k)}/N)$] that one would observe in the pure state if independence and continuity are fulfilled. If, through adequate retrospective questions, the exact duration at each event elapsed since event-origin has been recorded the average duration at event $E^{(k)}$ can be computed as usual by the weighted average of durations using $\varepsilon_i^{(k)}/P_\beta$ in place of the unknown reduced events $e_i^{(k)}/N$. P_β denotes the *whole* population of the cohort interviewed at time β, as was also the case above for renewable events. If there is *no selection*, due to disturbances (e.g., mortality, migration), the subcohort P_β interviewed at bound β can be considered to have experienced the process studied in a pure state.[50]

As a conclusion, one can state that the necessary conditions for an adequate *retrospective* analysis are also those required for *continuous* analysis of the process studied, i.e., analysis based on vital statistics. It is therefore possible[51] to replace observations based on continuous registration of vital events by census-type observations including retrospective questions. Furthermore, censuses and especially surveys supply more diversified data than continuous registration of vital events; census-type data also have the advantage of combing events and population numbers from the same universe (in the statistical meaning), which is not the case when one combines statistics on current population with data on population change. It is therefore understandable that any detailed analysis of a particular demographic phenomenon will usually be dealt with through census-type data instead of vital statistics.

1.3.3. Phenomena Excluding Population from Observation

In the preceding section, demographic phenomena were considered that did not exclude population from observation, i.e., natality and nuptiality.[52] In the present section, on the contrary, the argument will be restricted to demographic phenomena that exclude members of the cohort from observation, either through death or emigration. The former phenomena

---

[50]Remember that this is often not the case (see Section 1.3.2.2); measures obtained through retrospective questions are therefore usually biased.

[51]Except for the study of processes excluding persons from observation (mortality, emigration), as noted above.

[52]The study of nuptiality is related to the study of natality, as noted in the Introduction to this textbook.

considered in Section 1.3.2 made people pass from one state to another,[53] e.g., from the state of spinster to the state of ever-married, but the number of members of the cohort remained the same, except by attrition through disturbances. In the case of mortality or emigration, however, persons not only change states but are *excluded* from the cohort; it is therefore impossible to have recourse to the methods outlined in Sections 1.3.2.2 and 1.3.2.3 based on reduced events.

In order to measure the type of phenomenon under consideration, one has to fall back on corrected *attrition probabilities* as developed in Section 1.3.2.2, Eq. (1.5).

Having computed the attrition probabilities for each duration i, using formulas similar to relation (1.5), one proceeds to set up the attrition table (Section, 1.2.5); from the number of events in this table, it is easy to compute the average intensity and tempo of the phenomenon, as in Section 1.2.2. One can also use the following relation; in the attrition table without disturbances, one can write

$$e_i = N_i q_i$$

where e_i is the number of (nonrenewable) events in the table, N_i the number of "survivors" at exact (or completed) duration i, and q_i the attrition probability from duration i to $i + 1$.[54] Hence

$$e_i = \left[N_0 \prod_{j=0}^{i-1} (1 - q_j) \right] q_i$$

where the symbol $\prod$ indicates multiplication. Finally,

$$e_i / N_0 = q_i \prod_{j=0}^{i-1} (1 - q_j)$$

from which it is easy to derive the usual indexes $\bar{e}$ and $\bar{\imath}$ (Section 1.2.2). One should notice, however, that the reduced events thus obtained are entirely derived from the prior knowledge of the attrition probabilities; this method should therefore not be confused with the approach presented in Section 1.3.2.2, where reduced events without disturbances were estimated by observed reduced events; it has already been noted above that the latter method cannot be applied in the case of phenomena excluding persons from observation.

---

[53]If renewable event E is subdivided into a series of nonrenewable events $E^{(k)}$, as in Section 1.3.2.2.

[54]The argument can easily be extended to durations i to $i + n$.

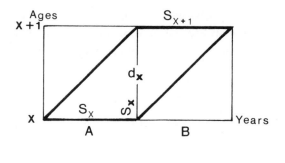

FIGURE 1.13

Another approach is to have recourse to *exposure rates*, as defined in Section 1.2.7. This is sometimes advantageous when one does not have data on the number of survivors at exact duration i, but rather on the number at *completed* duration **i**.[55] Instead of estimating the number of survivors at exact duration i, in order to compute attrition probabilities, one can also compute the corresponding exposure rate and convert it into a probability using the conversion formulas developed in Section 1.2.8 (as in example, Section 1.3.5.2).

Consider, for example (Fig. 1.13), the case of mortality of spinsters disturbed by the influence of nuptiality.[56] It has been shown in Section 1.3.2.2 that the corrected probability of *mortality* for spinsters is

$$q_x = d'_x/[S_x(1-0.5n_x)]$$

where d'_x represents the number of deaths of spinsters actually observed between exact ages x and $x+1$; S_x the number of surviving spinsters at exact age x; and n_x the probability of first marriage between x and $x+1$, in the absence of mortality. The death rate of spinsters can then be written as

$$t_x = d'_x/S_x = d'_x/S_{x+0.5}$$

if events are uniformly distributed from x to $x+1$. As one has

$$d'_x = q_x S_x(1-0.5n_x)$$

$$t_x = [q_x S_x(1-0.5n_x)]/S_{x+0.5}$$

[55]This is usually the case when population figures are obtained by current population statistics (census or survey).

[56]The opposite case has been envisaged in Section 1.3.2.2; various formulas developed previously in this respect can be taken up again here. As before, the condition of *independence* between mortality of spinsters and first marriage is assumed, i.e., the absence of selection.

Let $p_{\alpha,x}$ represent the probability of remaining a spinster between ages α and x, and $s_{\alpha,x}$ the probability of a spinster surviving until age x, knowing she was alive at age α. If N is the initial cohort figure at age α, then

$$t_x = \frac{N p_{\alpha,x} s_{\alpha,x}(1-0.5n_x)q_x}{N p_{\alpha,x+0.5} s_{\alpha,x+0.5}}$$

if the condition of independence is fulfilled. Therefore

$$t_x = e_x / N s_{\alpha,x+0.5}$$

$$= e_x / N_{x+0.5}$$

since $p_{\alpha,x}(1-0.5n_x) \cong p_{\alpha,x+0.5}$ and $s_{\alpha,x}q_x = e_x / N$, where e_x / N is the number of reduced deaths in the absence of disturbances (i.e., nuptiality) and $N_{x+0.5}$ is the number of survivors (to death) in the pure state (without nuptiality). One notices that when the condition of independence is satisfied, the exposure rate in the cohort with disturbances is equal to the rate one would have observed in the absence of disturbances. Assuming that events are evenly distributed between x and $x+1$, one can then evaluate attrition probabilities using the transformation formula

$$q_x = 2t_x / (2+t_x)$$

which has been established in the absence of disturbances (Section 1.2.8).

An advantage of this method is that it requires no data on the number of disturbing events (in this case, first marriages) but only on the number of events characterizing the process studied (i.e., on the number of deaths); this is not the case when attrition probabilities are directly computed, as the number of first marriages (m'_x) are included in the denominator of the probability as a correction factor, i.e.,

$$q_x = d'_x / (S_x - 0.5 m'_x)$$

When events are not uniformly distributed between ages x and $x+1$, the use of the linear transformation formula

$$q_x = 2t_x / (2+t_x)$$

introduces a bias in the estimation of attrition probabilities. The bias due to a nonuniform distribution of the events studied has been previously established (Section 1.2.8). One can show that if the disturbing events are also uniformly distributed between ages x and $x+1$, the probability obtained by the above-mentioned transformation formula is equal to the "corrected" probability obtained by a formula of type (1.5),[57] the latter being a close approximation to the true attrition probability. When disturbing events are not uniformly distributed, all three formulas differ; however, the "corrected" probability given by Eq. (1.5) does not constitute a better approximation of the true probability than the probability obtained by transformation of rates[58]; as the latter requires less data, as noted above, it is at least as satisfactory as the "corrected" probability [Eq. (1.5)].

1.3.4. Final Comments

The fundamental measures of intensity and tempo are usually obtained from observed reduced events in the case of phenomena that do not exclude members of the cohort from observation (natality, nuptiality), events being renewable or not and observation being continuous or retrospective. The method of reduced events is quite adequate as long as the conditions of independence and of continuity are more or less fulfilled. If discontinuity is important, it is better to have recourse to attrition probabilities, which only require the condition of independence to be satisfied; however, the data requirements in this case are heavier than in the case of reduced events.

Considering phenomena that exclude cohort members from observation, the method of observed reduced events is no longer applicable. One must once more fall back on attrition probabilities corrected for the influence of disturbances; the basic measures of intensity and tempo are then derived from these probabilities, most often through the intermediary of the attrition table. It will often be easier to evaluate attrition probabilities by transformation of rates, if studied and disturbing events are evenly distributed over the period considered.

Finally, one has observed in this chapter how cohort analysis relates demographic events to the lifespan of a cohort, between bounds α and β. No attention has been paid up to now to the population itself during a particular year, i.e., the aggregate of the various cohorts observed during that year. As Ryder (1964) has pointed out, demographic analysis moves from individual acts (procreation, death, migration) to cohort processes (fertility, mortality, spatial mobility), and thence to cohorts classified according to the duration elapsed since event-origin. These can be viewed, at any moment in time, as a cross section of cohorts stacked each atop its successor in time, as in a Lexis

---

[57]In the case of spinster mortality, the "corrected" probability is equal to $q_x = d'_x/(S_x - 0.5m'_x)$.

[58]Assuming that the events studied are uniformly distributed over the period.

diagram. This constitutes the composition of the population at that particular moment which, combined with the fertility, mortality, and spatial mobility of the cohorts at that time, yields the number of births, deaths, and migrations that change the size of the population. Cohort analysis is only concerned with the first stages of these processes; period analysis (to be examined in Chapter 2) deals instead with the latter stages.

1.3.5. Examples

1.3.5.1. Attrition Probabilities. Consider the study of adoption and legitimation of illegitimate children disturbed by the extraneous influence of death of illegitimate children. Table 1.6 gives the attrition of 10,000 illegitimate children due to adoption, legitimation, and death.[59]

The corresponding probabilities q_x of attrition by legitimation and adoption, corrected for the influence of mortality, can be computed as outlined in Section 1.3.2.2:

$$q_0 = 0$$

$$q_1 = 615 \Big/ \left(8748 - \frac{181}{2}\right) = 0.0710$$

$$q_2 = 845 \Big/ \left(7952 - \frac{60}{2}\right) = 0.1067$$

$$q_3 = 997 \Big/ \left(7047 - \frac{31}{2}\right) = 0.1418$$

and so on.

1.3.5.2. Exposure Rates. From the same data as above, and supposing uniform distribution of events between exact ages x and $x + 1$, the rate t_x of exposure to legitimation and adoption can be computed as

$$t_0 = 0$$
$$t_1 = 615/[\tfrac{1}{2}(8748 + 7952)] = 0.07365$$
$$t_2 = 845/[\tfrac{1}{2}(7952 + 7047)] = 0.11268$$
$$t_3 = 997/[\tfrac{1}{2}(7047 + 6019)] = 0.15261$$

[59]Adapted from the *Registrar General's Statistical Review of England and Wales for the Year 1965* (Part III). London: H.M.S.O., Table 36A, p. 87.

TABLE 1.6

Age (years)	Number of illegitimate children	Legitimations and adoptions	Deaths of illegitimate children
0	10,000	0	1,252
1	8,748	615	181
2	7,952	845	60
3	7,047	997	31
4	6,019	1,116	24

Transforming rates into probabilities by the formula $q_x = 2t_x/(2 + t_x)$ gives the same results as those computed in Section 1.3.5.1.

1.3.5.3. Reduced Events. Consider now the *total* population of the above cohort, legitimized or not, at each exact age (Table 1.7). According to Section 1.3.2.2, if legitimation (and adoption) and death are considered as independent events, reduced events r_x can be computed by dividing the number of legitimations and adoptions by the total population of the cohort, legitimized or still illegitimate, escaping mortality.

$$r_0 = 0$$

$$r_1 = 615/[\tfrac{1}{2}(8748 + 8554)] = 0.07110$$

$$r_2 = 845/[\tfrac{1}{2}(8554 + 8488)] = 0.09917$$

$$r_3 = 997/[\tfrac{1}{2}(8488 + 8453)] = 0.11770$$

1.3.5.4. Comparison of Results. From Section 1.3.5.1, one can draw up the attrition table (Table 1.8) due to legitimation and adoption in the absence of mortality. Multiplying the number of reduced events in Section 1.3.5.3 by 10,000 gives the number of legitimations and adoptions in the

TABLE 1.7

Exact age (years)	Children surviving to death (legitimized or not)
0	10,000
1	8,748
2	8,554
3	8,488
4	8,453

TABLE 1.8

Age (years)	Illegitimate children	Attrition probabilities	Legitimations and adoptions
0	10,000	0	0
1	10,000	0.0710	710
2	9,290	0.1067	991
3	8,299	0.1418	1,177

TABLE 1.9

Age (years)	Legitimations and adoptions
0	0
1	711
2	992
3	1,177

absence of mortality (Table 1.9). Results derived from reduced events are quite close, in this case, to those obtained by the more elaborate method of setting up an attrition table based on corrected attrition probabilities.

1.4. REFERENCES AND SUPPLEMENTARY BIBLIOGRAPHY

Duchêne, J., & Wijewickrema, S. Note sur les hypothèses d'indépendance et de continuité en démographie. Une approche probabiliste. *Population et Famille*, 1973, *3*, 93–111.

Henry, L. Theoretical research in demography. In *Cold Spring Harbor Symposia on Quantitative Biology* (Vol. XXII). New York: Cold Spring Harbor, 1957, pp. 105–108.

Henry, L. D'un problème fondamental de l'analyse démographique. *Population*, 1959, *14*(1), 9–32.

Henry, L. Approximations et erreurs dans les tables de nuptialité des générations. *Population*, 1963, *18*(4), 737–776.

Henry, L. Analyse et mesure des phénomènes démographiques par cohortes. *Population*, 1966, *21*(3), 465–482.

Henry, L. *Démographie. Analyse et Modèles*. Paris: Librairie Larousse, 1972, p. 341.

Péron, Y. La construction de tables de mortalité abrégées: comparaison de trois méthodes usuelles. *Population*, 1971, *26*(6), 1125–1130.

Pressat, R. *L'Analyse Démographique* (1st ed.). Paris: Presses Universitaires de France, 1961, p. 402.

Pressat, R. *L'Analyse Démographique* (2nd ed.). Paris: Presses Universitaires de France, 1969, p. 321.

Pressat, R. *Demographic Analysis.* Chicago: Aldine Publishing Co., 1972, p. 544. (A translation by J. Matras of the first French edition with a supplementary section on population mathematics translated from the second French edition.)

Reed, A. J., & Merrell, M. A short method for constructing an abridged life table. *The American Journal of Hygiene*, 1939, *30*(2), 33–62.

Ryder, N. B. Notes on the concept of a population. *The American Journal of Sociology*, 1964, *LXIX*(5), 447–463.

Ryder, N. B. The cohort as a concept in the study of social change. *American Sociological Review*, 1965, *30*(6), 843–861.

Ryder, N. B. Cohort analysis. In D. E. Sills (Ed.) *International Encyclopedia of the Social Sciences* (Vol. 2). New York: Macmillan, 1968, pp. 546–550.

Sheps, M. C. On the person years concept in epidemiology and demography. *Milbank Memorial Fund Quarterly*, 1966, *XLIV*(1), 69–91.

Wunsch, G. *Les Mesures de la Natalité*, Department de Démographie, Louvain, 1967, Appendix Tables II–VII.

Wunsch, G. La théorie des événements réduits: application aux principaux phénomènes démographiques. *Recherches Economiques de Louvain*, 1968, *XXXIV*(4), 391–409.

Wunsch, G. L'utilisation des mariages réduits. Étude des perturbations introduites par la mortalité et la mobilité spatiale. *Population et Famille*, 1970, *21*, 1–14.

BASIC PRINCIPLES OF PERIOD ANALYSIS

2

2.1. THE DOUBLE PURPOSE OF PERIOD ANALYSIS

2.1.1. Population Structures

In the present chapter, an approach fundamentally different but complementary to cohort analysis will be presented, i.e., *period analysis* of population change during one or more calendar periods such as years, months, etc.

As stated at the end of Chapter 1, period analysis is concerned with populations, and not with particular cohorts. Populations change in size and composition over time, and one of the major purposes of period analysis is to discern how these changes come about. Changes in population size, as we noted at the end of Chapter 1, are the result of the composition or *structure* of the population at a particular time and of the cohort processes at that time. A major task of period analysis is to discriminate between these two factors in order to measure their respective impact on population change. As we shall also see, a secondary task (of more doubtful value) is to evaluate the intensity and tempo of the cohort processes themselves.

Consider a number of cohorts observed during a calendar period j (a particular year, for example); at each duration i in these cohorts, one can compute rates or reduced events, depending on the process studied, such as (Fig. 2.1)

$$f_i(j) = \varepsilon_i(j)/P_i(j)$$

where $f_i(j)$ represents the rate or reduced events at duration i during year j, $\varepsilon_i(j)$ the number of events (deaths, births, etc.) actually observed in the cohort between completed durations $i-1$ and i during year j, and $P_i(j)$ the average population of the cohort during the year j. The total number of

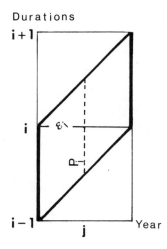

Durations

FIGURE 2.1

events observed during year j will be equal to[1]

$$\sum_i \varepsilon_i(j) = \sum_i P_i(j) f_i(j)$$

The number of events observed during year j is thus equal to the sum of products of average populations at each duration i by the rate or reduced events at this duration, or, in other words, the inner product of a population vector by a frequency vector.

The population vector $(P_0 P_1 \cdots P_\omega)$ will be called the *absolute population structure* at midpoint of year j, i.e., the population distributed according to duration i at a particular point θ in time. One may therefore speak, for example, of the population structure according to age (the age structure)[2] on the 1st of January, the 30th of June, the 31st of December, etc. Often, various population compositions by status are superimposed on structures

[1]In vector notation

$$\sum_i \varepsilon_i = (P_0 P_1 \cdots P_\omega) \begin{pmatrix} f_0 \\ f_1 \\ \vdots \\ f_\omega \end{pmatrix}$$

at time j, or briefly $\sum_i \varepsilon_i(j) = \langle P_i(j) \rangle \langle f_i(j) \rangle$.

[2]The age structure is often represented by a *population pyramid*, i.e., a histogram giving the absolute numbers (or proportions) of males and females by age or age groups (see example, Section 2.5.6).

by durations, giving multiple classifications by age, marital status, profession, etc. Moreover, population structures are often expressed in proportions, giving the *relative population structure*[3] or vector

$$(1/\sum_i P_i)(P_0 P_1 \cdots P_\omega) \quad \text{at time } \theta$$

2.1.2. Standardization and Translation

When one observes during a certain calendar period, j, a total number of events $\sum_i \varepsilon_i = \langle P_i \rangle \langle f_i \rangle$ (in vector notation), two basic questions come to mind:

(1) What is the respective impact of vector $\langle P_i \rangle$ and vector $\langle f_i \rangle$ on the total number of events observed during the period? Demographic analysis must therefore separate, in the study of population change, the impact due to population structure from the impact due to frequencies (rates or reduced events). This will be called hereafter the *standardization approach* in period analysis.

(2) To what extent do the observed frequencies $f_i(j)$ relating to period j reflect the fundamental behavior of the cohorts, i.e., the intensity and tempo of the phenomena considered? This requires the *translation*[4] of period measures into cohort measures.

This double approach in period analysis will be examined in Sections 2.2 and 2.3.

2.2. THE STANDARDIZATION APPROACH AND THE PROBLEM OF SUMMARY INDEXES

The following sections deal with various methods used in the standardization approach that attempt to hold the effect of structures constant. When structure-specific frequencies can be computed (that is, when events are classified according to the relevant durations and the corresponding population structures are available), one can have recourse to such methods as "direct standardization," frequency averaging, or "principal components"

---

[3]Very often, when one speaks of population structures, one implicitly refers to *relative* structures.

[4]The term has been brought into demography by Ryder (1964a).

analysis. When events are not classified according to the composition of the population but the population structure is known, "indirect standardization" can be used. In the worst case, when only the total numbers of events and population are known, one has to fall back on an unsophisticated index called the "crude rate" of occurrence. Finally, the respective impact of both composition and frequencies can be evaluated through "double standardization" techniques.

2.2.1. Direct Standardization

When the necessary data are available, the standardization problem is easily solved by computing the frequencies $f_i(j)$ (rates or reduced events) specific for each duration i during calendar period j. The sequence of duration-specific frequencies $f_i(j) = \varepsilon_i(j)/P_i(j)$ is obviously independent of the population structure[5] at time j. In view of comparing various sequences of frequencies at different points in time (or for different areas), the sequence can be summarized by the sum $\sum_{i=\alpha}^{\beta} f_i(j)$ at time[6] j, where α and β are, as before, the bounds of variability of the phenomenon considered (Section 1.1.2). When various duration intervals are used between α and β, frequencies should be weighted by the corresponding interval $\sum_{i=\alpha}^{\beta} n_n f_i(j)$.

Notice that the sum $\sum_i f_i(j)$ can be considered as the inner product $\langle 1 \rangle \langle f_i(j) \rangle$, i.e., as the application of the vector of frequencies $\langle f_i(j) \rangle$ to the population vector $\langle 1 \rangle$, i.e., a *"rectangular" population structure* comprised of one person at each duration. This arbitrary population is called a *standard population* and the method is called *direct standardization* of frequencies $f_i(j)$. The argument can be extended to include any arbitrary standard population (see example, Section 2.5.3).

For example, populations A and B exhibit, respectively, sequences f_i and ψ_i at time j; these sequences can be compared by their sums $\sum_{i=\alpha}^{\beta} f_i(j)$ and $\sum_{i=\alpha}^{\beta} \psi_i(j)$, but one may also choose an arbitrary[7] population structure K_i and compare the standardized indexes[8] $\sum_i K_i f_i(j)$ and $\sum_i K_i \psi_i(j)$. The choice of the standard population being arbitrary, different standards will

---

[5] The frequency $_n f_i = {}_n\varepsilon_i/{}_nP_i$ is, however, dependent on the population structure at durations i to $i+n$. For small values of n, this problem can be neglected.

[6] Notice that this sum is a *period* measure: it is not computed for a particular cohort as in Chapter 1.

[7] Theoretically, it is irrelevant which structure is chosen. Usually, one takes as standard a population structure similar to the populations considered.

[8] Usually one compares $\sum K_i f_i(j)/\sum K_i$ to $\sum K_i \psi_i(j)/\sum K_i$. The denominator being the same, this further refinement is, however, superfluous.

yield different comparisons[9]; it is therefore quite adequate to compare solely sums of frequencies instead of weighting by a standard (nonrectangular) population, unless one particularly wishes to give more importance to frequencies at particular durations. Standardized "rates" have no intrinsic value (as the standard population is arbitrary) and are used for comparative purposes only.

2.2.2. Frequency Averaging

Instead of having recourse to direct standardization, it is quite satisfactory to compare the averages of the frequency sequences. Using the same example as in Section 2.2.1, one may compute, among others, the *arithmetic mean* of the frequencies $f_i(j)$ and $\psi_i(j)$ and compare these averages, i.e., $\sum_i f_i(j)/m$, where m indicates the number of frequencies computed between bounds α and β. The method can easily be extended to cover observations with variable duration intervals[10] i to $i+n$.

Other types of means (see example, Section 2.5.2) can sometimes be preferred[11]; furthermore, complementary measures such as the variance of the distributions can also be compared in addition to the averages.

Notice that, in the case of arithmetic averages, the method yields a summary index very similar to a directly standardized index. The direct standardization method would imply comparison between $\sum_i f_i(j)$ and $\sum_i \psi_i(j)$, using a "rectangular" standard population; the arithmetic average method compares $\sum_i f_i(j)/m$ to $\sum_i \psi_i(j)/m$. The *ratio* of summary indexes is thus the same in this case, as the numerators of the measures are identical in both methods. Arithmetic averaging in this case involves a superfluous division by the number of frequencies.

2.2.3. Principal Components Analysis

A more theoretically sound approach to summarizing data standardized for population structures is to apply *principal components analysis* to the set of frequency sequences. Consider, for example, n areas for which one has computed a sequence of frequencies $f_i(j)$ at a specified period of time, j

---

[9]See, e.g., Wunsch (1969). For a thorough discussion of standardization, see Kitagawa (1964).
[10]The method consists, in that case, in computing the weighted arithmetic mean of the frequencies, weights being the various duration intervals n.
[11]In this case of mortality, for instance, there are good reasons for preferring the *geometric* mean as a summational index of mortality; see Schoen (1970), who has introduced an index based on the geometric mean of ratios of corresponding rates.

TABLE 2.1. Frequencies (Variables)

Areas	Scores			
	f_0	f_1	$\ldots$	f_ω
1	$f_0(1)$	$f_1(1)$	$\ldots$	$f_\omega(1)$
2	$f_0(2)$	$f_1(2)$	$\ldots$	$f_\omega(2)$
3	$f_0(3)$	$f_1(3)$	$\ldots$	$f_\omega(3)$
$\vdots$	$\vdots$	$\vdots$		$\vdots$
n	$f_0(n)$	$f_1(n)$	$\ldots$	$f_\omega(n)$

indicating this time a particular area.[12] This set of sequences can be presented in a *data matrix* of the type presented in Table 2.1.

The various frequencies at each duration can be considered as a set of scores for each area from which *principal components*[13] (i.e., linear combinations of variables) can be derived, such as $F = a_0 f_0 + a_1 f_1 + \cdots + a_\omega f_\omega$. Having identified the principal components by routine procedures, one can retain only the most significant variables (i.e., those highly correlated with the principal axes) for area comparisons.[14] This method does away with the arbitrary choice of variables vitiating standardizing and averaging techniques presented in the preceding sections. These theoretical advantages are, however, compensated for by the cumbersome amount of work involved in deriving principal components. Contrary to the more traditional methods of Sections 2.2.1 and 2.2.2, principal components analysis practically implies having resort to a computer; moreover, the method is usually not recommended when the number n of areas is small with respect to the number of variables (frequencies).[15]

2.2.4. Crude Rates; Indirect Standardization

Suppose now that available data are not adequate for the computation of frequencies: the population structure is known but only the *total* number of events has been recorded during the calendar period considered. As these

[12] j varies therefore from 1 to n.

[13] Principal components are pairwise uncorrelated; a small number of components usually account for a large proportion of the variance of the variables.

[14] For examples in fertility and mortality analysis see Le Bras (1971, 1972).

[15] For a discussion of this problem see Rummel (1970, pp. 219–220). This reference also contains a good description of the various techniques.

events are not distributed by duration, it is impossible to evaluate rates or reduced events. One can, however, take the ratio of the total number of events to the total midperiod population $E(j)/\sum_i P_i(j)$, where $E(j)$ denotes the total number of events $\sum_i \varepsilon_i(j)$ observed during calendar period j. This ratio is called in demographic analysis a *crude "rate,"* the term "rate" being understood here as "ratio"[16] and not in the strict meaning defined in Section 1.2.7.

These crude "rates" are, however, inadequate when trying to distin-guish the respective influences of frequencies and population structure on population change; their sole advantage is to standardize for the *total* population figure in area or period comparisons. Usually crude "rates" are expressed as the number of events (births, deaths, etc.) per "1000 persons" during the specified period, i.e., the ratio $E(j)/\sum_i P_i(j)$ is multiplied by 1000, the choice of 1000 persons being perfectly arbitrary.

Taking into account the separate influences of frequencies and struc-tures in spatial or temporal comparisons, one can resort to a method known as *indirect standardization.* As above, only the total number of events and the midperiod population structure[17] are known. Let E and E' represent the total number of events recorded for two populations A and B with respective population structures P_i and L_i. Choose an *arbitrary* sequence of frequencies g_i (the *standard* frequency sequence) and compute the ratios of actual to hypothetical events

$$E/\sum_i P_i g_i, \qquad E'/\sum_i L_i g_i \qquad (2.1)$$

These ratios can be written as

$$\frac{\sum_i P_i f_i}{\sum_i P_i} \bigg/ \frac{\sum_i P_i g_i}{\sum_i P_i}$$

and

$$\frac{\sum_i L_i \psi_i}{\sum_i L_i} \bigg/ \frac{\sum_i L_i g_i}{\sum_i L_i}$$

where f_i and ψ_i represent the unknown sequences of frequencies for

[16] As noted in Section 1.2.7, when this is the case, the term "rate" will be put in quotation marks.
[17] If the population structure is not known [i.e., if only the *total* population $P = \sum_i P_i(j)$ is enumerated], indirect standardization is impossible: only crude "rates" can be computed.

populations A and B. One notices that the indirectly standardized indexes[18] [Eq. (2.1)] correspond to the ratio of weighted averages of actual to standard frequencies, weights being the actual population structures. Indirect standardization, therefore, enables one to compare the sequences of actual (but unknown) frequencies f_i and ψ_i in terms of a sequence of standard frequencies. It is important to note that in relation (2.1) the ratios have no specific meaning, as the choice of the standard frequencies g_i is arbitrary; as in the case of direct standardization, indirect standardization yields solely *comparative indexes* of no intrinsic value (see example, Section 2.5.4). Once again, as in the case of direct standardization, various standards yield different comparisons. Indirect standardization is, however, a valuable tool when available data are inadequate for computing frequencies; in this case, comparisons between indirectly standardized indexes are much less influenced by differences in population structures than comparisons between crude "rates." Indirectly standardized indexes are also recommended when population figures are small. In this case, even if it is possible to compute the frequency sequence from available data, the computed rates or reduced events may be highly erratic due to the small numbers; indirectly standardized measures may therefore sometimes be preferred to the actual frequencies in spatial or temporal comparisons.

2.2.5. Double Standardization Techniques

In Sections 2.2.1–2.2.4, various methods were presented whose purposes were to eliminate the influence of population structures on the study of population change by holding these structures constant from one period of time to the other or from one area to the other. One may also adopt the converse point of view: frequencies can be held constant, in spatial or temporal comparisons, in view of studying the sole impact of population structures on population movement.

As before, for two populations A and B, let E and E' represent the total number of events observed during a certain period of time. Let P_i and L_i be the corresponding population structures, f_i and ψ_i the frequencies for populations A and B. The sole influence of differential frequencies will be given by[19] $\sum_i P_i f_i$ and $\sum_i P_i \psi_i$; the sole influence of differential population

---

[18]Usually, ratios (2.1) are multiplied by the crude "rate" in the *standard* population; this procedure is, however, superfluous.

[19]One can also write $\sum_i L_i f_i$ and $\sum_i L_i \psi_i$ or use any other standard population.

structures is expressed by the comparison between $\sum_i P_i \psi_i$ and $\sum_i L_i \psi_i$.[20] Multiply both *relative* differences between standardized indexes to yield

$$\frac{E'}{E} = \left(\frac{\sum_i P_i \psi_i}{\sum_i P_i f_i} \right) \left(\frac{\sum_i L_i \psi_i}{\sum_i P_i \psi_i} \right) \tag{2.2}$$

Since $\sum_i P_i f_i = E$ and $\sum_i L_i \psi_i = E'$, i.e., the number of events observed in populations A and B, the above product yields the relative difference between the total number of events observed E'/E. The above multiplication can thus be considered as a *double standardization* for structures and frequencies[21]; the relative difference between the total number of events can thus be decomposed into two parts, the first $(\sum P_i \psi_i / \sum P_i f_i)$ indicating the relative difference of frequencies, and the second $(\sum L_i \psi_i / \sum P_i \psi_i)$ the relative difference of population structures.

Instead of applying double standardization to the relative differences between the total number of events observed, one can also resort to double standardization of the *absolute difference* between the number of events. One can derive the following expressions[22]:

$$\begin{aligned} E' - E &= \sum_i L_i \psi_i - \sum_i P_i f_i \\ &= \sum_i \psi_i (L_i - P_i) + \sum_i P_i (\psi_i - f_i) \end{aligned} \tag{2.3}$$

The first sum represents the component due to differential population structures and the second sum the component due to differential frequencies. This method can easily be extended to measure the components of a difference between two crude "rates" (Kitagawa, 1955). Let $P = \sum_i P_i$ and

---

[20]This may also be expressed as a comparison between $\sum_i P_i g_i$ and $\sum_i L_i g_i$ for any standard set of frequencies.

[21]Formula (2.2) can also be considered as the product of the ratio of frequencies *indirectly* standardized (ψ_i being used as standard) by the ratio of structures *directly standardized* (ψ_i again being used as standard):

$$\frac{(\sum L_i \psi_i / \sum L_i \psi_i)}{(\sum P_i f_i / \sum P_i \psi_i)} (\sum L_i \psi_i / \sum P_i \psi_i) = E'/E$$

[22]Writing $\psi_i = f_i + \alpha_i$ and $L_i = P_i + \beta_i$, another approach is to use $E' - E = \sum (P_i + \beta_i)(f_i + \alpha_i) - \sum P_i f_i$, i.e., $\sum (L_i - P_i) f_i + \sum (\psi_i - f_i) P_i + \sum \alpha_i \beta_i$. Neglecting $\sum \alpha_i \beta_i$ one then breaks the difference $E' - E$ into the two components $\sum (L_i - P_i) f_i$ and $\sum (\psi_i - f_i) P_i$.

$L = \sum_i L_i$, then

$$\frac{E'}{L} - \frac{E}{P} = \sum_i \psi_i \left(\frac{L_i}{L} - \frac{P_i}{P} \right) + \sum_i \frac{P_i}{P}(\psi_i - f_i)$$

$$= \sum_i 0.5(\psi_i + f_i)\left(\frac{L_i}{L} - \frac{P_i}{P} \right) + \sum_i 0.5\left(\frac{P_i}{P} + \frac{L_i}{L} \right)(\psi_i - f_i)$$

with the last expression using the *average* frequencies and structures as standards.

Equations (2.2) and (2.3) above are quite general, as is the extension to the difference between crude "rates."[23] Knowing frequencies and population structures, it is therefore always possible to decompose population change during a certain period of time into two components taking into account the differences (relative or absolute) between frequencies on the one hand, and the difference between structures on the other hand.

2.3. THE TRANSLATION APPROACH

2.3.1. The Fictitious Cohort Method

During a certain period of time j (a calendar year, for example), one has computed for the phenomenon considered the sequence of frequencies $f_i(j)$ for all durations i between bounds α and β. These frequencies relate to all the cohorts observed between bounds α and β during period j (see Fig. 2.2), i.e., to a number $(\beta - \alpha) + 1$ of cohorts (Section 1.1.6). The basic question in the *translation* approach is the following: can one deduce the average intensity and tempo of the process studied from the frequencies (reduced events, rates) computed during period j, or in other words, can one translate period measures into cohort measures?

The traditional answer to this question has been to apply the period frequencies to a *fictitious cohort*[24] composed of an arbitrary number of persons (e.g., 1,000 or 10,000) at event-origin. For example, if frequencies

---

[23]Relation (2.2) can be extended to take into account the *relative* difference between crude "rates" as follows:

$$\frac{E'/L}{E/P} = \frac{\sum_i (P_i/P)\psi_i \sum_i (L_i/L)\psi_i}{\sum_i (P_i/P)f_i \sum_i (P_i/P)\psi_i}$$

[24]Synonyms are hypothetical cohort and synthetic cohort, and corresponding measures will be called *synthetic measures*.

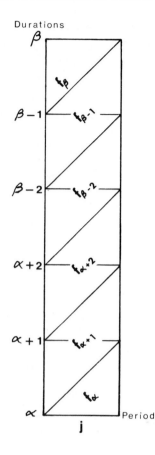

Durations

FIGURE 2.2

$f_i(j)$ are reduced events, an estimate of the average intensity and tempo of the process is obtained by the usual cohort procedure seen in Section 1.3.2, i.e.,

$$\hat{\bar{e}} = \sum_i f_i(j) \qquad \text{and} \qquad \hat{\bar{t}} = \sum_i if_i(j)/\hat{\bar{e}}$$

where the symbol $\hat{\ }$ denotes an estimate.

If $f_i(j)$ is a rate (as defined in Section 1.2.7), an estimate of the average intensity and tempo is obtained by constructing a fictitious attrition table, using the same procedure as defined in Section 1.3.3.

The fictitious cohort method is, however, open to criticism. First, period j might be badly chosen. For example, synthetic measures of fertility computed during wartime do not reflect the actual experience of a cohort observed through life, as couples usually tend to postpone births under these circumstances.[25] Wartime experience cannot be considered as representative of the experience of a real cohort observed between bounds α and β.

Second, even if the period of time is not peculiar, period synthetic measures of intensity, which summarize the behavior of many cohorts, usually do not adequately reflect the true cohort intensity, as the period measures are also dependent on the tempo of events (as defined in Section 1.2.1.1) in the cohorts considered (see example, Section 2.5.5). Conversely, synthetic period tempo measures do not usually correspond to true cohort measures, as they are also influenced by cohort intensities.[26] This bias, called "*distributional distortion*" by Ryder,[27] is the topic of the following section.

2.3.2. Distributional Distortion and Translation Models

In view of showing the impact of distributional distortion, consider a situation where the average intensity $\bar{e}$ is constant from one cohort to the other; only the cohort tempo of events is variable. For example, the average number of children per woman is constant, but the timing of births differs from one birth-cohort to another. Denote

$$\bar{e} = \sum_{x=0}^{\omega} \frac{e_{xg}}{Ng}$$

where e_{xg}/Ng is the number of reduced events at age x for cohort g. The tempo of the process is characterized, for each cohort g, by the distribution of reduced events e_{xg}/Ng by duration elapsed since event-origin, age in this case, or (what amounts to the same) by the distribution of *relative* reduced events $(e_{xg}/N_g)/\bar{e}$, which will be denoted by the expression k_{xg}.

Suppose now that the ratios k_{xg} vary in a linear way[28] from one cohort to the other; one can therefore write $k_{xg} = a_x + b_x g$ (*a* and *b* being constant

[25] Period measures of fertility computed during the Great Depression in the thirties yielded quite alarming conclusions on the future population in developed countries; these measures were, however, drastically influenced by temporary postponement of births during that period.

[26] It is only in a strictly stationary situation (constant intensity and tempo) that period measures would correspond to cohort measures.

[27] The problem considered here has been thoroughly studied by Ryder in a number of articles, especially in Ryder (1956).

[28] The present model is adapted from Pressat (1969).

for each age x). Then

$$\sum_x k_{xg} = \sum_x a_x + g \sum_x b_x$$

and as $\sum_x k_{xg} = 1$, one has $\sum_x a_x + g\sum_x b_x = 1$ for all g.

This condition is satisfied if $\sum_x a_x = 1$ and $\sum_x b_x = 0$. Computing the average duration μ for cohort g gives

$$\mu = \sum_x xk_{xg}$$

$$= \sum_x xa_x + g \sum_x xb_x$$

Using the *derivative* with respect to g

$$\mu' = \sum_x xb_x \qquad \text{of constant value}$$

Consider now reduced events in period analysis; during a certain calendar period, one can compute the average synthetic *period* intensity $\bar{E}$ by the fictitious cohort method:

$$\bar{E} = \sum_{x=0}^{\omega} \bar{e}k_{xg}$$

$$= \bar{e} \sum_{x=0}^{\omega} (a_x + gb_x)$$

Denoting the most recent cohort as $g = 0$, and the immediately preceding cohort as $g = -1$, etc., the above expression can be written as

$$\bar{E} = \bar{e} \sum_{x=0}^{\omega} (a_x - xb_x)$$

as cohort $g = 0$ is observed at age 0, cohort $g = -1$ at age $1, \ldots$, cohort $g = -x$ at age x. It has been shown that $\sum_x a_x = 1$ and $\sum_x xb_x = \mu'$; therefore the synthetic period intensity $\bar{E}$ becomes

$$\bar{E} = \bar{e}(1 - \mu')$$

When the average duration μ decreases from one cohort to another, its derivative μ' is negative and therefore $\bar{E} > \bar{e}$; the converse is true when μ is increasing.

One can therefore write $\bar{E} = \Delta\bar{e}$. When the cohort average duration is decreasing, Δ will be greater than 1 and $\bar{E} > \bar{e}$. The symbol Δ in this case represents the distributional distortion due to changing cohort tempos. A similar model could be derived in order to show that synthetic tempo measures are influenced by changing cohort intensities.

Though quite crude, the above *translation model* shows that fictitious period measures can be misleading due to distributional distortions. When basic cohort trends are known, it is possible to construct more sophisticated translation models (see, e.g., Ryder, 1964) enabling one to translate period measures into cohort measures (or vice versa), taking into account a correction factor eliminating distributional distortions. This approach is quite adequate for historical studies where cohort and period data are available; as one is never quite sure of future cohort trends, however, translation models do not necessarily yield adequate population forecasts.

As a final comment, one should in any case abandon, in the translation approach, the sole use of synthetic measures based on the fictitious cohort method. The translation approach of evaluating cohort behavior from period measures can never be quite conclusive; one should in any case derive period measures over a sufficiently long period of time, in order to eliminate *temporary* changes in the behavior of cohorts (e.g., temporary postponement of births). Moreover, even elaborate translation models are only second best to a true cohort approach in view of evaluating the actual intensity and tempo of a process. Synthetic measures may, however, be used in what we have formerly called the standardization approach (Section 2.2). In this case, they measure the behavior of the population during a particular period, holding the impact of population structures constant, and can be used as any standardized index with no reference whatever to cohort intensity or tempo.

2.3.3. The Identification Problem

In Section 2.3.2, it was shown that a particular dependent variable (i.e., the number of reduced events at a certain age) is not only influenced by period effects but also by duration effects. This problem can now be generalized further by stating that most if not all demographic phenomena are the result of period, cohort, and duration effects. For example, marital fertility in a marriage-cohort depends at a certain point in time on the particular conditions of the period in question (an economic depression, for example, would tend to lower the fertility rate), on the duration of marriage (a high duration is usually associated with an achieved desired family size, among others, and therefore fertility rates at this duration would tend to be low), and on the particular marriage-cohort if one assumes, following Ryder, that members of a cohort tend to behave somewhat similarly as their marital life evolves in the same socioeconomic context. These three effects are, however, confounded and the basic principles of demographic analysis developed up to now do not enable one to distinguish the separate effects of cohort, duration, and period on the dependent variable, even though one knows that they may be operating.

The way to resolve this problem is to place constraints on the model, i.e., to specify one effect (one parameter) in order to estimate the other two. There is, however, no general solution[29]: it all depends on the specification of the parameter one wishes to adopt. In some cases, one could ignore one of the effects, for example, suppose that there is no cohort effect; this solution is inadequate, however, if we consider the three effects as distinct. A more satisfactory solution is to define a model specifying the effect of the three variables and their possible interaction on the dependent variable. One could consider, for example, that adjacent cohorts do not present different cohort effects, as they evolve practically in the same socioeconomic context; in that case, divergent rates are due solely to duration and/or period effects. Another approach would be to specify the trend of the cohort intensity of the process, considering changes in cohort effects to be slow; changes in rates could therefore once again be related to duration and period effects. One could also set the pattern of the relationship between the dependent variable and duration, such as fitting a gamma function to age-specific fertility rates (reduced births), thus specifying the duration effect in this particular case. Unless one is willing to make these strong assumptions, the nature of which depend on the problem under study, it is impossible to disentangle the various time effects on the dependent variable. Unfortunately, as Mason *et al.* (1973) have shown, estimates derived from different models can be quite distinct and can therefore lead to different conclusions about the separate effects of the three parameters.

2.4. POPULATION STRUCTURES AND MOVEMENT

2.4.1. Generalized Period Frequencies

Until now, period frequencies have been limited to rates (in the strict meaning) or reduced events. However, *in the standardization approach* this restriction is unnecessary. Let P_i and P_{i+1} represent a population

---

[29]For a recent discussion, see Mason *et al.* (1973).

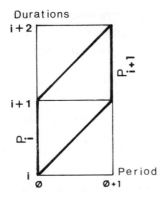

FIGURE 2.3

enumerated at completed durations **i** and **i+1** at point of time ϕ and $\phi+1$ (see Fig. 2.3). One can obviously write $P_{i+1} = P_i - \sum_y \varepsilon_{i+1,y}$ where $\varepsilon_{i+1,y}$ is the number of demographic events of type y (e.g., deaths, in- and out-migration) observed at average duration $i+1$ in the cohort. Denoting $P_{i+0.5}$ as the average population of the cohort between completed durations **i** and **i+1**, a *generalized period frequency* can now be defined as $f_{i+1,y} = \varepsilon_{i+1,y}/P_{i+0.5}$ for a specified y. This measure simply indicates the relative population change due to events $\varepsilon_{i+1,y}$ between completed durations **i** and **i+1**. As before, one can write $\sum_i \sum_y \varepsilon_{i,y} = \sum_i \sum_y f_{i,y} P_i$, the total number of events is the product sum of frequencies by population structures. Whatever the type of event, one can therefore always distinguish, in the standardization approach, the respective impact of structures and frequencies on population change. Frequencies $f_{i,y}$ can always be summarized, moreover, by one of the methods presented in Section 2.2.

It is important to note, however, that these period frequencies can be converted into the usual cohort measures (*the translation approach*) only if they correspond to rates or reduced events. For example, one can compute period immigration frequencies by dividing the number of immigrants recorded during a specified period of time by the average population during that period. These immigration frequencies, however, have no cohort counterparts,[30] as immigration is an extraneous process to the cohort considered. One can therefore compute adequate period measures in the

---

[30]That is to say, immigration cannot be studied in a cohort by the traditional methods presented in Chapter 1 (attrition probabilities, exposure rates, reduced events). See also Section 6.5.1 for a further treatment of this issue.

standardization approach that have no sense in the translation approach or in a true cohort approach. This is because at the present state of demographic analysis the two approaches of cohort analysis remain basically different in purpose[31]: the former is a tool for deriving the intensity and tempo of the process, the latter is a method of marking out the respective impact of populations structures and frequencies upon change. Both approaches are equally necessary but they have remained irreducible to each other up to now. A solution to this problem would consist in extending cohort analysis to incorporate the *whole* experience of a cohort with respect to the components of population change, i.e., to include immigration as well. Cohort replacement (or *reproduction* ·as it is called) would then not only cover birth and death[32] but also in- and out-migration. Period analysis could then be considered as the study of segmented cohort experiences over specified periods of time, and population *projections* would consist in extending cohort experience into the future. One could therefore make use of the *same* type of measures (indexes) in cohort and period analysis, as well as in population projections.

This goal, however, has not yet been attained,[33] and one therefore encounters different types of measures in cohort and period analysis, and in population projections.

2.4.2. Period Frequencies, Rates, and Reduced Events

It has been noted in the previous section that period frequencies do not necessarily correspond to rates or reduced events as defined in Chapter 1. In many cases, however, period frequencies do correspond to rates or reduced events, though slight adaptations are sometimes necessary. Consider, for example, Fig. 2.4a. Let M_{x+1} represent the number of first marriages actually observed between completed ages x and $x+1$ during period j, where C_x and C_{x+1} represents the number of spinsters recorded at those ages. Period frequency $M_{x+1}/0.5(C_x + C_{x+1})$ can be considered as a true marriage rate.[34] The same is true in Fig. 2.4b: period frequency $M_{x+1}/0.5(P_x + P_{x+1})$ can be considered as true reduced marriages[35] if P_x and P_{x+1} denote the total population (spinsters and ever-marrieds) at completed durations i and $i+1$.

---

[31]That is, if one neglects the translation approach which is, as a matter of fact, only a substitute for cohort analysis.
[32]As in the case of traditional measures of *gross and net reproduction* (see Section 5.2.4).
[33]For a good overview of this problem, see Ryder (1964, especially pp. 453–456).
[34]If events are evenly distributed and if the condition of independence is satisfied.
[35]If the supplementary condition of continuity is fulfilled.

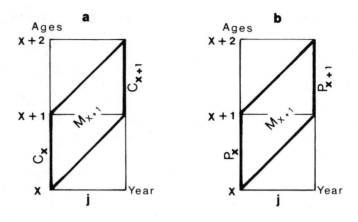

FIGURE 2.4

Consider now Figs. 2.5a and b. Marriages are here recorded by age only and not by cohort, and populations are given at completed age **x** at the beginning and end of the year. These population numbers obviously refer to different cohorts; however, period frequencies can nevertheless be computed by the expressions

$$\frac{M_{x+0.5}}{0.5(C'_x + C''_x)} \quad \text{and} \quad \frac{M_{x+0.5}}{0.5(P'_x + P''_x)}$$

Strictly speaking, these measures are not equivalent any more to a particular cohort rate or reduced events, as the above indexes refer to two cohorts. If cohort experiences do not differ too much, one can very often assume that the period frequencies computed above are approximately equal to a true rate or reduced events in a cohort observed between *exact* ages x to $x + 1$. As

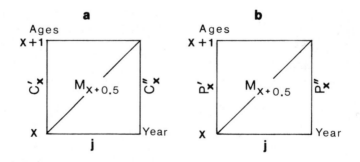

FIGURE 2.5

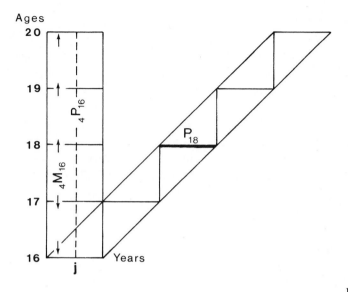

FIGURE 2.6

events are very often not recorded by duration *and* cohort, one is frequently forced to compute the *hybrid-type* rate or reduced events presented here.

Another problem consists in translating period frequencies computed over *groups* of durations into rates or reduced events. Consider, for instance, Fig. 2.6. The number of first marriages between exact ages 16 and 20, during calendar year j, is denoted $_4M_{16}$, and the midyear population (spinsters and ever-marrieds) aged 16 to 20 is represented by $_4P_{16}$. Period first-marriage frequency for exact ages 16 to 20 is computed by the ratio $_4f_{16} = {_4M_{16}}/{_4P_{16}}$. Suppose now that the fictitious cohort approach is adopted. In order to compute reduced first marriages in the hypothetical cohort between ages 16 and 20 one divides the number of first marriages by the mean population[36] in the age group, i.e., P_{18} (see Section 1.3.2.2): $_4r_{16} = {_4M_{16}}/P_{18}$. Now P_{18} is more or less equal to one-fourth of $_4P_{16}$; therefore, in order to estimate fictitious *reduced events* from period frequencies, one has to multiply the latter by the interval of the age group, in this case four $_4r_{16} \cong 4 _4f_{16}$. In general, one can therefore write $_nr_x = n _nf_x$; the synthetic average intensity is thus equal to

$$\hat{e} = \sum_x {_nr_x} = \sum_x n_x \, {_nf_x}$$

[36]Considering that events are uniformly distributed over the period.

If a constant interval n (e.g., five-year age groups) is used between bounds α and β, one can also write $\hat{\bar{e}} = n \sum_x {}_n f_x$.

When period frequencies correspond to *rates* (in the strict meaning), there is no problem of this sort. Denoting ${}_4C_{16}$ as the midyear population of spinsters during calendar year j, the synthetic first-marriage rate is equivalent to the period frequency of first marriages ${}_4M_{16}/{}_4C_{16}$, since the denominator ${}_4C_{16}$ can be considered approximately equal to the number of person-years of exposure to first marriage[37] between exact ages 16 and 20. Remember, however, that (in all usual cases) application of the fictitious cohort method is subject to the restrictions outlined in Sections 2.3.1 and 2.3.2.

2.5. EXAMPLES

2.5.1. Types of Rates

Consider the data[38] in Table 2.2. The following types of rates can be computed:

(a) the "hybrid" rate at completed age 0 (Fig. 2.7):

$$t_0 = \frac{481 + 2,603}{\frac{1}{2}(143,300 + 139,387)}$$

$$= 0.02182$$

(b) the "true" rate between exact ages (Fig. 2.8):

$$t_0 = \frac{2,893 + 481}{143,300}$$

$$= 0.02355$$

(c) the "true" rate between completed ages (Fig. 2.9):

$$t_1 = \frac{481 + 122}{\frac{1}{2}(143,300 + 142,697)}$$

$$= 0.00422$$

---

[37]In the fictitious cohort, the number of person-years of exposure is equal to $\int_{16}^{20} C_t \, dt$; this definite integral is approximately equivalent to $\sum_{16}^{20} C_i$, i.e., ${}_4C_{16}$.

[38]Source: *Annuaire Statistique de la Belgique* (Vols. 90 and 91), Institut National de Statistique, Brussels, 1970.

TABLE 2.2

Year	Completed age (years)	Birth cohort	Deaths	Survivors[a]
1967	0	1967	2,893	143,300
1968	0	1968	2,603	139,387
1968	0	1967	481	—
1968	1	1967	122	142,697

[a] On December 31st.

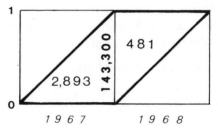

FIGURE 2.7

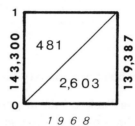

FIGURE 2.8

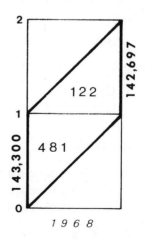

FIGURE 2.9

TABLE 2.3. Age-Specific General Fertility Rates

Age groups (in completed years)	USA (×1000)	Ireland (×1000)
15–19	68.9	13.4
20–24	174.0	127.1
25–29	142.6	230.6
30–34	79.3	211.3
35–39	38.5	143.2
40–44	10.6	54.5
45–49	0.7	4.2

2.5.2. The Problem of Summary Indexes

Consider in Table 2.3 the age-specific general fertility "rates," i.e., the ratio of births in a particular age group and calendar year to the average number of females in the age groups during the year, for the USA, 1967 and for Ireland 1966.[39]

In order to compare the average fertility between the USA and Ireland, the following summary indexes can be computed (Sections 2.2.1 and 2.2.2):

(a) the sum of "rates" (×1000):

USA: 514.6
Ireland: 784.3   ratio: $\dfrac{784.3}{514.6} = 1.5241$

(b) the arithmetic average of "rates" (×1000):

USA: 73.51
Ireland: 112.04   ratio: $\dfrac{112.04}{73.51} = 1.5241$

(c) the geometric average of "rates" (×1000):

USA: 32.55
Ireland: 59.75   ratio: $\dfrac{59.75}{32.55} = 1.8356$

2.5.3. Direct Standardization

In addition to the above-mentioned age-specific general fertility "rates," consider the *relative* population structures for the female populations of the USA and Ireland (Table 2.4).

[39]Source: *United Nations Demographic Yearbook*, New York: United Nations, 1968 and 1969.

TABLE 2.4. Proportion of Females

Age groups (in completed years)	USA (×10,000)	Ireland (×10,000)
15–19	868	878
20–24	744	631
25–29	601	517
30–34	547	507
35–39	582	542
40–44	626	574
45–49	602	577
All ages 0 to ω	10,000	10,000

Direct standardization (as in Section 2.2.1) for population structures (inner product of "rates" by the standard population vector) yields the following results (×1000):

(a) USA structure as a standard:

USA: 34.78
Ireland: 48.04   ratio: $\dfrac{48.04}{34.78} = 1.3813$

(b) Ireland structure as a standard:

USA: 31.16
Ireland: 42.96   ratio: $\dfrac{42.96}{31.16} = 1.3787$

2.5.4. Indirect Standardization

With data from Sections 2.5.3 and 2.5.4, it is possible to compare Irish and American fertility, using American age-specific general fertility rates as a standard by having recourse to the indirect standardization method seen in Section 2.2.4. The inner product of population structures by the standard vector of American fertility "rates" gives the following results:

USA: $\dfrac{0.03478}{0.03478} = 1$

ratio: 1.3787

Ireland: $\dfrac{0.04296}{0.03116} = 1.3787$

Comparison of the results derived in Sections 2.5.2, 2.5.3, and 2.5.4 shows that in all cases the average fertility of Irish women is higher than the average

TABLE 2.5

Ages (years)	First marriages	Mean population	Reduced marriages (×10,000)	Ages (years)	First marriages	Mean population	Reduced marriages (×10,000)
15	77	68,120	11	33	345	66,451	52
16	470	70,516	67	34	275	67,726	41
17	1,548	70,054	221	35	227	64,431	35
18	3,814	70,725	539	36	208	64,726	32
19	5,943	60,699	979	37	196	63,882	31
20	8,240	60,554	1,361	38	157	65,618	24
21	9,173	57,927	1,584	39	139	67,114	21
22	7,013	50,794	1,381	40	118	67,054	18
23	5,111	47,399	1,078	41	138	67,467	20
24	4,260	53,016	804	42	97	66,239	15
25	3,395	58,931	576	43	91	68,083	13
26	2,379	60,491	393	44	95	68,581	14
27	1,545	58,297	265	45	59	51,538	11
28	1,085	58,068	187	46	38	37,068	10
29	805	58,549	137	47	35	37,282	9
30	643	60,715	106	48	40	41,655	10
31	502	61,083	82	49	52	50,983	10
32	385	64,936	59	50	31	60,843	5

fertility of American women. However, the proportional difference between fertility schedules varies from 38% (direct and indirect standardization) to 83% (geometric average of "rates"). Different methods will thus yield different comparisons; there are, however, no particular reasons for preferring one method to another.

2.5.5. Distributional Distortion

Distributional distortion affecting period measures adopting the fictitious cohort method was introduced in Section 2.3.2. As an example, consider the number of reduced female first marriages (Table 2.5) computed for the year 1964 in Belgium.[40]

The number of reduced marriages are obtained for each age by dividing the number of first marriages recorded at that age by the average female population married or not. In a fictitious cohort, the sum of these reduced marriages should represent the average number of first marriages per head in a female birth-cohort. This average is equal here to 1.0201, an obvious

[40]Source: *Statistiques Démographiques.* Belgium: Institut National de Statistique, 1964.

TABLE 2.6

Age (in completed years)	Population numbers (December 31, 1961)	
	Males	Females
0	79,481	75,702
1	77,830	73,863
2	79,254	75,774
3	78,105	74,281
4	77,128	73,376
Total population (all ages)	4,496,860	4,692,881

impossibility in a true cohort. The "error" is due to shifting tempos of marriage, from cohort to cohort, toward a lower average age at marriage.

2.5.6. The Population Pyramid

In Section 2.1.1 we noted that the age structure of a population is often represented by a histogram, called the *population pyramid*. Consider, for example, the data in Table 2.6 drawn from the 1961 census of Belgium.[41]

These data can be represented by a histogram, where population figures are specified on the horizontal axis and completed ages on the vertical axis. The number of males is represented on the left of the vertical axis by a *rectangle* whose surface is *proportional* to the actual population figure; similarly, the figure for females is shown on the right of the vertical axis. The above data can then be represented as in Fig. 2.10.

Suppose now that the data are given by five-year age groups; for example, the figure for males aged 0–4 in completed years is equal to 391,798. Dividing this figure by the number of years in the age group (5 in this case) gives 78,359.6. This figure is represented on the histogram by a rectangle whose base is equal to 78,359.6 (rounded to 78,360) and height equal to 5. The surface of this rectangle is $78,359.6 \times 5 = 391,798$, i.e., the number of males in the age group. On the histogram drawn above, this five-year rectangle is represented by the surface limited by the dotted line and can be compared to the one-year rectangles, as all surfaces are proportional to the actual population numbers.

[41]Source: G. Masuy-Stroobant: *ABC de la Démographie Belge*. Brussels: Société Belge de Démographie, 1974, from which the charts are taken.

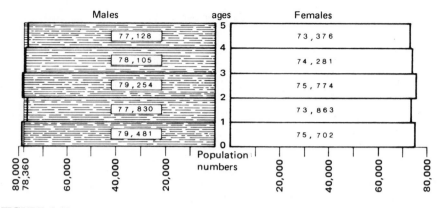

FIGURE 2.10

To compare age–sex structures of populations with different total population figures, it is useful to standardize for this total. One divides the number of males or females in each age group by the total population of males *and* females,[42] and multiplies the result by a multiple of 10 (e.g., 10,000). With the above data, one obtains the *relative* structure, as in Table 2.7.

The histograms of Figs. 2.11 and 2.12 compare the relative structure of the 1961 Belgian population to the relative structure of the Belgian population in 1900; both charts were obtained by the procedure outlined above.

One first notices the different shape of both "pyramids." This is due to the fact that the pyramid for 1900 reflects the high fertility of the Belgian population during the nineteenth century. On the contrary, the 1961

TABLE 2.7

Age (in completed years)	Relative population numbers (×10,000)	
	Males	Females
0	86	82
1	85	80
2	86	82
3	85	81
4	84	80

[42]Dividing by the total population (all ages) of males and females maintains the *sex differentials* in population numbers by age.

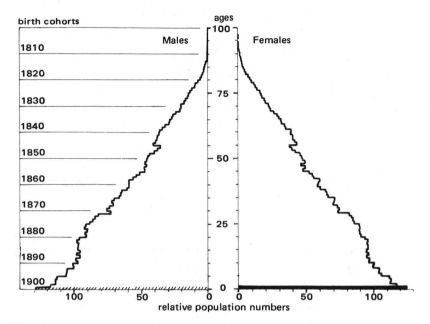

FIGURE 2.11. Population pyramid of Belgium 1900 (for 10,000 inhabitants, both sexes).

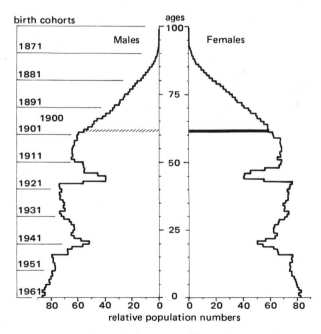

FIGURE 2.12. Population pyramid of Belgium 1961 (for 10,000 inhabitants, both sexes).

population structure reflects the transition to a low fertility, which occurred during the first decades of the twentieth century. Other characteristics can be observed: the greater number of males at young ages [due to the excess of males at birth (see Section 5.2.4)] and of females at higher ages [due to lower mortality (see Section 3.2.1.2)], the postponement of natality during the two world wars and the Great Depression during the thirties, and the increased number of births after both wars. One can also follow the aging of a cohort by comparing, for example, the cohort aged 0 (in completed years) in 1900 to the survivors of the same cohort in 1961 (hatched regions on both pyramids). Incidentally, looking at the shape of the histogram for the year 1900, one now understands why the term "pyramid" has been coined for this type of chart.

2.6. REFERENCES AND SUPPLEMENTARY BIBLIOGRAPHY

Frinking, G. L'utilisation des formules de translation dans les modèles de prévision. Liège: I.U.S.S.P. *International Population Conference* (Vol. I), 1969, pp. 65–72.

Hunter, A. A. Factorial ecology: A critique and some suggestions. *Demography*, 1972, *9*(1), 107–117.

Kitagawa, E. M. Components of a difference between two rates. *Journal of the American Statistical Association*, 1955, *50*(272), 1168–1194.

Kitagawa, E. M. Standardized comparisons in population research. *Demography*, 1964 *I*(1), 296–315.

Le Bras, H. Géographie de la fécondité française depuis 1921. *Population*, 1971, *26*(6), 1093–1124.

Le Bras, H. La mortalité actuelle en Europe. (I) Présentation et représentation des données. *Population*, 1972, *27*(2), 271–293.

Mason, K. O. *et al*. Some methodological issues in cohort analysis of archival data. *American Sociological Review*, 1973, *38*(2), 242–258.

Pressat, R. *L'Analyse Démographique*. Paris: Presses Universitaires de France, 1969.

Rummel, R. G. *Applied Factor Analysis*, Evanston: Northwestern University Press, 1970.

Ryder, N. B. *The cohort approach: essays in the measurement of temporal variations in demographic behaviour*, 1951 (University Microfilms, Ann Arbor, No. 11,015).

Ryder, N. B. La mesure des variations de la fécondité au cours du temps. *Population*, 1956, *7*(1), 29–46.

Ryder, N. B. The process of demographic translation. *Demography*, 1964a, *I*(1), 74–82.

Ryder, N. B. Notes on the concept of a population. *The American Journal of Sociology*, 1964b, *LXIX*(5), 447–463.

Schoen, R. The geometric mean of the age-specific death rates as a summary index of mortality. *Demography*, 1970, *7*(3), 317–324.

Shryock, H. S. *et al*. *The methods and materials of demography* (2 volumes). Washington: US Department of Commerce, Bureau of the Census, 1971.

Wolfenden, H. H. On the theoretical and practical considerations underlying the direct and indirect standardization of death rates. *Population Studies*, 1962, *16*(2), 188–190.

Wunsch, G. Indices standardisés et indices résumés d'une distribution de taux d'éventualité. *Recherches Economiques de Louvain*, 1969, *XXXV*(4), 289–308.

THE ANALYSIS OF MORTALITY

3

3.1. INFANT MORTALITY

3.1.1. The Infant Mortality "Rate"

The *infant mortality "rate"* measures the risk of dying during the first year of life, i.e., from birth to exact age 1; though the term "rate" is commonly used, the measure in fact represents a *probability* of dying, and will therefore be called the *infant probability of dying*.

Consider the data presented in the Lexis diagram of Fig. 3.1. Let N_0 and N_1 be the number of births observed during two specified years j_0 and j_1. Let d_0 and d_1 be the number of infant deaths recorded in the two Lexis triangles during year j_0, and d_2 and d_3 the corresponding number of deaths during the year j_1. If there are no disturbances[1] (i.e., migrations), the probability of dying between exact ages 0 and 1 for cohort N_0 will simply be

$$q_0 = (d_1 + d_2)/N_0 \qquad (3.1)$$

As noted in Section 1.1.5, the events are distributed over *two* calendar years, years j_0 and j_1.

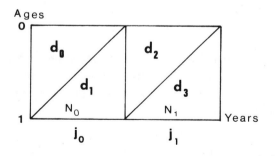

FIGURE 3.1

[1]If migration intervenes, a *corrected* attrition probability can be computed, as in Section 1.3.3. See also Section 3.2.2.1.

Suppose now that one is interested in knowing the impact of the conditions of a specified year on infant mortality, for example, year j_1. The above measure cannot be considered, as it covers two calendar years. However, one can decompose the probability of *surviving* between exact ages 0 and 1 during year j_1 into two components: the probability p'_0 of surviving until the end of the year, and the probability p''_0 of surviving from the beginning of the year until the first birthday.[2] With the data from Fig. 3.1, one can write

$$p'_0 = \frac{N_1 - d_3}{N_1}$$

$$p''_0 = \frac{(N_0 - d_1) - d_2}{N_0 - d_1}$$

If the condition expressed in the previous footnote is fulfilled, one can then obtain the probability of surviving from exact ages 0 to 1 during year j_1 by the product $p'_0 p''_0$,

$$p_0 = \left(\frac{N_1 - d_3}{N_1}\right)\left(\frac{N_0 - d_1 - d_2}{N_0 - d_1}\right)$$

The probability of *dying* between birth and exact age one during year j_1 is thus equal to $1 - p_0$, i.e.,

$$q_0 = 1 - \left(\frac{N_1 - d_3}{N_1}\right)\left(\frac{N_0 - d_1 - d_2}{N_0 - d_1}\right) \tag{3.2}$$

Data in relation (3.2) relate to *one* calendar year but to *two* birth-cohorts. Some approximations to relation (3.2) can easily be derived (see example, Section 3.1.3.1). First, one can write

$$q_0 \cong \frac{d_2 + d_3}{N_1} \tag{3.3}$$

This approximation is biased when cohort numbers N_0 and N_1 are very different from each other, the number of deaths d_2 depends partly on the initial number of births N_0. A better approximation can therefore be obtained by the relation

$$q_0 \cong \frac{d_2}{N_0} + \frac{d_3}{N_1} \tag{3.4}$$

[2]If the two cohorts N_0 and N_1 experience the same risk of dying between exact ages 0 and 1, one can consider p''_0 as the probability of dying from the *end* of year j_1 to exact age 1.

Note that relation (3.4) is equivalent to relation (3.1) if $d_3/N_1 = d_1/N_0$; moreover, relation (3.4) is equivalent to relation (3.2) if $N_0 = N_1$ and $d_3 = d_1$. Usually, the last condition is not fulfilled, but nevertheless relation (3.4) yields a good approximation to relation (3.2) and is more easily computed.

If infant deaths are not recorded by age *and* birth-cohort, the above methods cannot be used. However, one can easily derive an approximate attrition probability as follows: Let $d = d_2 + d_3$ be the number of infant deaths recorded during year j_1. If d_2 and d_3 are known, one could write

$$d = N_0(d_2/N_0) + N_1(d_3/N_1)$$

The problem is to find a denominator N in order to have $q_0 = d/N$. One can therefore write

$$N = d/q_0$$
$$= \frac{N_0(d_2/N_0) + N_1(d_3/N_1)}{d_3/N_1 + d_2/N_0}$$

where q_0 has been estimated by relation (3.4).

The number of births N required for computing the infant probability of death during year j_1, is therefore equal to a *weighted average* of births N_0 and N_1 recorded during years j_0 and j_1, weights being d_2/N_0 and d_3/N_1, respectively. One can therefore obtain two *separation factors* k'' and k' by using

$$k'' = \frac{d_2/N_0}{d_3/N_1 + d_2/N_0} \quad \text{and} \quad k' = \frac{d_3/N_1}{d_3/N_1 + d_2/N_0}$$

An approximate probability of dying for year j_1 can thus be computed by the relation

$$q_0 = \frac{d}{k'N_1 + k''N_0} \tag{3.5}$$

When infant mortality is low (i.e., roughly a probability of dying of 100‰ or less), the separation factors are approximately[3] equal to $k' = \frac{3}{4}$ and $k'' = \frac{1}{4}$. When infant mortality is high, better separation factors can be obtained by taking $k' = \frac{2}{3}$ and $k'' = \frac{1}{3}$.

In an attempt to grasp the meaning of these factors, let $N_0 = N_1$. Therefore $k' = d_3/(d_3 + d_2)$ and $k'' = d_2/(d_3 + d_2)$. In other words, $\frac{3}{4}$ (or $\frac{2}{3}$) of infant deaths occur in the first triangle of the Lexis diagram (i.e., from birth

---

[3]For better approximations, see Section 3.1.3.1 and Shryock, *et al.* (1971, p. 414).

until 6 months of age on average) and $\frac{1}{4}$ (or $\frac{1}{3}$) during the last 6 months of the 1st year of life. This is attributable to the fact that, due to congenital malformations and diseases of the newborn, most deaths occur during the first few days after birth; deaths are therefore definitely *not* distributed uniformly over the 1st year of life.[4]

3.1.2. Endogenous and Exogenous Infant Mortality

It has just been noted above that infant deaths occur most often in the few days or weeks following birth, due to specific causes. A gross classification of the latter is the dichotomy between *endogenous* and *exogenous* infant deaths, endogenous deaths arising from congenital malformations and from circumstances related to confinement, and exogenous deaths from environmental causes (diseases or accidents). J. Bourgeois-Pichat (1952) has devised a biometric method enabling one to distinguish between endogenous and exogenous infant deaths through the sole use of infant deaths classified by day and month of occurrence, without having to resort to statistics on causes of deaths. When the latter are available, a detailed analysis of death by cause is preferable.

The method is based on the assumption that all deaths during the last 11 months of the 1st year of life are exogenous. Let $d_1, d_2, \ldots, d_{11}$ represent the *proportion* of deaths occurring during the 2nd, 3rd, . . . , 12th month to the total number of deaths from the 2nd to the 12th month. These proportions are more or less independent of the level of mortality; as they relate to exogenous deaths, Bourgeois-Pichat assumes that during the 1st month of life the proportion d_0 of *exogenous* deaths is also independent of the level of mortality. By trial and error he has shown that a good approximation to the proportions d_n is given by the relation

$$d_n = \frac{\log_{10}^3 [30.5(n+1)+1] - \log_{10}^3 [30.5n+1]}{\log_{10}^3 366 - \log_{10}^3 31.5}$$

Grossly then d_0 is more or less equal[5] to 0.25, i.e., the proportion of *exogenous* deaths during the 1st month of life is more or less equal to 25% of all (exogenous) deaths from the 2nd to the 12th month of life. Therefore, if d represents the *number* of infant deaths during the whole year, and D represents the number of deaths occurring from the second to the 12th

---

[4]Incidentally, the linear transform function of rates into probabilities (Section 1.2.8) should therefore not be used for transforming a true infant mortality rate into the infant probability of dying (Section 3.2.2.1).

[5]$d_0 = \log_{10}^3 31.5 / (\log_{10}^3 366 - \log_{10}^3 31.5) \cong 0.249$.

month, the number of exogenous deaths during the 1st month of life will be equal to 0.25 D. Therefore, the number of *endogenous* deaths during the 1st month of life is equal to $d - 0.25\,D - D$ or $d - 1.25\,D$ (see example, Section 3.1.3.2).

Bourgeois-Pichat (1951a,b) has also devised a graphic method yielding the number of endogenous and exogenous infant deaths, which may sometimes be preferred to the above method in cases of exogenous surmortality.

Finally, note that in some demographic studies, one finds the term *perinatal mortality*: this usually comprises stillbirths and endogenous deaths, though the latter are sometimes replaced by the number of deaths occurring during the first 28 days of life,[6] including, therefore, exogenous deaths as well. The expression *fetal mortality* covers miscarriages, abortions, and stillbirths; a synonym is *intrauterine mortality* (see also Section 5.5.1.4 for the measurement of fetal mortality).

3.1.3. Examples

3.1.3.1. Types of Infant Mortality "Rates." The data in Table 3.1 have been recorded[7] for calendar years 1967 and 1968. As seen in Section 3.1.1, various probabilities of infant mortality can be computed. Assuming the impact of migration negligible, one obtains the following:

(a) The "true" probability of dying between exact ages 0 and 1 for birth-cohort 1967 is $q_0 = (2{,}893 + 481)/142{,}471 = 0.02368$.

(b) The probabilities of dying during year 1968:

(1) $\quad q_0 = 1 - \left(\dfrac{138{,}214 - 2{,}603}{138{,}214}\right)\left(\dfrac{142{,}471 - 2{,}893 - 481}{142{,}471 - 2{,}893}\right) = 0.02222$

(2) $\quad q_0 = \dfrac{(481 + 2{,}603)}{138{,}214} = 0.02231$

(3) $\quad q_0 = \dfrac{481}{142{,}471} + \dfrac{2{,}603}{138{,}214} = 0.02221$

(4) $\quad q_0 = \dfrac{(481 + 2{,}603)}{0.25(142{,}471) + 0.75(138{,}214)} = 0.02214$

---

[6]The term neonatal mortality is used for these deaths; the period of 4 weeks is sometimes replaced by a month.
[7]Source: *Annuaire Statistique de la Belgique* (Vols. 90 and 91), Brussels, Institut National de Statistique, 1970 and 1971.

TABLE 3.1

Year	Birth-cohort	Age (years)	Deaths	Births
1967	1967	0	2,893	142,471
1968	1967	0	481	—
1968	1968	0	2,603	138,214

Although method (1) is theoretically more sound than (2), (3), and (4) when computing a probability for the sole calendar year 1968, all methods in this case give similar results. A variant of method (4) is obtained by using weights other than 0.75 and 0.25. A standard set of weights, with respect to the level of infant mortality, is presented in Table 3.2 (Shryock *et al.*, 1971, p. 414).

Using 0.85 and 0.15 as standard weights, according to the presumed level of infant mortality, one obtains a new estimate using method (4):

$$q_0 = \frac{(481 + 2,603)}{0.15(142,471) + 0.85(138,214)} = 0.02220$$

Once again, the observed difference is not very significant.

3.1.3.2. Endogenous and Exogenous Infant Mortality. Out of the 3,374 infant deaths (see Table 3.1) relating to birth-cohort 1967, 2,306 were recorded during the 1st month of life. According to Bourgeois-Pichat's method (Section 3.1.2), all deaths recorded during the 2nd to the 12th month of life are due to exogenous causes. The number of endogenous deaths is thus equal to $3,374 - 1.25 (1,068) = 2,039$. The endogenous and

TABLE 3.2

Infant mortality probability (‰)	Weights (%)	
	k'	k''
200	60	40
150	67	33
100	75	25
50	80	20
25	85	15
15	95	5

exogenous infant mortality probabilities are therefore, respectively, equal to 2,039/142,471 and 1,335/142,471, i.e., 0 01431 and 0.00937.

3.2. PERIOD MEASURES OF MORTALITY

3.2.1. The Standardization Approach

3.2.1.1. Crude Death "Rate." As noted in Section 2.1.2, two approaches can be adopted in the study of period mortality: standardization or translation. This section is devoted to the former approach, the separation of the respective impact of structures and frequencies upon population change. The various measures introduced in Section 2.2 will be briefly reviewed.

First, a *crude annual death "rate"* can be computed by dividing the total number of deaths recorded during a specified year,[8] by the midyear population or the average of population numbers on January 1st and December 31st.

This ratio is usually multiplied by 1000 in order to express the result as the annual number of deaths per 1000 persons on the average. The only use this measure has is to standardize for different *total* populations, in temporal or spatial comparisons.

3.2.1.2. Age–Sex-Specific Period Frequencies or Rates. Since the risk of death is highly dependent upon age, any refined measure of mortality must necessarily take the age structure into account. If deaths are recorded annually by age- and birth-cohort, *age-specific*[9] *death rates* can be computed by dividing the number of deaths observed in a birth-cohort during a specified year by the average population of the cohort during the year. Consider Fig. 3.2; deaths in cohort $j-(x+1)$ during year j are denoted d_x and d_{x+1} at completed ages x and $x+1$. The total population of the birth-cohort observed on the first and last days of the year is represented by P_x and P_{x+1}. The age-specific period frequency (a true rate in this case[10]) is equal to

$$t_{x+1} = \frac{d_x + d_{x+1}}{0.5(P_x + P_{x+1})} \qquad \text{at exact age } x+1 \text{ on average}$$

---

[8]The procedure can easily be extended to two or more years by dividing the average of deaths recorded during the time period by the total population at midperiod.

[9]Since risks of mortality differ also by sex (males usually having higher risks), death rates are usually also *sex specific*.

[10]The average population is expressed as the number of person-years of exposure to the risk of dying during the year.

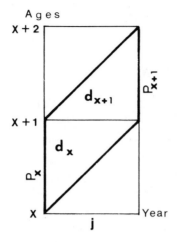

FIGURE 3.2

One could also compute a death rate at a specified age covering two calendar years. In Fig. 3.3, d_x' and d_x'' represent the number of deaths observed in cohort $j-x$ during years j and $j+1$, P_x being the population figure of the cohort on December 31, year j. The age-specific death rate (at exact age $x+0.5$ on average) will then be equal to

$$t_{x+0.5} = \frac{d_x'+d_x''}{P_x}$$

since P_x is more or less equal to the average population of the cohort observed during the year.

Finally, if deaths are not recorded by age- and birth-cohort, a hybrid rate of mortality relating to two cohorts can be computed as in Section 2.4.1.

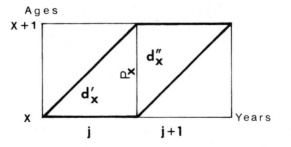

FIGURE 3.3

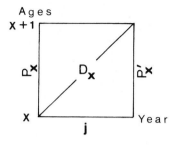

FIGURE 3.4

In Fig. 3.4, D_x represents the number of deaths recorded at completed age x during year j, and P_x and P'_x represent the population figures of cohorts $j - (x + 1)$ and $j - x$ at the beginning and end of year j. The corresponding hybrid death rate is

$$t_{x+0.5} = \frac{D_x}{0.5(P_x + P'_x)} \quad \text{at average exact age } x + 0.5$$

It should be stressed that the sole purpose of these rates, in the standardization approach, is for studying the yearly variations in mortality irrespective of the effect of the age and sex structure of the population. All three rates described above can be interpreted in the above way. Differential mortality between males and females can be studied by the ratio of the male rate to the female rate at a particular age; Schoen (1970) has shown that the sequence of these ratios by age can be advantageously summarized by their geometric mean.

3.2.1.3. Death Rates by Age Groups. The above methods can be extended to the case when age *groups* are considered, instead of single years of age. Considering five-year age groups, for example, the following types of death rates can be computed (see example, Section 3.2.1.5). First, one can compute a death rate relating to five cohorts observed during a single calendar year j (see Fig. 3.5). The total number of deaths observed during year j in the five cohorts is divided by the average of the population aged x to $x + 4$ (completed years) on January 1st and the population aged $x + 1$ to $x + 5$ (completed years) on December 31st.

Though unusual, a second type of five-year age-group death rate can be computed (see Fig. 3.6) by dividing the number of deaths observed during two years j and $j + 1$ in five cohorts by the (average) population at the end of year j aged x to $x + 4$ in completed years.

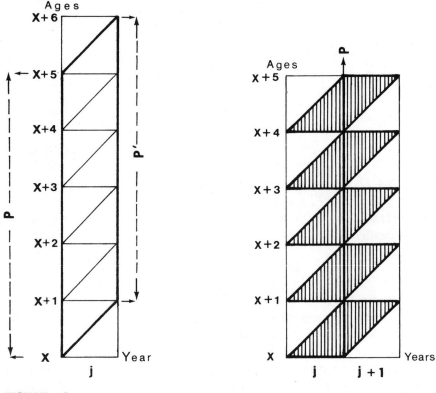

FIGURE 3.5   **FIGURE 3.6**

Finally, a third (hybrid) type of rate can be computed (Fig. 3.7) by dividing the number of deaths observed during year j at completed ages x to $x + 4$, by the average population aged x to $x + 4$ in completed years, i.e., the average of populations aged x to $x + 4$ at the beginning and end of the year. Note that this last rate concerns *six* cohorts and not five as for the two other types of rates.

3.2.1.4. Standardized Death Rates. For spatial or temporal comparisons independent of the influence of population structures, period death rates by age or age groups can be summarized by the methods developed in Section 2.2.

If n rates t_x have been computed between bounds 0 and ω for different periods of time $j, j + i, j + m, \ldots$, for example, the sequences can be summarized by their arithmetic average $\sum_0^\omega (t_x/n)$ or their geometric

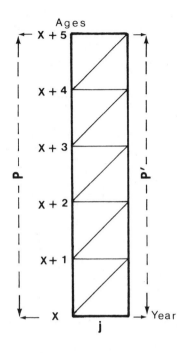

average $(\prod_0^\omega t_x)^{1/n}$, or simply by their *sum* $\sum_0^\omega t_x$. The latter expression corresponds to a *direct standardization*; as seen in Section 2.2.1 any other standard population can also be used.[11]

If the distribution of deaths by age is unknown, one may have recourse to the *indirect standardization* method (Section 2.2.4), any sequence of death rates being used as a standard. For example, in a study of mortality differentials by occupation, the age–sex-specific death rates for the whole population can be used as a standard. Remember also that indirect standardization is recommended when population numbers are small, since computed death rates tend therefore to be erratic.

3.2.1.5. Examples. The following Lexis diagrams (Figs. 3.8a, b, and c show various ways of computing mortality rates by age groups, as seen in Section 3.2.1.3. The examples all relate to the first 5 years (or birth-cohorts) of life in period analysis for calendar years 1967–1968.[12] From Fig. 3.8a one

---

[11]The choice depends on the weights one wants to apply to the rates by age or age groups.

[12]Source: *Annuaire Statistique de la Belgique* (Vols. 89 to 91), Brussels, Institut National de Statistique, 1968–1971.

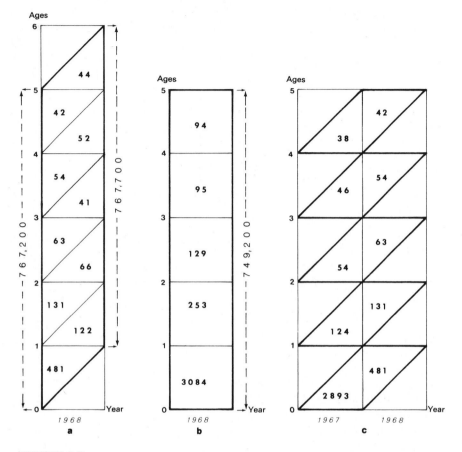

FIGURE 3.8

computes the death rate for average exact age 3 by the ratio

$$t_3 = \frac{1,096}{0.5(767,200 + 767,700)}$$

$$= 0.00143$$

Death rates derived from Fig. 3.8b and c are, respectively, equal to

$$t_{2.5} = \frac{3,655}{0.5(767,200 + 749,200)}$$

$$= 0.00482$$

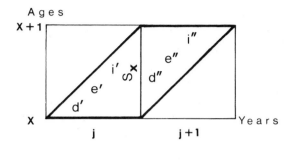

FIGURE 3.9

and

$$t_{2.5} = \frac{3,926}{767,200}$$

$$= 0.00512$$

The latter death rates are higher than the former, since they take into account infant mortality during the first months of life, an age at which the risk of dying is especially high.

3.2.2. The Translation Approach: The Period Life Table

3.2.2.1. The Life-Table Functions

a. *Probability of Dying* $_nq_x$. It is in the field of mortality that the concept of the attrition table (Section 1.2.5) has been widely developed under the name of *life table*. In this section, only the period life table will be considered, having access to the fictitious cohort method (Section 2.3.1); for an example, see Section 3.2.2.6a.

Consider the general case of computing probabilities of dying q_x from exact age x to exact age $x + 1$ in the various cohorts observed during two calendar years[13] j and $j + 1$ (see Fig. 3.9). Let d', d'', e', e'', and i', i'', respectively, represent the number of deaths, out-migrants, and in-migrants affecting the cohort size between exact ages x and $x + 1$ during years j and $j + 1$. Moreover, let S_x be the population at exact age x, and S_x (or $S_{x+0.5}$) be the population enumerated on the 31st December, year j.

---

[13]In practice, period probabilities of dying—forming the basis of the life table—are sometimes computed over a period of several years to avoid erratic fluctuations from year to year in the risks of dying.

In order to obtain the probability of dying *corrected for disturbances* (in- and out-migration), one can resort to the approximate relation developed in Section 1.3.2.2 and write

$$q_x \cong \frac{1}{S_x}[d' + d'' + 0.5q_x(e' + e'') - 0.5q_x(i' + i'')]$$

Therefore, one has approximately

$$q_x = \frac{d' + d''}{S_x - 0.5(e' + e'') + 0.5(i' + i'')}$$

$$= \frac{d' + d''}{S_x - 0.5E_x + 0.5I_x} \tag{3.6}$$

where

$$e' + e'' = E_x \qquad \text{and} \qquad i' + i'' = I_x.$$

Since S_x represents the midyear population (on December 31st, year j), one has $S_x = S_x + d' + e' - i'$. Writing $S_{x+0.5}$ for S_x, in order to avoid confusion, the corrected probability of dying can also be expressed as

$$q_x = \frac{d' + d''}{S_{x+0.5} + d' - \frac{1}{2}(e'' - e') + \frac{1}{2}(i'' - i')} \tag{3.7}$$

If there is no *net migration* (i.e., if $E_x = I_x$), relation (3.6) simply becomes equal to

$$q_x = \frac{d' + d''}{S_x}$$

$$= \frac{d' + d''}{S_{x+0.5} + d' + e' - i'}$$

If, furthermore $e' = i'$, the above relation is reduced to

$$q_x = \frac{d' + d''}{S_{x+0.5} + d'} \tag{3.8}$$

Relation (3.8) is also obtained if in relation (3.7) one has $e' = e''$ and $i' = i''$, i.e., if migration is uniformly spread out between exact ages x and $x + 1$. Since this can often be assumed over short periods of time, relation (3.8) can be considered as a good approximation to the probability of dying, without disturbances.

The above relations can easily be extended to the case of probabilities of dying between exact ages x and $x + n$. When n is large, relation (3.7) is preferred over (3.8) since migration is not necessarily uniformly distributed over long periods of time.[14]

Finally, when deaths are not classified by age and birth-cohort one can compute death *rates* $_n t_x$ between ages x and $x + n$ during year j and convert these into probabilities using, for example, the linear transform functions of Section 1.2.8:

$$_n q_x = 2n\,_n t_x / (2 + n\,_n t_x)$$

Probabilities of death usually constitute the starting point of the life table. In many actuarial and demographic studies this function is *graduated* beforehand in order to remove peculiar indexes and obtain a smoothed curve of attrition probabilities.[16] Graduation is justified when one wants to remove sampling errors from the set of data; very often, however, especially when the probability sequence is computed for a large population, peculiarities observed at some ages are not due to random errors but to intrinsic factors of the population considered.[17] In this case, graduation actually removes interesting information from the data and should not be applied. Generally speaking, except when sample errors are large, or when inadequate data are used, demographic indexes should *not* be graduated; a smoothed curve, even if aesthetically more satisfying, often removes non-random "errors" that are of particular interest for the demographer. The viewpoint of the latter is therefore somewhat different from current actuarial practice.

b. Functions of Survival and Death l_x and d_x. Having computed the probabilities of death from $x = 0$ to $x = \omega - 1$, assuming that there are no survivors after age ω,[18] one can assume that a *fictitious cohort without disturbances* is subjected to these risks of dying during its lifetime. Let l_0

[14]This is the case when migration is strongly correlated with the business cycle, for example.

[15]Better approximations for $_1 q_0$ and $_4 q_1$ are obtained by the relations

$$_1 q_0 = \frac{2\,_1 t_0}{2 + 1.82\,_1 t_0} \qquad _4 q_1 = \frac{8\,_4 t_1}{2 + 4.88\,_4 t_1}$$

adapted from C. L. Chiang (1972).

[16]See, for example, Wolfenden (1954, Chap. VII), or Benjamin and Haycocks (1970, Chaps. 11–16).

[17]We are always assuming that there are no errors due to inadequate *data collection*, though these must sometimes be taken into account, even in countries with a long experience in census-taking and vital registration.

[18]Therefore $q_{\omega-1} = 1$.

represent the number of births in this hypothetical cohort[19]; the number of deaths d_0 between birth and exact age 1 is equal to $d_0 = l_0 q_0$. The number of survivors at exact age 1, l_1, is therefore equal to $l_1 = l_0 - d_0$.

One can therefore derive the survivorship function l_x and the function of life-table deaths d_x by the following algorithm

$$l_x q_x = d_x$$

$$l_{x+1} = l_x - d_x$$

until one finally obtains $l_\omega = l_{\omega-1} - d_{\omega-1} = 0$

c. *Probability of Survival* p_x. The probability of survival from exact age x to exact age $x+1$ is obviously equal to $p_x = 1 - q_x$. Since $q_x = (l_x - l_{x+1})/l_x$, one can also write $p_x = l_{x+1}/l_x$. The probability of surviving from exact age x to exact age $x+n$ is similarly obtained by $_n p_x = l_{x+n}/l_x$. But $l_{x+n} = l_x \prod_x^{x+n-1} p_i$; therefore, one also has $_n p_x = \prod_x^{x+n-1} p_i$. For example,

$$_x p_0 = l_x / l_0$$

$$= \prod_0^{x-1} p_i$$

$$= \prod_0^{x-1} (1 - q_i)$$

As a corollary, the probability of dying between exact ages x and $x+n$ can be written as

$$_n q_x = {}_n d_x / l_x$$

$$= 1 - {}_n p_x$$

$$= 1 - \prod_x^{x+n-1} (1 - q_i)$$

d. *Number of Person-Years* L_x. The number of person-years lived by the hypothetical cohort between exact ages x and $x+1$ is equal to $L_x = \int_x^{x+1} l_i di$ (Section 1.2.7). If the survivorship function is *linear*, one has $L_x = 0.5 (l_x + l_{x+1})$. Generally speaking, the number of person-years lived by the survivors between exact ages x and $x+n$ is equal to

$$_n L_x = \int_x^{x+n} l_i \, di$$

$$= (l_x + l_{x+n})(n/2)$$

---

[19] l_0, or *radix* of the life table, is usually expressed as a multiple of 10 (e.g., 100,000 persons).

assuming the survivorship function is linear from x to $x+n$. The latter assumption is not adequate when n is large; furthermore, even when $n = 1$ it has already been noted (Section 3.1.1) that the survivorship function is not linear between exact ages 0 and 1. For the first year of age, a better approximation of the number of person-years lived[20] is

$$L_0 = k''l_0 + k'l_1$$

where constants k' and k'' have the same meaning as in Section 3.1.1, i.e., $k'' = \frac{1}{4}$ or $\frac{1}{3}$ and $k' = \frac{3}{4}$ or $\frac{2}{3}$ depending on low or high mortality levels.

The function L_x can be considered otherwise. Suppose that all hypothetical cohorts of identical radix are subjected to the same sequence of survival probabilities[21]; as by assumption there is no migration, $_nL_x$ represents the stationary population figure aged **x** to **x+n−1** in completed years at any point of time. The $_nL_x$ function can therefore be considered either as the number of person-years of exposure to risk or as the stationary population number between exact ages x and $x+n$.

e. Total After Lifetime T_x. Total after lifetime is the total number of person-years lived by the cohort after exact age x. It is thus equal to

$$T_x = \int_x^\omega l_i \, di$$

$$= \sum_x^{\omega-1} L_i$$

In the stationary population corresponding to the life table T_x is therefore the total population number aged x and over.

If one considers the approximation $L_x = 0.5(l_x + l_{x+1})$, T_x can also be written as

$$T_x = \sum_{i=x}^{\omega-1} 0.5(l_i + l_{i+1})$$

[20] An even better approximation of L_0 would be the following:

$$L_0 = l_1 + 0.25 k' d_0 + 0.75 k'' d_0$$
$$= l_1 + (l_0 - l_1)(0.25 \, k' + 0.75 \, k'')$$

The absolute difference between the two approximations is, however, usually small, being equal to $0.25 \, d_0(k' - k'')$.

[21] If all synthetic cohorts experience the same mortality, and have the same radix, cohort and period observations are identical. This particular model is called the *stationary population* corresponding to the life table.

f. Life Expectancy e_x. The *expectation of life* or *life expectancy*[22] at exact age x represents the average after lifetime at age x, i.e., the average number of years lived by the fictitious cohort after age x. Since the number of survivors at age x is equal to l_x, the life expectancy is

$$e_x = \frac{T_x}{l_x}$$

Taking into account the above expression for T_x, one can also write

$$e_x = \frac{\sum\limits_{x}^{\omega-1} L_i}{l_x}$$

For ages where the survivorship function is approximately linear between i and $i+1$, one has $L_i = 0.5(l_i + l_{i+1})$. Therefore, the life expectancy can also be written:

$$e_x = \frac{\sum\limits_{x}^{\omega-1} 0.5(l_i + l_{i+1})}{l_x}$$

$$= 0.5 + \frac{1}{l_x}(l_{x+1} + l_{x+2} + l_{x+3} + \cdots + l_\omega)$$

This last relation should not be used for the expectation of life at birth (also called the *mean length of life*), since the survivorship function is not linear from birth to exact age one. Having recourse once more to the separation factors k' and k'' introduced in Section 3.1.1, a better approximation[23] to the mean length of life is equal to

$$e_0 = k'' + \frac{1}{l_0}\left[l_1(k' + 0.5) + \sum\limits_{2}^{\omega} l_x\right]$$

with k' being equal, as before, to $\frac{2}{3}$ or $\frac{3}{4}$ and k'' to $\frac{1}{3}$ or $\frac{1}{4}$.

It can easily be shown, from the above formula, that the mean length of life is also equal to the average age at death for the synthetic cohort subjected to mortality alone. Disregarding the problem of the first age

[22]In actuarial works, the symbol $\overset{\circ}{e}_x$ usually represents the "complete" life expectancy at exact age x. The standard European practice of writing e_x instead has been adopted here.
[23]This approximation is obtained from $e_0 = T_0/l_0$ using $L_0 = k''l_0 + k'l_1$, and $L_i = 0.5(l_i + l_{i+1})$ for $i \neq 0$.

group, one can write

$$e_0 = \frac{1}{l_0}\left[\sum_0^\omega (x+0.5)(l_x - l_{x+1})\right]$$

as derived from the approximation

$$e_0 = \frac{1}{l_0}\left[\sum_x 0.5(l_x + l_{x+1})\right]$$

As $l_x - l_{x+1} = d_x$, the mean length of life is equal to $(1/l_0)[\sum_x(x+0.5)d_x]$, i.e., the average age at death. It is, however, important to note that, in an actual population observed during a certain period of time, the average age at death is *not* equal to the mean length of life, due to the impact of migration, differential mortality experiences, and, especially differential cohort population numbers. Only in a stationary population are the two measures identical.[24]

g. *Survival "Rate" P_x.* The survival "rate" P_x is, in fact, the *probability* of surviving between two *completed* years, or between two groups of completed years. Expressing P_x as a function of survivors L_x at completed age **x**, one can write

$$P_x = L_{x+1}/L_x$$

and generally,

$$_nP_x = \frac{_nL_{x+n}}{_nL_x}$$

Again, using L_i equal to $0.5(l_i + l_{i+1})$, one can write

$$P_x = \frac{l_{x+1} + l_{x+2}}{l_x + l_{x+1}}$$

Similarly,

$$_nP_x = \frac{l_{x+n} + l_{x+2n}}{l_x + l_{x+n}}$$

For the first age group, nonlinearity in the survivorship function has to be taken into account once more, writing $k''l_0 + k'l_1$ as L_0. With relation to

---

[24]Furthermore, in a *stationary* population, the crude death rate is equal to l_0/T_0, i.e., the reciprocal of the mean length of life.

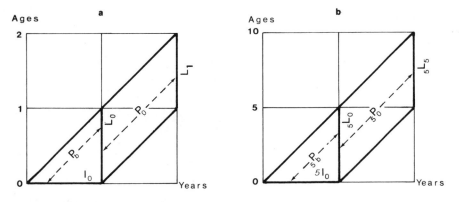

FIGURE 3.10

the first age groups, there is also a problem of notation. One has $P_0 = L_1/L_0$ and $_nP_0 = {_nL_n}/{_nL_0}$. The probability of survival from birth will be expressed by the expression P_b and is equal to $P_b = L_0/l_0$ or $_5P_b = {_5L_0}/{5l_0}$. This difference is easily observed in Fig. 3.10a and b.

Survival probabilities (improperly called "rates") between completed years are commonly used in population projections. The complement to unity of the survival "rate" is the probability of dying between completed years (as in Section 1.2.6).

3.2.2.2. Life-Table Functions for the Last Age Interval. For the older ages the probabilities of dying tend to be erratic, since they are computed from small population figures. Generally, therefore, the probabilities of dying at an old age are obtained by graduation methods.[26] However, it is also quite adequate to end the life table with an open age interval, say 70 years and over, without estimating the probabilities of dying, and other life table functions, at high ages (over 70).

Denoting by k the terminal exact age chosen for the life table, it is, however, necessary to estimate the total after lifetime T_k in order to compute the total after lifetimes and life expectancies at ages lower than k. Various methods are employed, of which two are given below.

a. *First Method of Estimating T_k.* In the life table, denote by m_x the *death rate* between exact ages x and $x + 1$. Following Section 1.2.7, one can write

$$m_x = \frac{d_x}{L_x} \quad \text{and therefore} \quad L_x = \frac{d_x}{m_x}$$

[26]For a brief account, see Spiegelman (1968, pp. 127–128).

This result can be extended to the open age interval $k+$, noting that $L_{k+} = T_k$,

$$T_k = \frac{d_{k+}}{m_{k+}}$$

The number of deaths d_{k+} is equal to l_k, survivors at exact age k. The life table death rate is unknown but it can be estimated by the death rate M_{k+} for the actual population.[27] Therefore, an estimate of the total after lifetime T_k is given by

$$T_k = l_k/M_{k+}$$

The value of the life expectancy at age k is equal to

$$e_k = T_k/l_k$$
$$= l_k/l_k M_{k+} \qquad \text{where } m_{k+} \cong M_{k+}$$
$$= 1/M_{k+}$$

The life expectancy of the open age interval is therefore equal to the reciprocal of the death rate.[28] Life expectancies at lower ages are computed by the usual relations, taking into account that $T_k = l_k/M_{k+}$.

 b. Second Method of Estimating T_k. If k is, as before, the terminal age chosen, one can write

$$T_k = e_k l_k$$

Assuming that the values of e_k at high ages do not differ too much from one population to another,[29] an estimate $\hat{e}_k$ of the unknown life expectancy at age k enables one to derive an estimate of T_k. Table 3.3 summarizes various values of e_k corresponding to different values of q_0; estimates of e_k can be obtained by linear interpolation between the values in the table.[30]

[27]Obtained by dividing the number of deaths of age k and over during a specified year by the midyear population aged k and over.

[28]For $k = 0$, one finds that $e_0 = 1/M_{0+}$, a result already noted above for the *stationary* population, as M_{0+} is equal to the crude death rate.

[29]This assumption is probably valid at very high ages but becomes less and less adequate as the terminal age k decreases.

[30]Source of table values: A. J. Coale and P. Demeny (1966), West model, levels 17, 19, 21, and 24. Values for "both sexes" have been computed assuming a sex ratio at birth of 105 males to 100 females.

TABLE 3.3. Values of e_k Corresponding to Different Values of q_0

Sex	$q_0(\times 1000)$	$k = 70$	$k = 75$	$k = 80$
Females	71	9.8	7.3	5.2
	50	10.4	7.7	5.5
	31	11.0	8.2	5.9
	9	12.6	9.4	6.9
Males	86	8.9	6.7	4.7
	63	9.4	7.0	5.0
	41	9.8	7.4	5.3
	13	11.2	8.4	6.2
Both sexes	79	9.4	7.0	5.0
	57	9.9	7.4	5.3
	36	10.4	7.8	5.6
	11	12.0	9.0	6.6

For a specified value of $\hat{e}_k$, using the relation $e_x = 0.5 + [(\sum_{x+1}^{\omega} l_i)/l_x]$ yields the approximate formula (for $x < k$):

$$e_x = 0.5 + \frac{1}{l_x}\left[\sum_{x+1}^{k} l_i + (\hat{e}_k - 0.5)l_k\right]$$

since

$$\hat{e}_k = 0.5 + \frac{1}{l_k}\left(\sum_{k+1}^{\omega} l_i\right)$$

3.2.2.3. Mortality by Cause of Death. The formula for corrected attrition probabilities (Section 1.3.3) can be extended to the study of death due to cause (i) in the absence[31] of all other causes of death $(\sim i)$ at completed age **x** (see example, Section 3.2.2.6c):

$$q_x(i) \cong \frac{D_x(i)}{S_x - D_x(\sim i)/2}$$

where S_x is the population surviving at exact age x, $D_x(i)$ represents the number of deaths due to cause (i), and $D_x(\sim i)$ the number of deaths due to all *other* causes.[32] As before, a life table can be set up for the sole cause of death (i) starting from the sequence of probabilities $q_x(i)$.

[31]Other causes of death act as disturbances.
[32]In the absence of migration.

Another way to proceed is to start from the actual proportions $V_x(i) = D_x(i)/D_x$ of deaths due to cause (i) to the total number of deaths (all causes) at age x.[33] Assuming that these proportions also hold for the general life table population (*all* causes of deaths), one derives the life table deaths due to cause (i) at completed age x by the product $d_x(i) = d_x V_x(i)$, where d_x represents the number of life table deaths due to all causes of death. The probability of dying after exact age x due to cause (i) can then be written as

$$\frac{\sum\limits_{x}^{\omega} d_x(i)}{l_x} = \frac{l_x(i)}{l_x}$$

One can also consider the problem the other way around and compute the probability of dying in the *absence* of cause (i), i.e., the probability of dying due to all causes other than (i). With the above notation one has, assuming no migration,

$$q_x(\sim i) = \frac{D_x(\sim i)}{S_x - D_x(i)/2}$$

$$= \frac{D_x - D_x(i)}{S_x - D_x(i)/2}$$

Again one derives the life table relating to all causes of death other than (i) from these probabilities; the difference between the mean lengths of life computed for the general life table (all causes of death) and for the life table relating to causes other than (i) represents the gain in life expectancy if cause of death (i) were eliminated.

Various problems should, however, be pointed out here, though they lie somewhat outside the scope of this book. First, applying actual proportions of deaths $V_x(i)$ to the number of life-table deaths d_x for all causes of death in fact yields *multiple-decrement* life tables where each cause of death acts in the presence of the other causes. This leads to the additive properties of life-table deaths, survivors, and probabilities by cause. The use of corrected probabilities of dying by cause yields, on the contrary, *single-decrement* life tables by cause: in this case, each cause is considered to act alone, i.e.,

---

[33]Corrected probabilities at age x can then also be written, following Section 1.3.2.2,

$$q(i) = 1 + 0.5\,[V(i)q - V(\sim i)q] - \{1 + 0.5[V(i)q - V(\sim i)q]^2 - 2V(i)q\}^{1/2}$$

$$q(i) \cong V(i)q/[1 - 0.5\,V(\sim i)q]$$

where $q = D_x/S_x$ and $V(\sim i) = D_x(\sim i)/D_x$.

independently of the other causes of death. The additive property is replaced here by the multiplicative property of probabilities of survival by cause.[34]

Multiple-decrement tables are used when one wishes to take into account the various phenomena that cause cohort attrition, without privileging one particular cause and considering the others as disturbances. Single-decrement tables are used, on the other hand, when one determines the impact of a particular cause of attrition in a pure state; in this case, all other causes of attrition are considered as disturbances. For example, in the study of mortality by cause, taking simultaneous account of all the various causes of death (assuming no migration) would lead to a multiple-decrement life table by causes of death; the associated single-decrement life tables would consider, on the contrary, each cause of death acting alone, in the absence therefore of other causes of death.

Second, the gain in life expectancy if the cause of death (i) were eliminated, obtained by subtracting the mean length of life (all causes) from the mean length of life obtained by eliminating cause (i), leads to fallacious results when various causes are eliminated. In this case, the gain in life expectancy due to cause (i) will increase with the rank of elimination of (i) in the order of elimination of the various causes of death. If various causes were eliminated at the same time, one could not determine their respective contribution to the overall gain in life expectancy that would result from the disappearance of these causes of death (Baloche & Nizard, 1973).

3.2.2.4. Abridged Life Tables. Abridged life tables by *age groups* fulfill a double purpose: first, one can condense a complete life table computed as in Section 3.2.2.1 if values by age groups are deemed sufficient; second abridged life tables can be set up if data are not adequate to compute a complete life table.

Whatever the purpose, life-table functions in the abridged form are either identical or very similar to the concepts developed for the complete life table (Section 3.2.2.2). Indeed, the only functions that change are those relating to age *intervals*; variables l_x, T_x, and e_x at exact ages have the same meaning as before. The basic functions are briefly introduced below (see also the example in Section 3.2.2.6b).

a. Probability of Dying $_nq_x$. If the abridged life table condenses a complete one, the probabilities of dying between exact ages x and $x + n$ are

---

[34]For a full treatment of this subject, see Preston, Keyfitz, and Schoen (1972, Chap. II). An example of multiple-decrement is given in Section 6.5.2.

simply computed by the relation

$$_nq_x = 1 - (l_{x+n}/l_x)$$

where values l_x and l_{x+n} are drawn from the corresponding complete life table. Usually, one uses quinquennial age groups; the probability therefore becomes equal to $1 - (l_{x+5}/l_x)$ for each quinquennial age group.

If deaths and/or population numbers are classified by age groups x to $x + n$, or if data by single ages are affected by errors in age recording (as in most underdeveloped areas), a complete life table is either impossible to derive or is too sensitive to age misrecordings. In this case, one computes average period *death rates* over a certain number of years and transforms these rates into probabilities, having resort to a transform function as seen in Section 1.2.8. For example, suppose that deaths and population numbers are classified by sex and quinquennial age groups. An average *death rate* over a certain number f of calendar years (averaging reduces erratic fluctuations from year to year) can be computed from the data as follows:

$$_5t_x = \frac{(1/f)[_5D_x(a) + _5D_x(b) + \cdots]}{_5P_x}$$

where $_5D_x(a), _5D_x(b), \ldots$ represent the number of deaths recorded between exact ages x to $x + 5$ in the f calendar years $a, b, \ldots$, and $_5P_x$ represents the *midperiod* population aged x to $x + 5$.[35] The exposure rate $_5t_x$ can be transformed into a probability of dying by the usual relation

$$_5q_x = 10 \, _5t_x/(2 + 5 \, _5t_x)$$

or by another transform function if preferred.[36]

It should be noted that a double bias is involved here. A first bias is introduced when the l_i function between ages x and $x + n$ does not correspond to the form assumed (e.g., the linear form). A second bias appears when the observed death rate is used in place of the life table death rate in the transformation formula of rates into probabilities, as the age structure of the life-table population (the "stationary" population) is different from the actual one in the age interval x to $x + n$. For example, the transform function of $_5t_x$ into $_5q_x$ given above is based on the assumption that l_i decreases linearly between ages x and $x + n$ (Section 1.2.8), $_5t_x$ being the *life-table* exposure rate (i.e., $_nd_x/\int_x^{x+n} l_i \, di$). In practice, however, the actual exposure

---

[35]Another way of averaging would be to compute $_5t_x$ for *each* year $a, b, \ldots$ and take the average of these f rates. The two methods do not yield exactly the same results.

[36]Exponential transform or Greville's method (see Greville, 1943).

rate computed for the real population is used in place of the life-table rate; as noted above, there is a slight discrepancy between the two rates, due to different population structures in the age group considered.[37] This led L. J. Reed and M. Merrell (1939) to study directly the empirical relations between $_nt_x$ and $_nq_x$, that is, between the observed death rates and the probabilities of dying drawn from life tables[38] without an explicit assumption with regard to the l_x function. The equations fitting the empirical observations are the following:

$$_4q_1 = 1 - \exp\left(-4\,_4t_1 - 0.512\,_4t_1{}^2\right) \qquad \text{for ages 1 to 5}$$

$$_5q_x = 1 - \exp\left(-5\,_5t_x - _5t_x{}^2\right) \qquad \text{for ages } x \text{ to } x+5$$

$$_{10}q_x = 1 - \exp\left(-10\,_{10}t_x - 8\,_{10}t_x{}^2\right) \qquad \text{for ages } x \text{ to } x+10$$

These expressions are easily resolved with any calculator having an exponential subroutine, though tables of conversion have been computed and are presented in Pressat (1972). It seems that, up to very high ages, the Reed and Merrell formulas do not yield better evaluations of the probabilities of dying than the formula based on the linear assumption for l_x (Péron, 1971). It is only after age 75 or 80 that the Reed and Merrell formulas would be preferable, but computed rates at those ages are very erratic and not very trustworthy in any case. At high ages, nonconventional methods such as those developed by Vincent (1951) should be preferred.

b. *Functions of Survival and Death: l_x and $_nd_x$.* If one condenses a complete life table, l_x values at ages $i, i+n, i+2n, \ldots$ are simply read from the complete table. The number of life table deaths are derived either by the sum of deaths by single ages

$$_nd_x = \sum_{x}^{x+n-1} d_i$$

or by the difference $l_x - l_{x+n}$.

In the other approach, having computed $_nq_x$ from $_nt_x$, as above, one starts from an arbitrary radix l_0 and uses a similar algorithm as for the complete life table,

$$_nd_x = l_x\,_nq_x$$

$$l_{x+n} = l_x - _nd_x$$

---

[37]For an interesting discussion of this problem, see Qvist (1972).

[38]US data for 1910, 1920, and 1930 were used, and a best fit was obtained by an equation of the type $_nq_x = 1 - \exp(-n\,_nt_x - an^3\,_nt_x{}^2)$, where the constant a has been empirically evaluated as 0.008.

c. Probability of Survival $_np_x$. The probability of survival between exact ages x and $x+n$ is equal to the complement to unity of the probability of dying over the same age interval. It can also be computed by the ratio l_{x+n}/l_x.

d. Number of Person Years $_nL_x$. As seen before, the number of person-years lived between exact ages x and $x+n$ is approximately equal to $_nL_x = (n/2)(l_x + l_{x+n})$. For the first age interval, this formula is slightly biased. When $n=5$, a better approximation for $_5L_0$ is given by

$$_5L_0 = k''l_0 + (2+k')l_1 + 2l_5$$

when the value of l_1 is known, with $k'' = \frac{1}{4}$ or $\frac{1}{3}$ and $k' = \frac{3}{4}$ or $\frac{2}{3}$ as in Section 3.1.1.

e. Survival "Rate" $_nP_x$. As seen in Section 3.2.2.1, the probability of survival $_nP_x$ is equal to

$$_nP_x = \frac{_nL_{x+n}}{_nL_x}$$

or approximately

$$_nP_x = \frac{l_{x+n} + l_{x+2n}}{l_x + l_{x+n}}$$

f. Total after Lifetime and Life Expectancy: T_x and e_x. With $T_x = \sum_x {}_nL_x$ and $e_x = T_x/l_x$ as in the complete life table, and writing $_nL_x$ as a function of l_x, one has

$$e_x = \frac{n}{2} + \frac{n(l_{x+n} + l_{x+2n} + l_{x+3n} + \cdots)}{l_x}$$

3.2.2.5. Model Life Tables. Various authors have attempted to derive patterns of mortality by condensing the experience of actual populations as reflected in their life tables. The first major work in this field was published by the United Nations in 1955. Model life tables by age and sex were derived from a set of actual life tables for populations with adequate data, using chain parabolic regressions[39] of probabilities of dying starting from q_0. For example, one could find in the table the average value of $_5q_x$ (x specified) for an initial value of q_0. A few years later Coale and Demeny (1966) at the Office of Population Research at Princeton University elaborated four "families" of model life tables, representing four different patterns of mortality by age, combining for each family a double system of regression

---

[39]Gabriel and Ronen (1958) have shown that this method of chain regressions leads to biased estimates.

equations of the type $_nq_x = A_x + B_x e_{10}$ and $\log{_nq_x} = A'_x + B'_x e_{10}$. For one initial value of q_0 (for instance), one finds therefore four different values of $_5q_x$ (x specified) depending on the pattern (or "family") of mortality by age. More recently still Ledermann (1969), from the National Demographic Institute (I.N.E.D.) in Paris, has set up a system of life tables by a regression model based on one or two variables of the type

$$\log{_nq_x} = a_{x0} + a_{x1}\log{_nq_i}$$

and

$$\log{_nq_x} = b_{x0} + b_{x1}\log{_nq_i} + b_{x2}\log{_nq_j}$$

Table A.1 in the Appendix presents the sets of coefficients a_{xi} and b_{xi} (males and females) for the one-entry model table based on $_nq_i = {_5q_0}$ (males and females) and for the two-entry model table based on $_nq_i = {_5q_0}$ (males and females) and $_nq_j = {_{20}q_{45}}$ (males and females). The use of both sets is explained in the example in Section 3.2.2.6d.

Various initial values $_nq_i$ are used, as an estimate of $_nq_x$, knowing q_0 (for example) is slightly biased if the regression equation is based, for instance, on $_nq_i = {_5q_0}$.[40] Furthermore, the set of model life tables based on *two* "entries" $_nq_i$ and $_nq_j$ has the great advantage of considerably reducing the variance of the estimate of $_nq_x$.

Ledermann's tables are presently the most refined set of model life tables available. A complete treatment of the subject is, however, outside the scope of this book; the reader is referred to Ledermann's book (1969), which also contains a thorough discussion of previous model life tables.

Access to model life tables is obviously useful in circumstances where actual life tables are impossible to compute due to incomplete or defective data.[41] However, it is important to note that models currently available are all based on the experience of presently developed countries, the only group having a time series of life tables of good quality. Developing countries might present other patterns of mortality not taken into account in the present models; this somewhat limits the usefulness of model life tables, though in the absence of adequate data for computing actual life tables they remain the best alternative.

---

[40]This bias affects estimates derived from Coale and Demeny's tables using another "entry" than e_{10}.

[41]In this respect, see Coale and Demeny (1967). Other types of model life tables are also available (see Brass, 1971).

TABLE 3.4

Age (in completed years)	Midyear population	Deaths (male + female)	Death rate	Age (in completed years)	Midyear population	Deaths (male + female)	Death rate
0	63,589	1,552	0.02441	36	30,229	51	0.00169
1	64,182	93	0.00145	37	30,738	45	0.00146
2	63,534	80	0.00126	38	30,236	56	0.00185
3	63,111	34	0.00054	39	32,740	82	0.00250
4	61,515	31	0.00050	40	31,452	81	0.00258
5	61,970	33	0.00053	41	32,532	65	0.00200
6	60,896	29	0.00048	42	31,986	105	0.00328
7	59,455	19	0.00032	43	34,361	92	0.00268
8	58,252	17	0.00029	44	33,031	120	0.00363
9	58,417	27	0.00046	45	34,142	172	0.00504
10	57,180	18	0.00031	46	33,990	133	0.00391
11	58,394	21	0.00036	47	33,137	123	0.00371
12	56,448	20	0.00035	48	29,476	142	0.00482
13	58,176	20	0.00034	49	35,772	161	0.00450
14	55,277	17	0.00031	50	32,930	293	0.00890
15	55,731	22	0.00039	51	34,181	188	0.00550
16	54,571	26	0.00048	52	31,501	341	0.01083
17	53,396	34	0.00064	53	34,319	265	0.00772
18	49,784	32	0.00064	54	32,026	321	0.01002
19	45,874	38	0.00082	55	33,389	334	0.01000
20	43,724	34	0.00078	56	29,825	364	0.01220
21	39,490	25	0.00063	57	29,230	339	0.01160
22	36,388	33	0.00091	58	26,501	412	0.01554
23	34,898	20	0.00057	59	28,119	380	0.01351
24	30,789	19	0.00062	60	26,383	563	0.02134
25	30,200	25	0.00083	61	25,464	397	0.01560
26	30,849	26	0.00084	62	24,561	561	0.02284
27	29,861	33	0.00110	63	24,269	544	0.02242
28	28,241	26	0.00092	64	23,163	619	0.02672
29	30,166	30	0.00099	65	27,633	815	0.02949
30	29,403	33	0.00112	66	22,845	736	0.03222
31	28,717	26	0.00091	67	22,285	627	0.02813
32	28,654	33	0.00115	68	19,721	850	0.04310
33	31,216	32	0.00103	69	21,742	825	0.03794
34	28,635	36	0.00126	70+	208,831	21,276	0.10188
35	30,329	47	0.00155				

3.2.2.6. Examples

a. The Complete Life Table. Table 3.4 gives the number of deaths by age and the midyear[42] population of both sexes, for Ireland during calendar

[42] Actually, the population refers to April 17th, 1966; no conversion to June 30th has, however, been attempted here.

TABLE 3.5. Life Table for Ireland (Both Sexes)

Age (years)	q_x ($\times 10^6$)	p_x ($\times 10^6$)	l_x	d_x	L_x	P_x ($\times 10^6$)	T_x	e_x
0	24,115	975,885	1,000,000	24,115	987,942	987,080^a	69,917,963	69.92
1	1,448	998,552	975,885	1,414	975,178	998,645	68,930,021	70.63
2	1,259	998,741	974,471	1,227	973,857	999,100	67,954,843	69.74
3	539	999,461	973,244	525	972,981	999,480	66,980,986	68.82
4	499	999,501	972,719	486	972,476	999,484	66,008,005	67.86
5	529	999,471	972,233	515	971,975	999,495	65,035,529	66.89
6	479	999,521	971,718	466	971,485	999,600	64,063,554	65.93
7	319	999,681	971,252	310	971,097	999,695	63,092,069	64.96
8	289	999,711	970,942	281	970,801	999,626	62,120,972	63.98
9	459	999,541	970,661	446	970,438	999,615	61,150,171	63.00
10	309	999,691	970,215	300	970,065	999,664	60,179,733	62.03
11	359	999,641	969,915	349	969,740	999,645	59,209,668	61.05
12	349	999,651	969,566	339	969,396	999,655	58,239,928	60.07
13	339	999,661	969,227	329	969,062	999,675	57,270,532	59.09
14	309	999,691	968,898	300	968,748	999,650	56,301,470	58.11
15	389	999,611	968,598	377	968,409	999,566	55,332,722	57.13
16	479	999,521	968,221	464	967,989	999,440	54,364,313	56.15
17	639	999,361	967,757	619	967,447	999,360	53,396,324	55.18
18	639	999,361	967,138	619	966,828	999,270	52,428,877	54.21
19	819	999,181	966,519	792	966,123	999,199	51,462,049	53.25
20	779	999,221	965,727	753	965,350	999,295	50,495,926	52.29
21	629	999,371	964,974	607	964,670	999,230	49,530,576	51.33
22	909	999,091	964,367	877	963,928	999,260	48,565,906	50.36
23	569	999,431	963,490	549	963,215	999,405	47,601,978	49.41
24	619	999,381	962,941	597	962,642	999,275	46,638,763	48.43
25	829	999,171	962,344	798	961,945	999,165	45,676,121	47.46
26	839	999,161	961,546	807	961,142	999,031	44,714,176	46.50
27	1,099	998,901	960,739	1,056	960,211	998,990	43,753,034	45.54
28	919	999,081	959,683	882	959,242	999,045	42,792,823	44.59
29	989	999,011	958,801	949	958,326	998,946	41,833,581	43.63
30	1,119	998,881	957,852	1,072	957,316	998,985	40,875,255	42.67
31	909	999,091	956,780	870	956,345	998,970	39,917,939	41.72
32	1,149	998,581	955,910	1,099	955,360	998,910	38,961,594	40.76
33	1,029	998,971	954,811	983	954,319	998,855	38,006,234	39.81
34	1,259	998,741	953,828	1,201	953,227	998,596	37,051,915	38.85
35	1,548	998,452	952,627	1,475	951,889	998,382	36,098,688	37.89
36	1,688	998,312	951,152	1,606	950,349	998,425	35,146,799	36.95
37	1,458	998,542	949,546	1,385	948,853	998,346	34,196,450	36.01
38	1,848	998,152	948,161	1,753	947,284	997,827	33,247,597	35.07
39	2,496	997,504	946,408	2,363	945,226	997,464	32,300,313	34.13
40	2,576	997,424	944,045	2,432	942,829	997,712	31,355,087	33.21
41	1,998	998,002	941,613	1,882	940,672	997,363	30,412,258	32.30
42	3,274	996,726	939,731	3,077	938,192	997,024	29,471,586	31.36
43	2,676	997,324	936,654	2,507	935,400	996,850	28,533,394	30.46

TABLE 3.5 (*Continued*)

Age (years)	q_x ($\times 10^6$)	p_x ($\times 10^6$)	l_x	d_x	L_x	P_x ($\times 10^6$)	T_x	e_x
44	3,623	996,377	934,147	3,385	932,454	995,675	27,597,994	29.54
45	5,027	994,973	930,762	4,679	928,422	995,534	26,665,540	28.65
46	3,902	996,098	926,083	3,614	924,276	996,197	25,737,118	27.79
47	3,703	996,297	922,469	3,416	920,761	995,744	24,812,842	26.90
48	4,808	995,192	919,053	4,419	916,843	995,351	23,892,081	26.00
49	4,489	995,511	914,634	4,106	912,581	993,329	22,975,238	25.12
50	8,860	991,140	910,528	8,068	906,494	992,819	22,062,657	24.23
51	5,484	994,516	902,460	4,950	899,985	991,878	21,156,163	23.44
52	10,771	989,229	897,510	9,668	892,676	990,760	20,256,178	22.57
53	7,690	992,310	887,842	6,828	884,428	991,173	19,363,502	21.81
54	9,970	990,030	881,014	8,784	876,622	990,039	18,479,074	20.98
55	9,950	990,050	872,230	8,679	867,890	988,967	17,602,452	20.18
56	12,126	987,874	863,551	10,472	858,315	988,167	16,734,562	19.38
57	11,533	988,467	853,079	9,839	848,159	986,534	15,876,247	18.61
58	15,420	984,580	843,240	13,003	836,738	985,572	15,028,088	17.82
59	13,419	986,581	830,237	11,141	824,666	982,759	14,191,350	17.09
60	21,114	978,886	819,096	17,295	810,448	981,673	13,366,684	16.32
61	15,479	984,521	801,801	12,412	795,595	980,996	12,556,236	15.66
62	22,582	977,418	789,389	17,826	780,476	977,620	11,760,641	14.90
63	22,171	977,829	771,563	17,107	763,009	975,753	10,980,165	14.23
64	26,367	973,633	754,456	19,893	744,509	972,303	10,217,156	13.54
65	29,061	970,939	734,563	21,348	723,889	969,633	9,472,647	12.90
66	31,709	968,291	713,215	22,616	701,907	970,242	8,748,758	12.27
67	27,739	972,261	690,599	19,157	681,020	965,136	8,046,851	11.65
68	42,190	957,810	671,442	28,329	657,277	960,234	7,365,831	10.97
69	37,233	962,767	643,113	23,946	631,140	—	6,708,554	10.43
70	—	—	619,167	—	—	—	6,077,414	9.82

$^aP_b = 987,942.$

year 1966.[43] Age-specific death rates are easily obtained by dividing the number of deaths at each age by the midyear population, the latter being more or less equal to the person-years of exposure to risk. Death rates t_x are then converted to probabilities of dying q_x by the approximate relation.[44]

$$q_x = 2t_x/(2+t_x)$$

From the sequence of age-specific probabilities of dying, the complete life table is then computed (Table 3.5).

[43]Source: *Report on Vital Statistics 1966, and Census of Ireland 1966* (Vol. II), G.P.O. Dublin 1, 1966.
[44]For q_0, a better approximation is given by $2t_0/(2+1.82\,t_0)$, or 0.02388, as seen in Section 3.2.2.1.

The various life-table functions were computed by the following relations:

$$p_x = 1 - q_x, \qquad P_x = L_{x+1}/L_x$$

$$l_{x+1} = l_x p_x, \qquad P_b = L_0/l_0$$

$$d_x = l_x q_x, \qquad T_x = \sum_x^\omega L_x$$

$$L_x = 0.5(l_x + l_{x+1}), \qquad e_x = T_x/l_x$$

Two variants for L_0 may be computed,

$$L_0 = 975,885 + (1,000,000 - 975,885)[0.25(0.75) + 0.75(0.25)]$$
$$= 984,928$$

or

$$L_0 = 0.25(1,000,000) + 0.75(975,885)$$
$$= 981,914$$

Both constitute better approximations to person-years of exposure than the stated value in the table obtained by taking the arithmetic average of l_0 and l_1.

Values of T_{70} have been computed by the two methods suggested in Section 3.2.2.2:

(a) Since $M_{70+} = 0.10188$, one has approximately $T_{70} = 619,167/0.10188$ or $6,077,414$ person-years, and $e_{70} = 1/0.10188$, i.e., 9.815 years.

(b) Using the standard set of e_x values given in Section 3.2.2.2, one finds by interpolation that e_{70} equals 11.2; T_{70} will then be equal to 11.2 (619,167), i.e., 6,934,670 person-years.

As one sees, the discrepancy between both estimates is rather wide in the present case; method (a), based on the rate really observed over age 70, should probably be preferred and has been used in the life table above.

   b. The Abridged Life Table. The complete life table computed in the above section has been abridged into five-year groups (Table 3.6) according

TABLE 3.6. Abridged Life Table for Ireland 1966

Age (years)	$_5q_x$ ($\times 10^6$)	$_5p_x$ ($\times 10^6$)	l_x	$_5d_x$	$_5L_x$	$_5P_x$ ($\times 10^6$)	T_x	e_x
0	27,767	972,233	1,000,000	27,767	4,930,583	984,898^a	69,929,435	69.93
5	2,076	997,924	972,233	2,018	4,856,120	998,129	64,998,852	66.86
10	1,667	998,333	970,215	1,617	4,847,033	997,685	60,142,732	61.99
15	2,964	997,036	968,598	2,871	4,835,813	996,767	55,295,699	57.09
20	3,503	996,497	965,727	3,383	4,820,178	995,916	50,459,886	52.25
25	4,668	995,332	962,344	4,492	4,800,490	994,940	45,639,708	47.43
30	5,455	995,445	957,852	5,225	4,776,198	992,773	40,839,218	42.64
35	9,009	990,991	952,627	8,582	4,741,680	988,472	36,063,020	37.86
40	14,070	985,930	944,045	13,283	4,687,018	982,122	31,321,340	33.18
45	21,739	978,261	930,762	20,234	4,603,225	968,211	26,634,322	28.62
50	42,061	957,939	910,528	38,298	4,456,895	948,713	22,031,097	24.20
55	60,917	939,083	872,230	53,134	4,228,315	918,604	17,574,202	20.15
60	103,203	896,797	819,096	84,533	3,884,148	871,317	13,345,887	16.29
65	157,095	842,905	734,563	115,396	3,384,325	—	9,461,739	12.88
70	—	—	619,167	—	—	—	6,077,414	9.82

$^a{}_5P_b = 986,117.$

to the following relations:

$$_5d_x = l_x - l_{x+5}, \qquad _5P_x = {}_5L_{x+5}/{}_5L_x$$

$$_5q_x = {}_5d_x/l_x, \qquad _5P_b = {}_5L_0/5l_0$$

$$_5p_x = l - {}_5q_x, \qquad T_x = \sum_x^\omega {}_5L_x$$

$$_5L_x = 2.5(l_x + l_{x+5}), \qquad e_x = T_x/l_x$$

It should be pointed out that life tables should be computed for both males and females, in order to take into account differential mortality by sex. If one wants to take into account the sex ratio at birth (grossly 105 male births for 100 female births), the radix of the male life table can be multiplied by 1.05, that is, l_0 (males) is expressed as 1.05 l_0 (females).

c. *Mortality by Cause of Death.* For 100,000 live births consider the attrition due to congenital malformations and to other causes of death[45] (Table 3.7). The corrected probabilities of dying due to congenital

---

[45] Source: adapted from *Report on Vital Statistics 1966, and Census of Ireland 1960* (Vol. II). G.P.O. Dublin 1, 1966.

TABLE 3.7

Age (years)	Survivors	Causes of death		Total
		Congenital malformations	Other	
0	100,000	640	1,772	2,412
1	97,588	28	110	138
2	97,450	17	105	122
3	97,328	4	49	53
4	97,275	2	47	49

malformations are equal to

$$q_0' = 640/(100,000 - \tfrac{1}{2}1,772) = 0.00646$$

$$q_1' = 28/(97,588 - \tfrac{1}{2}110) = 0.00029$$

The probabilities of dying due to other causes of death are

$$q_0'' = 1,772/(100,000 - \tfrac{1}{2}640) = 0.01778$$

$$q_1'' = 110/(97,588 - \tfrac{1}{2}28) = 0.00113$$

The probability of dying from all causes of death is then

$$q_0 = 1 - (1 - q_0')(1 - q_0'')$$

$$= 0.02413, \text{ approximately } 2,412/100,000$$

$$q_1 = 1 - (1 - q_1')(1 - q_1'')$$

$$= 0.00142, \text{ approximately } 138/97,588$$

etc.

d. Ledermann's Model Life Tables. The following probabilities of death of both sexes are known[46]: $_5q_0 = 30.1(‰)$ and $_{20}q_{45} = 221.3(‰)$. Estimate the probability of dying (both sexes) $_5q_{50}$ using Ledermann's model life tables (Section 3.2.2.5 and Table A.1 in the Appendix). The one-entry table gives the following estimate: using $\log_{10} 30.1 = 1.47857$, one has $\log_{10} {}_5q_{50} = 0.95183 + 0.40564(1.47857)$ and $_5q_{50} = 35.61(‰)$. Since $\log_{10} 221.3 = 2.34498$, the two-entry table gives the following estimate: $\log_{10} {}_5q_{50} = -1.30096 + 0.01336(1.47857) + 1.24950(2.34498)$ and $_5q_{50} = 44.55(‰)$.

---

[46]In the Ledermann approach, all probabilities are expressed *in "per thousand,"* i.e., $_5q_x \times 1000$.

As the logarithms of the probabilities are assumed to be distributed according to a normal law around the central value estimated above, 95% of the cases will be within two standard deviations of the mean, i.e., $\log_{10} {}_5q_{50} \pm 2\sigma$. The last column of Table A.1. gives the value of K, the antilogarithm of 2σ; the interval is therefore defined by the confidence limits ${}_5q_{50}/K$ and ${}_5q_{50}K$ corresponding, respectively, to $\log_{10} {}_5q_{50} - 2\sigma$ and $\log_{10} {}_5q_{50} + 2\sigma$. In this example, one obtains the 95% confidence intervals: $35.61/1.413 = 25.202$ to $35.61(1.413) = 50.317$ for the one-entry model, and $44.55/1.074 = 41.480$ to $44.55(1.074) = 47.847$ for the two-entry model.

One notices how incorporating a second entry increases the precision of the estimate; one should therefore always use the two-entry model life tables if adequate data are available.

3.3. SOME COMMENTS ON COHORT MEASURES OF MORTALITY

Compared to other demographic phenomena, the study of mortality is relatively simple: all persons die and therefore the intensity of the process is always equal to unity in every cohort. As to the tempo of events, humanity has tried, in general, to raise the expectation of life. Period analysis of mortality therefore reflects period conditions, since current measures of mortality are only slightly affected by the distributional distortion effect (noted in Section 2.3.2), which biases most period measures of other demographic processes. Period death rates, for example, quite adequately reflect the mortality conditions of the period, cleared from the influence of age–sex structures. This sequence of rates can then be condensed by one of the methods seen in Section 2.2.

The period life table, in the translation approach, also reflects period conditions; the mean length of life of the fictitious cohort even represents a good synthetic measure of period mortality. However, a period life table cannot be considered as representing the experience of a birth-cohort[47]: if, at young ages, mortality in an actual cohort is quite similar to the conditions described by the period life table computed for the calendar year of birth of the cohort, the differences between the latter life table and the cohort life table tend to increase with age due to the decrease of mortality observed at least since the 19th century in developed countries.

[47]The following comments are based on work by Légaré (1966) and Vallin (1973).

Other differences can also be noted between cohort and period life tables. Considering cohort life tables computed in Great Britain, Légaré has shown that the reduction of mortality seems different depending on the use of cohort or period life tables. For the older birth-cohorts, the relative decrease in the probabilities of dying from one cohort to the other between ages 20 and 60 is independent of age; this observation is not valid for recent birth-cohorts where the relative decrease of probabilities of dying for males slackens after age 45 and is thus dependent upon age. In period life tables, on the contrary, the relative decrease of probabilities of dying slackens after 35 years of age, a fact which is only valid for recent cohorts as noted above.

Finally, cohort life tables would partly enable one to explain the increase in the risks of dying for males recently observed in various developed nations. Different factors can be called upon: a change in causes of death,[48] a generation effect,[48] a reverse selection effect[49]; up to now, no definitive explanation has been advanced due, among other things, to the lack of studies of mortality by cohort.

Cohort analysis of mortality is therefore a real necessity, even if period measures of mortality are useful for studying the conditions of particular calendar years. Unfortunately, long time-series of data on mortality are available for very few countries; this partly explains the lack of studies in this field.[50]

3.4. REFERENCES AND SUPPLEMENTARY BIBLIOGRAPHY

Baloche, C., & Nizard, A. *Evolution de la Mortalité par Type de Causes de Décès en France, 1950–1967. Essai d'une Nouvelle Mesure de la Mortalité* (Vol. 3). Liège: I.U.S.S.P. International Population Conference, 1973, pp. 185–217.

Benjamin, B., & Haycocks, H. W. *The Analysis of Mortality and Other Actuarial Statistics.* London: Cambridge University Press, 1970.

Bourgeois-Pichat, J. La mesure de la mortalité infantile. *Population,* 1951, *6*(2), 233–248; *6*(3), 459–480.

Bourgeois-Pichat, J. Analyse de la mortalité infantile. *Bulletin Démographique (Nations Unies),* 1952, *2*, 1–14.

Brass, W. On the scale of mortality. In W. Brass (Ed.), *Biological Aspects of Demography.* London: Taylor & Francis, 1971, pp. 69–110.

Calot, G. *L'Analyse de la Mortalité Différentielle* (Vol. II). Liège: I.U.S.S.P. International Population Conference, 1969, pp. 942–949.

---

[48]For example, the influence of the 1914–1918 war on older males.

[49]Formerly, only healthy persons survived until old age and formed therefore a highly selected group.

[50]Another factor that certainly comes into play is the lack of interest of many demographers for cohort studies of mortality, with period analysis dominating the field.

Chiang, C. L. On constructing current life tables. *Journal of the American Statistical Association*, 1972, *67*(339), 538–541.

Coale, A., & Demeny, P. *Regional Model Life Tables and Stable Populations.* Princeton: Princeton University Press, 1966.

Coale, A., & Demeny, P. *Methods of estimating basic demographic measures from incomplete data.* United Nations ST/SOA/Series A/42, 1967.

Gabriel, K. R., & Ronen, I. Estimates of mortality from infant mortality rates. *Population Studies*, 1958, *XII*(2), 164–169.

Greville, T. N. E. Short methods of constructing abridged life tables. *The Record of the American Institute of Actuaries*, 1943, *XXXII*(65), Part 1, 29–42.

Jacobson, P. H. Cohort survival for generations since 1840. *The Milbank Memorial Fund Quarterly*, 1964, *42*(3), Part 1, 36–51.

Keyfitz, N. *Introduction to the Mathematics of Population.* Reading: Addison–Wesley Publishing Co., 1968, Chapter 1.

Kitagawa, E. M. Theoretical considerations in the selection of a mortality index, and some empirical comparisons. *Human Biology*, 1966, *38*(3), 293–305.

Ledermann, S. *Nouvelles Tables-Types de Mortalité.* Paris: Presses Universitaires de France, 1969.

Ledermann, S., & Bréas, J. Les dimensions de la mortalité. *Population*, 1959, *14*(4), 637–682.

Légaré, J. Quelques considérations sur les tables de mortalité de génération. *Population*, 1966, *21*(5), 915–938.

Logan, W. P. D. *The measurement of infant mortality. United Nations Population Bulletin* No. 3, ST/SOA/Ser. N/3, 1953, pp. 30–67.

Péron, Y. La construction de tables de mortalité abrégées: comparaison de trois méthodes usuelles. *Population*, 1971, *26*(6), 1125–1130.

Pressat, R. *Demographic Analysis.* Chicago: Aldine Publishing Co., 1972.

Preston, S. H., Keyfitz, N., & Schoen, R. *Causes of Death. Life Tables for National Populations.* New York: Seminar Press, 1972.

Qvist, J. On the construction of abridged life tables. *Statistisk Tidskrift*, 1972, (3), 200–208.

Reed, L. J., & Merrell, M. A short method for constructing an abridged life table. *The American Journal of Hygiene*, 1939, *30*(2), 33–62.

Schoen, R. The geometric mean of the age-specific death rates as a summary index of mortality. *Demography*, 1970, *7*(3), 317–324.

Schwartz, D., & Lazar, Ph. Taux de mortalité par une cause donnée de décès en tenant compte des autres causes de décès ou de disparition. *Revue de l'Institut International de Statistique*, 1961, *29*(3), 44–56.

Shryock, H. S. *et al. The methods and materials of demography* (2 volumes) Washington, D.C.: US Department of Commerce, Bureau of the Census, 1971.

Spiegelman, M. *Introduction to Demography* (Rev. ed.). Cambridge, Massachusetts: Harvard University Press, 1968.

Spiegelman, M. Segmented generation mortality. *Demography*, 1969, *6*(2), 117–123.

United Nations. *Age and sex patterns of mortality: model life tables for underdeveloped countries.* New York: ST/SOA/Ser. A/22, 1955.

Vallin, J. *La Mortalité par Génération en France, Depuis 1899.* Paris: I.N.E.D., P.U.F., 1973.

Vincent, P. La mortalité des vieillards. *Population*, 1951, *6*(2), 181–204.

Wolfenden, H. H. *Population Statistics and Their Compilation.* Chicago: The University of Chicago Press, 1954.

THE ANALYSIS OF NUPTIALITY 4

4.1. ANALYSIS BASED ON STATISTICS OF POPULATION CHANGE

As noted in the Introduction, the analysis of nuptiality is often a prerequisite for the study of fertility. Though not a "true" demographic phenomenon, in the sense that it does not contribute directly to population change, nuptiality is, however, such an important component of natality that it deserves a separate chapter in this textbook.

Two types of analyses will be outlined in this chapter: first, analysis of nuptiality based on statistics of population change combined with data on population structures; second, analysis of nuptiality through the sole use of census-type material, i.e., current population statistics including often retrospective questions. This section is devoted to the first approach using statistics of population change; as usual, analysis may be based on period or cohort data.

4.1.1. Period Analysis

The two specific approaches of standardization or translation can be adopted here.

4.1.1.1. Standardization. In attempting to distinguish the influence of population structures on the number of events (marriages, marriage dissolutions) observed during a certain period of time, one may compute exposure rates or reduced events in the standardization approach. In the field of *first marriage*, for example, one may compute nuptiality rates in the strict sense (Section 1.2.7). From Fig. 4.1, a *first marriage rate* can be obtained by dividing the number of first marriages observed in a female[1] birth-cohort at

---

[1]The same holds true for a male birth-cohort. See Section 4.3 for the general problem of combining male *and* female populations for the study of marriage.

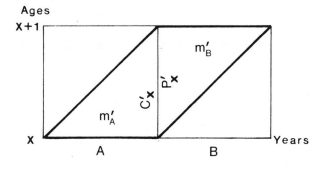

FIGURE 4.1

completed age $x(m'_A + m'_B)$ by the number of person-years lived in spinster-hood between exact ages x and $x + 1$, the denominator being approximately equal to the number of spinsters C'_x actually recorded at completed age x (i.e., on December 31st, year A). The first marriage rate t_x is thus equal to

$$t_x = (m'_A + m'_B)/C'_x$$

and covers two calendar years, A and B. The sequence of similar rates computed from, e.g., ages 15 to 50[2] can be summarized, among others, by their sum $\sum_{15}^{50} t_x$ or by other methods of standardization.

Reduced first marriages could also be computed; with the data in Fig. 4.1, the number of reduced first marriages can be computed by the formula

$$M_x = (m'_A + m'_B)/P'_x$$

where P'_x stands for the total population (spinsters and ever-marrieds) aged x in completed years, i.e., at the end of year A. Once again, the sequence of indexes can be summarized by routine standardization procedures (Section 2.2).

Rates or reduced events could also be computed for the calendar year A (see Fig. 4.2) either by deriving rates or reduced marriages for each cohort observed during year A between bounds 15 and 50 (Fig. 4.2a) or by computing hybrid rates or reduced events covering two cohorts, as in Fig. 4.2b. Once again, these rates can be summarized by standardization. These standardized indexes reflect period conditions of nuptiality excluding the impact of population structures.

[2]Female marriages after age 50 have no impact on fertility; as to the lower bound, it depends on custom and legal dispositions.

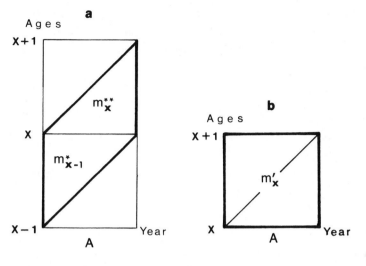

FIGURE 4.2

The same methods can be used in the study of *marriage dissolutions* and *remarriages*. Rates or reduced events can be computed for specific calendar periods in view of eliminating the impact of population structures by age and marital status, usually at census time.[3] These period indexes can then be summarized, in view of spatial or temporal comparisons, by their sum, their average, or other standardization procedures. During intercensal periods, however, population structures are frequently not known; it is therefore impossible to compute true rates or reduced events. If the age–sex structure is estimated, age–sex-specific frequencies of marriage dissolutions or remarriages can be computed by dividing the number of events at age x by the average male or female population at that age. These indexes, eliminating the influence of the age and sex population structure, can once again be condensed into a summary index by the usual methods.[4]

When only the total number of events (marriages and marriage dissolutions) is known, one may compute *crude rates* by dividing the total number of events observed during a specified calendar period by the midperiod total population. If population structures are known it is also possible to compute *indirectly standardized* indexes, using a standard set of frequencies as developed in Section 2.2.4.

[3]Population structures by marital status are usually known only at time of census.
[4]It is important to note that these summary indexes do not necessarily have a meaning in the *translation* approach.

Finally, double standardization for structures and frequencies (Section 2.2.5) can be introduced if, for example, one wishes to know the respective impact of population structures and nuptiality frequencies on the number of events observed during a specified period of time.

4.1.1.2. Translation. Starting with the case of *first marriages,* one can compute *first marriage rates* t_x or *reduced first marriages* M_x as above during a certain time period (see example, Section 4.1.3.2). Using the *fictitious cohort method* (Section 2.3.1), reduced first marriages can be summed between bounds α and β (e.g., 15 and 50 for females, 15 and 60 for males) in order to derive the *fictitious mean number of first marriages* per female or male:

$$\bar{e} = \sum_x M_x$$

The *fictitious mean age at marriage* is equal to the weighted average of ages at marriage, weights being the number of reduced first marriages at each age. If data conform to Fig. 4.1, the average age at first marriage is equal to

$$\bar{x} = \frac{1}{\bar{e}} \sum_x (x + 0.5) M_x$$

With data as in Fig. 4.2a, one has

$$\bar{x} = \frac{1}{\bar{e}} \sum_x (x) M_x$$

and with data as in Fig. 4.2b

$$\bar{x} = \frac{1}{\bar{e}} \sum_x (x + 0.5) M_x$$

always considering that marriages are evenly distributed between exact ages considered.

If first marriage rates have been computed instead, these can be transformed into *first marriage probabilities* using a transformation formula as seen in Section 1.2.8, for example,

$$n_x = 2t_x / (2 + t_x)$$

It is easy, thereafter, to set up the *period first marriage table*[5] (see example, Section 4.1.3.1). With reference to the general theory of attrition tables (Section 1.2.5), and assuming that the lower and upper bounds correspond,

[5] *Double decrement tables,* taking mortality also into account, are sometimes computed: these tables are of doubtful utility, as they should include migration too.

respectively, to exact ages 15 and 50, select an arbitrary radix C_{15} of spinsters or bachelors at exact age 15; the first marriage table is set up using the algorithm

$$C_x n_x = m_x$$

$$C_x - m_x = C_{x+1}$$

where n_x denotes the period probability of first marriage between exact ages x and $x + 1$; C_x represents the number of spinsters or bachelors at exact age x in the nuptiality table; and m_x holds for the number of first marriages at completed age x in the table.

The period average intensity of first marriage is then equal to[6]

$$\bar{e} = \frac{1}{C_{15}} \sum_{15}^{49} m_x$$

the fictitious average age at first marriage being

$$\bar{x} = \frac{\sum_{15}^{49} (x + 0.5) m_x}{\sum_{15}^{49} m_x}$$

As noted in Section 4.1.1.1, period measures of *marriage dissolution and remarriage* can usually only be obtained at census time; during intercensal periods, the adequate population structures are indeed not known. It is therefore generally impossible to compute rates or reduced events relating to marriage dissolutions and remarriages during intercensal periods. L. Henry has, however, devised a method of obtaining a period *mean number of divorces per marriage*, which will be briefly outlined below[7]; for an example see Section 4.1.3.3.

Let M_i represent the number of marriages observed during year i, d_i the average number of divorces per marriage in this marriage-cohort, and S_j the proportion of divorces that occur in the marriage-cohort j years after marriage. Assuming S_j constant from cohort to cohort, one may write $D = (d_0 M_0) S_0 + (d_1 M_1) S_1 + (d_2 M_2) S_2 + \cdots$, where D is the actual number of divorces observed during a particular year A, and M_i are the number of marriages observed during year A and the preceding years. If d_i is

---

[6]Note that $C_{15} - C_{50} = \sum_{15}^{49} m_x$. Therefore, $\bar{e} = (C_{15} - C_{50})/C_{15}$ or $1 - C_{50}/C_{15}$; C_{50}/C_{15} represents the *proportion ultimately single*.

[7]For further reference, see Henry (1952). See also Preston (1975) for other methods.

independent of the marriage-cohort, an average number of divorces per marriage can be obtained from the relation

$$d = D/\sum S_i M_i$$

The problem consists therefore in deriving a weighted average of the number of marriages over a certain period of time, weights being equal to the *tempo* of divorce by marriage durations. Standard tables of separation factors S_j due to L. Henry and M. Van Houte-Minet,[8] are presented in the Appendix, Table A.2. This weighted average method could be extended to other components of nuptiality as long as the phenomenon under consideration is more or less stationary over time.[9]

One should note that all these fictitious measures of intensity and tempo of nuptiality are highly influenced by distributional distortion effects, as seen in Section 2.3.2. Measures of the average number of first marriages per head, for example, are not only dependent upon the true cohort number of marriages per head but also upon the shifts in age at marriage from one cohort to the other.[10] Recourse to translation models (Section 2.3.2) may sometimes improve estimates when trends are sufficiently well known. Often, however, one should not put too much emphasis on the value of these estimates; one should in any case be cautious when period measures are used for translation purposes instead of for the quite adequate standardization approach.

4.1.2. Cohort Analysis

4.1.2.1. First Marriage. When the necessary data are available, cohort analysis of first marriage will rely on the computation of *corrected probabilities of first marriage*. Consider Fig. 4.3, where C'_x represents the number of bachelors or spinsters actually observed at exact age x in a male or female birth-cohort; m'_x denotes the actual number of male or female first marriages observed at completed age x.

Writing d'_x, e'_x, and i'_x, respectively, for the number of deaths, out- and in-migration of bachelors or spinsters, the corrected probability of first

---

[8]M. Van Houte-Minet, unpublished data, 1969.

[9]Other applications of this method are given in Sections 5.3.1.2 and 5.4.1.2.

[10]In some cases, distributional distortion effects are so strong that the average number of *first* marriages per head (sum of period reduced first marriages) is greater than unity, an obvious impossibility in a real cohort.

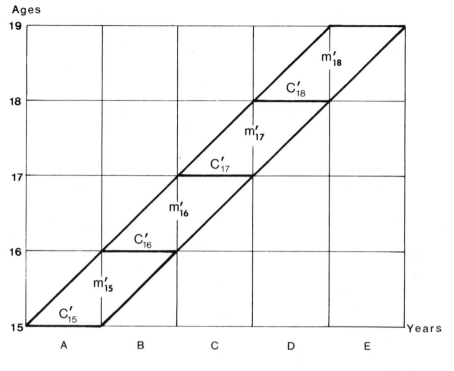

FIGURE 4.3

marriage will be approximately equal to

$$n_x = \frac{m_x'}{C_x' - d_x'/2 - e_x'/2 + i_x'/2}$$

following the general theory developed in Section 1.3.2.2. As the correction factor in the denominator is usually small with respect to C_x', the corrected probability of first marriage can often be taken simply as[11]

$$n_x = m_x'/C_x'$$

Having estimated by the above measures the probability of first marriage at each age for the male or female birth-cohort, a *cohort first-marriage table* can be set up using similar relations to those developed for the period

---

[11]Usually the number of bachelors or spinsters are estimated at the end of the year (i.e., at *completed* age x); writing C_x' for this estimate, the probability of first marriage becomes equal to $m_x'/(C_x' + \frac{1}{2}m_x')$. One may also compute first-marriage *rates* and transform the latter into probabilities, as in Section 4.1.1.2.

table (Section 4.1.1.2). Cohort intensity and tempo of first marriage can then be estimated from the number of marriages in the table.

The method of corrected probabilities, however, requires detailed data each year on the number of first marriages by age and birth-cohort,[12] and on the number of persons single by birth-cohort. The latter are usually not known unless one keeps track of attrition due to marriage, death, and migration. Cohort analysis resorting to corrected probabilities of first marriage can therefore only be performed for areas having detailed data on marriages, deaths, and migrations cross tabulated by birth-cohort and marital status.

If the method of corrected probabilities is not feasible, due to lack of data, one may have recourse to *cohort reduced marriages*, assuming that the condition of continuity is fulfilled.[13] Reduced first marriages are computed by the usual procedure (Section 1.3.2.2). In Fig. 4.4 let m_x' hold once again for the actual number of first marriages observed between exact ages x and $x+1$ in a birth-cohort, P_x' denoting this time the total population (ever married or not) at completed age x. The number of reduced first marriages M_x is simply expressed as

$$M_x = m_x'/P_x'$$

The average cohort intensity of first marriage (mean number of first marriages per head) will thus be equal to

$$\bar{e} = \sum_\alpha^\beta \frac{m_x'}{P_x'}$$

and the average cohort age at marriage will be

$$\bar{x} = \frac{1}{\bar{e}} \sum_\alpha^\beta (x+0.5)\frac{m_x'}{P_x'}$$

As just noted in the previous footnote, these two measures of intensity and tempo are usually biased due to discontinuities in mortality and migration between bachelors and ever-marrieds. If there is no migration, the true

---

[12] The classification by birth-cohort is sufficient; tabulation by age alone is inadequate as marriages then relate to *two* cohorts instead of one.

[13] As noted in Section 1.3.2.2, this is strictly not the case, due to differential mortality and migration between never- and ever-marrieds; estimates will therefore be biased. If there is no migration, observed reduced marriages will be slightly lower than those in a pure state, due to lower survival probabilities for never-marrieds; the intensity of first marriage will therefore underestimate the true value.

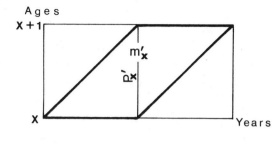

FIGURE 4.4

value of reduced first marriages is equal to

$$\frac{m'_x}{P'_x}\left(\frac{s'_{0,x+0.5}}{s_{0,x+0.5}}\right)$$

where the correction factor between parentheses represents the ratio of probabilities of survival of the total population to the never-married. If these ratios are known, better estimates of reduced first marriages can be derived. Table A.3 in the Appendix presents a standard set of correction factors based on recent differential mortality data,[14] for *exact ages* 15 to 50; correction factors for other ages can be obtained by linear interpolation. Correction factors are frequently much lower for females than for males; reduced first marriages without correction are therefore less biased for females than for males with respect to differential mortality by marital status.

When migration intervenes, discontinuities are often higher than for mortality alone and seem to affect the female population more this time; correction factors for spinsters and bachelors are, however, much more variable from country to country so that a standard set of correction factors for differential migration is impossible to derive.

Corrected probabilities of first marriage, on the other hand, though requiring elaborate data, only presume that the condition of independence is satisfied; they are not affected by differential mortality experience between never-marrieds and ever-marrieds. However, if the population remaining single has to be estimated from statistics on marriages, deaths, and migrations by marital status, evaluation errors might be more important than discontinuities in the case of reduced marriages. It is therefore doubtful that, in practice, corrected probabilities will lead to better estimates of nuptiality in a pure state than reduced first marriages.

[14]Average of correction factors for 13 populations (see Wunsch, 1970).

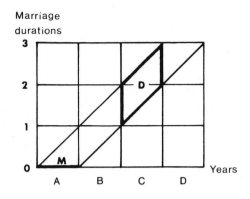

FIGURE 4.5

4.1.2.2. Marriage Dissolution and Remarriage. Even when *marriage dissolutions* are tabulated each year by marriage-cohort,[15] it is rarely possible to compute reduced events due to absence of data on the number of survivors in the cohort at each duration of marriage.

However, approximate measures can be obtained by dividing the number of dissolutions (D) observed in the marriage-cohort during a specified year by the *initial* number of marriages (M) in the cohort (see Fig. 4.5). Approximate measures of the average number of dissolutions per marriage and of the average duration of marriage at dissolution are then obtained by

$$\hat{\hat{e}} = \sum_0^\beta \frac{D_x}{M}$$

and

$$\hat{\hat{x}} = \frac{1}{\hat{e}} \sum_0^\beta x \frac{D_x}{M}$$

Bound β should cover the wife's reproductive ages.[16] If data are cross tabulated by age of spouses, summation can extend to wife's age 50 or husband's age 60, for example; if dissolutions are tabulated only by duration of marriage, summation will proceed until duration of marriage 30 or 35, covering practically all fertile ages.

[15]In theory, marriage dissolutions should be cross-tabulated by marriage-cohorts *and* birth-cohorts of spouses.
[16]Marriage dissolutions occurring after the wife's menopause are of no great interest to the demographer. As a practical measure, one could restrict the study to dissolutions of marriage concluded under age 50 for the wife.

It is important to note that these measures are biased: the denominator in the true number of reduced events is usually smaller than the initial population of the cohort, due to attrition; therefore, the above measures *underestimate* the true measures of intensity and tempo of marriage dissolution in the marriage-cohort.

A similar procedure can be used for the study of remarriage. Remarriages should be tabulated each year by cohort of widowhood or divorce and if possible by birth-cohort also. Again, surviving numbers of the cohort will be unknown and remarriages will be divided by the initial number of widows (widowers) and divorcé(e)s[17]; these frequencies will then be combined by the usual procedures in order to estimate the average number of remarriages per widow (widower) or divorced person and the average duration at remarriage elapsed since divorce or widowhood. These values will also be underestimated, for the reason given above.

Due to a lack of adequate data, studies of marriage dissolution and remarriage are unfortunately scarce. Frequently, it will be easier to study these phenomena through retrospective questions asked at census or survey rather than through statistics of population change.

4.1.3. Examples

4.1.3.1. The Period First Marriage Table. Table 4.1 presents the number of first marriages by age groups recorded in Canada during 1966, as well as the population of spinsters by age groups enumerated on the first of June 1966.[18] Considering the latter as the number of person-years of exposure to the "risk" of marriage, first marriage rates are easily computed.

Transforming marriage rates $_5N_x$ into first marriage probabilities $_5n_x$ by the usual relation

$$_5n_x = 10\,_5N_x/(2 + 5\,_5N_x)$$

gives the nuptiality table (Section 4.1.1.2) of Table 4.2. Table 4.2 has been computed using the relations

$$C_x\,_5n_x = \,_5m_x$$

and

$$C_x - \,_5m_x = C_{x+5}$$

[17]Once again, the study could be restricted to remarriages during reproductive ages.

[18]Source: *Demographic Yearbook 1968*, New York: United Nations, 1969. No correction has been made in order to estimate the population of spinsters on June 30th, instead of June 1st.

TABLE 4.1

Age groups (in completed years)	Number of first marriages	Midyear population of spinsters	First marriage rates
15–19	47,636	839,812	0.05672
20–24	72,058	324,762	0.22188
25–29	14,337	97,738	0.14669
30–34	3,875	56,940	0.06805
35–39	1,802	50,355	0.03579
40–44	1,019	48,073	0.02120
45–49	583	43,227	0.01349

TABLE 4.2

Exact age x (years)	Spinsters C_x	Marriages $_5m_x$	First marriage probability $_5n_x$ ($\times 1000$)
15	100,000	24,838	248.38
20	75,162	53,634	713.58
25	21,528	11,553	536.65
30	9,975	2,901	290.78
35	7,074	1,162	164.25
40	5,912	595	100.66
45	5,317	347	65.25
50	4,970	—	—
		95,030	

The radix C_{15} of the table is perfectly arbitrary, and was chosen here as being equal to 100,000 spinsters. The mean number of marriages per head is equal to

$$\frac{100,000 - 4,970}{100,000} = 0.95$$

The average age at marriage of 22.5 years can be obtained by either of the two following formulas:

$$17.5 + \frac{5(C_{20} + C_{25} + \cdots + C_{45}) - 30C_{50}}{C_{15} - C_{50}}$$

$$= 17.5 + \frac{5(124,968) - 149,100}{95,030} \qquad \text{since } _5m_x = C_x - C_{x+5}$$

TABLE 4.3

Birth-cohorts	First marriages in 1956	Average female population, 1956	Reduced first marriages
1941–1937	5,671	228,947	0.1238
1936–1932	22,200	213,393	0.5202
1931–1927	10,799	230,078	0.2347
1926–1922	3,750	256,232	0.0732
1921–1917	1,506	273,400	0.0275
1916–1912	767	265,795	0.0144
1911–1907	512	267,419	0.0096

or

$$[17.5(24,838)+22.5(53,634)+\cdots+47.5(347)]\frac{1}{95,030}$$

$$= 2,138,765/95,030$$

4.1.3.2. Period Reduced First Marriages. As an example of computation of period reduced first marriages, consider the data for Sweden, 1956,[19] given in Table 4.3. Period reduced first marriages are obtained by dividing the number of first marriages by age group by one-fifth of the population in each age group (Section 2.4.2).

The fictitious mean number of first marriages per head is obtained by the sum of reduced first marriages, i.e., 1.0034. In this case, it is obvious that distributional distortion effects bias the estimated average intensity, as the latter is greater than unity.

Taking into account the fact that marriages are distributed here according to birth-cohorts, the fictitious mean age at marriage is obtained by the weighted average:

$$\frac{1}{1.0034}[17(0.1238)+22(0.5202)+\cdots+47(0.0096)] = 24.22 \text{ years}$$

4.1.3.3. Average Number of Divorces per Couple. In Section 4.1.1.2, an approximate method for estimating the period (fictitious) average number of divorces per head or couple has been developed. It is applied here to data on divorces in Great Britain for calendar year 1966 (Table 4.4). The number of marriages concluded between 1931 and 1966 are weighted by the standard

---

[19]Source: Adapted from *Befolknings Förändringar 1967, Del. 3,* Stockholm: Central Bureau of Statistics, 1969.

TABLE 4.4. Weighted Average of Marriages 1931–1966[a]

Year of marriage	Weights	Number of marriages	Year of marriage	Weights	Number of marriages
1966	0	437,083	1948	29	449,969
1965	3	422,054	1947	28	455,087
1964	6	410,165	1946	26	441,192
1963	15	401,142	1945	25	456,720
1962	64	397,818	1944	22	349,239
1961	82	391,101	1943	21	344,764
1960	82	393,598	1942	20	428,819
1959	77	390,178	1941	17	448,507
1958	71	390,356	1940	16	533,866
1957	64	398,955	1939	15	502,507
1956	56	406,266	1938	12	413,449
1955	50	410,630	1937	11	410,469
1954	44	392,859	1936	9	405,307
1953	40	395,316	1935	7	399,470
1952	38	399,762	1934	5	391,208
1951	36	411,399	1933	4	363,647
1950	33	408,033	1932	3	351,067
1949	31	425,965	1931	2	356,397

[a] Sources: *Demographic Yearbook*. New York: United Nations, 1958 and 1968; *Statistical Review of England and Wales 1966* (Part II). London: H.M.S.O., 1966.

calendar of divorce for Great Britain given in the Appendix, Table A.2. The average (fictitious) number of divorces per head or couple, 42,051 divorces being recorded in 1966, is therefore equal to $42,051/432,876 = 0.097$, i.e., 97 divorces per 1,000 marriages. Using the standard weights for France instead would have given $42,051/406,753$, i.e., 103 divorces per 1,000 marriages.

4.2. ANALYSIS BASED ON CENSUS-TYPE DATA

4.2.1. Use of Retrospective Questions

The present section will be devoted to census-type material incorporating retrospective questions on nuptiality experience. Section 4.2.2 will consider current population data without retrospective questions, i.e., data on population structures only.

The purpose of retrospective questions is to enable reconstruction of the "history" of persons interviewed with regard to nuptiality. As noted in

Section 1.3.2.3, obviously only persons surviving[20] at the time of the census or survey can be interviewed; however, if this group is not selected with respect to nuptiality, adequate measures of the intensity and tempo of nuptiality can be obtained nevertheless.

A question on marital status at the time of interview already allows the population to be classified according to the following status: (a) single, (b) married,[21] (c) divorced (and separated),[22] (d) widowed.

Since nuptiality experience after menopause is of no great interest for the study of population change, retrospective questions can be asked of married, divorced, and widowed women at the end of their reproductive period[23] in order to determine the average number of first marriages, remarriages, and marriage dissolutions per head. These indexes will characterize nuptiality in a pure state if the conditions of independence and continuity are fulfilled. The tempo of the various events can also be computed (truncated at age 50, for example) if one obtains the following data:

(a) date of birth;

(b) date of first marriage for all ever-marrieds;

(c) (α) date(s) of marriage dissolution(s); (β) date(s) of possible remarriage(s) for widowed, divorced, and remarried women.

With a cross tabulation of such data, it is possible to obtain, for the subgroups of surviving women,[24] the average age at first marriage [(a) and (b)], the average duration of first marriage at dissolution [(b) and (c)], and the average duration, at remarriage, elapsed since marriage dissolution [(c) α and (c) β].

In attempting to study *partial intensities* from cohort to cohort, i.e., intensities relating to women still in their reproductive period, similar questions may also be asked of women under age 50; the average (partial) intensities thus obtained may, however, possibly be affected by distortions due to changing *tempos* of events from cohort to cohort.[25] It is very often

---

[20]Surviving to death or to migration.

[21]*De jure* or possibly *de facto.* In some countries, there are several classifications of "married."

[22]In some censuses, separated persons are included with the married population instead; in this case, one should distinguish between married living with spouse and married not living with spouse.

[23]These questions can be combined with others in order to reconstruct the *fertility* history of these women (see Section 5.3.2).

[24]Due to increasing differential mortality with age, these measures might be considerably biased if data relating to older women are used.

[25]Increasing intensities of marriage before age 25, for example, from cohort to cohort, may be due either to decreasing proportions ultimately single or to decreasing age at marriage.

difficult to tell whether observed variations, from cohort to cohort, of partial intensities (at ages $x < \beta$) are due to changing tempos from one cohort to the other; often, however, after a certain age variations in partial intensities quite truly reflect trends in final intensities and therefore constitute interesting complementary material.

The battery of questions listed above is probably unsuitable for a census form and would require a special survey. However, demographers should take advantage of surveys conducted in other fields and include the necessary questions for a detailed analysis of nuptiality histories. It is, however, necessary that the survey samples the whole population, married or not; a fertility survey, for example, will usually select only married persons and therefore not be adequate.

4.2.2. Use of Population Structures by Marital Status

4.2.2.1. Proportions of Never-Married Persons. If retrospective questions have not been asked, but if the population structure by marital status and age is available, some approximate measures of *first marriage* can be derived.

If the conditions of independence and of continuity between nuptiality, mortality, and migration are satisfied, the proportion of persons single in a birth-cohort at a point of time will be identical to the proportion one would observe in a pure state, i.e., without mortality or migration.

Let S_{15} represent the (female[26]) population assumed still single aged **15** in completed years, and T_x the proportion of spinsters in this cohort at completed age **x**, in the *absence* of disturbances (mortality, for example). If the condition of *independence* is satisfied, the actual number of spinsters observed at completed age **x** will be equal to $S_{15}T_xL_x$, where L_x represents the probability of surviving until completed age x for the subpopulation of spinsters. The total population (ever married or not) is equal to $S_{15}L_x'$, the factor of S_{15} denoting the probability of survival for the whole population. The actual proportion T_x' of spinsters is therefore equal to

$$T_x' = S_{15}T_xL_x/S_{15}L_x'$$

Finally, $T_x' = T_x$ if $L_x = L_x'$, i.e., the condition of *continuity* if fulfilled.[27]

---

[26]The extension to the male population is immediate.

[27]As noted earlier, there is a slight discontinuity (higher for males than for females) due to differential mortality; discontinuity is greater when migration is also taken into account.

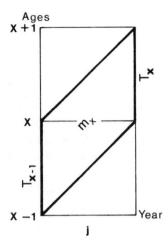

FIGURE 4.6

Therefore, if one has a series of censuses (or surveys) at close intervals, birth-cohorts can be followed from one census to another, attrition by first marriage being taken into account (Chasteland & Pressat, 1962). Proportions of spinsters T_{50} at age **50** will characterize the proportion ultimately single; $1 - T_{50}$ will therefore measure the average number of first marriages per head. Using T_{15} equal to 1, since the relative number of marriages m_x in the pure state is equal to $m_x = T_{x-1} - T_x$ (see Fig. 4.6), the average age at first marriage without disturbances is obtained by the relation

$$\bar{x} = \frac{\sum\limits_{16}^{50} x m_x}{\sum\limits_{16}^{50} m_x}$$

$$= \frac{\sum\limits_{16}^{50} x(T_{x-1} - T_x)}{\sum\limits_{16}^{50} (T_{x-1} - T_x)}$$

Since $\sum_{16}^{50} m_x = T_{15} - T_{50}$ and $\sum_{16}^{50} x(T_{x-1} - T_x)$ can be developed into $16T_{15} - 16T_{16} + 17T_{16} - 17T_{17} + \cdots + 50T_{49} - 50T_{50}$, the average age at first marriage becomes

$$\bar{x} = \frac{16T_{15} + \sum\limits_{16}^{49} T_x - 50T_{50}}{T_{15} - T_{50}}$$

or

$$\bar{x} = 16 + \frac{\sum\limits_{16}^{49} T_x - 34T_{50}}{1 - T_{50}}$$

Replacing T_x by its approximation T'_x yields the cohort average age at marriage derived from a succession of population structures by marital status and age. The above formula has to be adapted in practice, in order to take into account the actual durations of intercensal periods.

Frequently, proportions of persons single observed at *one* census are combined by the *fictitious cohort method* (Hajnal, 1953; see example, Section 4.2.3). The procedure is very similar to the one outlined above; however, computation is usually restricted to the proportions single by quinquennal age groups observed between *exact* ages 15 and 50. If the conditions of independence and continuity are satisfied, the proportion ultimately single at exact age 50 can be expressed as

$$T_{50} = ({}_5T_{45} + {}_5T_{50})/2$$

where ${}_5T_x$ represents the proportions single observed in five-year age groups at census. In the synthetic cohort the fictitious average mean age at first marriage will be equal to

$$\bar{x} = 15 + \frac{\sum\limits_{15}^{45} (5\ {}_5T_x - 35T_{50})}{1 - T_{50}}$$

In order to derive this formula, Hajnal considers that the mean age at first marriage is equal to the average number of years lived in the single state by those who marry before age 50. This average is equal to $\sum_{15}^{45} 5\ {}_5T_x$ person-years lived in the single state by the whole cohort between exact ages 15 and 50[28] plus $15T_{15}$ person-years lived in the single state by the whole cohort before exact age 15 (assuming marriages are not concluded before age 15, one has $T_{15} = 1$) minus $50T_{50}$ person-years lived by persons ultimately single, before their 50th birthday. Adding together these three subtotals gives the above relation for $\bar{x}$.

Though widely used, this measure only provides a synthetic estimate of the singulate mean age at marriage. Strictly speaking, this estimate is only

---

[28]Multiplication of ${}_5T_x$ by 5 derives from the fact that ${}_5T_x \cong (T_x + T_{x+5})/2$; the number of person-years lived single between x and $x+5$ is equal to $\int_x^{x+5} T_i\, di \cong 5T_{x+5} + (5/2)(T_x - T_{x+5}) = (5/2)(T_x + T_{x+5})$, i.e., $5\ {}_5T_x$.

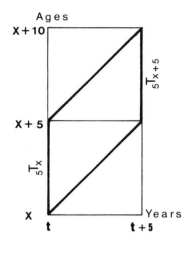

FIGURE 4.7

valid if all cohorts observed at census have experienced the same intensity and tempo of nuptiality; this condition will never be satisfied in practice. Even if mean ages at marriage are the same for each cohort, the period age at marriage may nevertheless be a biased estimate of true cohort tempos due to distributional distortion effects if cohort intensities are changing (Wattelar *et al.*, 1970). Hajnal's measure of the singulate mean age at marriage must therefore only be considered as a rough estimate of age at first marriage at census time.

Another approach to *period* analysis of first marriage, having access to the proportions single, is to compute probabilities of remaining single between ages x and $x + n$ from proportions single observed at *two* censuses at times t and $t + n$ (Agarwala, 1962; Kumar, 1967). For example, for an intercensal period of five years, the probability[29] of remaining single between completed age groups x, $x + 4$ to $x + 5$, $x + 9$ is equal to $_5T_{x+5}/_5T_x$ (see Fig. 4.7), where $_5T_i$ represents the proportion single in the age group i to $i + 5$. These probabilities can then be combined by the usual procedure for period first marriage tables (Section 4.1.1.2), as $1 - (_5T_{x+5}/_5T_x)$ represents the probability of first marriage between age groups considered. This method assumes that census errors are similar at times t and $t + n$; moreover, the nuptiality experience of the fictitious cohort in the nuptiality table is based on the conditions of the intercensal period—it is therefore subjected

---

[29] Assuming once more independence and continuity.

to all the restrictions of the fictitious cohort approach outlined in Section 2.3. It is interesting to note that in this method all cohorts experience the conditions of the *same* period (the intercensal period); in Hajnal's method, on the contrary, the proportions single reflect nuptiality histories of variable durations, the latter being low for young cohorts and higher for older cohorts. Hajnal's method is usually more biased by distributional distortion effects than the method based on two successive censuses, though the advantage of the latter approach is slight.

4.2.2.2. Proportions of Ever-Married Persons.

Comparisons between successive population structures by marital status cannot be extended to the study of marriage dissolutions or remarriages. The proportion of widowed or divorced persons to the married population, at a given point in time, depends not only on the risks of marriage dissolution but also on the chance of remarriage. Therefore, proportions of widowed and divorced persons vary from one census to the other, due not only to marriage dissolutions during the intercensal period but also to remarriages, which bring back a certain number of divorcées or widows into the married population. This problem did not affect the study of first marriage using the proportions single, as persons married do not become "single" again if their marriage is dissolved.

The proportion of persons married to the population ever-married thus behaves differently from the proportion single to the whole population, due to remarriages. Furthermore, risks of marriage dissolutions cannot be drawn from analysis of the proportions married and divorced, or married and widowed, to the population ever-married. In the study of widowhood, for example, the proportion of persons married and divorced to the population ever-married depends not only on the risks of becoming a widow during the intercensal period, but also on the impact of first marriages and remarriages[30] as well as of divorce, the latter preventing some marriages from being dissolved by death of a spouse.

Similarly, one cannot consider the proportions of ever-married (non-widowed) at census as the relative population escaping widowhood. Furthermore, the proportion of widowed and of ever-married (nonwidowed) in a cohort at a given age depends on the average age at marriage in the cohort, i.e., on the duration of exposure to widowhood: if age at marriage varies from one cohort to the other, the proportion widowed at a given age may change solely under the influence of differential periods of exposure to risk.

---

[30]Some widows during the period will reintegrate the category of married, and some persons single will become married.

In one case, however, proportions of ever-married can nevertheless be used; this is when census data distinguish between "first married" and "remarried" persons. When this is the case and if the conditions of independence and continuity are fulfilled, the proportions of first married change from one census to another under the sole influence of marriage dissolutions and first marriages. The latter can be inferred from changing of proportions single; therefore, it is easy to compute the frequency of marriage dissolution for *first married* persons. Indeed, consider two censuses at times t and $t+n$ and let FM_x, RM_x, WD_x, and S_x, respectively, denote the proportions of persons first married, remarried, widowed and divorced, and single at completed age x at time t, with respect to the total population. At age $x+n$ at time $t+n$, the corresponding proportions observed will be FM_{x+n}, RM_{x+n}, WD_{x+n}, and S_{x+n}. The relative number of first marriages, between t and $t+n$, is equal to $S_x - S_{x+n}$; the proportion of first marriage dissolutions is therefore equal to $FM_x - FM_{x+n} + (S_x - S_{x+n})$. The probability $_n\psi_x$ *of first marriage dissolution*[31] can therefore be computed by the relation

$$_n\psi_x = \frac{FM_x - FM_{x+n} + (S_x - S_{x+n})}{FM_x + (S_x - S_{x+n})/2}$$

The denominator of $_n\psi_x$ takes into account the fact that there is an "immigration" of first marriages into the first married category during the intercensal period. Note, however, that it is impossible to distinguish, even in this case, between risks of widowhood and divorce, as one does not know the respective impact of divorces and deaths of spouse on the population first married. Furthermore, it is impossible to compute the probability of marriage dissolution for the *remarried* population from the above data, as one cannot determine the relative number of remarriages during the intercensal period; there is also no possibility to derive the risks of remarriage by age.

4.2.3. Example

The present example illustrates Hajnal's method of estimating the average number of first marriages per head and the singulate mean age at marriage from the proportion of bachelors or spinsters observed at census.

---

[31]Ideally, one should also have to take duration of marriage into account, since marriage dissolution does not depend solely upon age.

TABLE 4.5

Age groups (completed years)	Proportion of bachelors
15–19	0.98686
20–24	0.69962
25–29	0.29336
30–34	0.16171
35–39	0.12741
40–44	0.10584
45–49	0.09480
50–54	0.09113

Table 4.5 gives the proportion of bachelors by five-year age groups observed in Australia on June 30, 1966.[32]

The estimated average number of first marriages per head is equal to: $1 - \frac{1}{2}(0.09480 + 0.09113) = 0.90703$. The singulate mean age at marriage is given by the formula

$$\bar{x} = 15 + \frac{5 \sum\limits_{15}^{45} {_5}T_x - 35 T_{50}}{1 - T_{50}}$$

where T_i stands for the proportions single at age i. One obtains in this case

$$\bar{x} = 15 + \frac{12.34800 - 3.25395}{0.90703}$$

$$= 25.03 \text{ years}$$

4.3. THE "MARRIAGE MARKET" PROBLEM

Up to now, in the present chapter, measures of first marriage have always been developed either for male or for female birth-cohorts. This approach neglects, however, the obvious fact that marriage is concluded between a male *and* a female.[33] A full study of first marriages requires

---

[32]Source: *Demographic Yearbook 1968*. United Nations, 1968. Since bachelors are taken into account instead of spinsters, an ultimate age at marriage higher than 50 should actually be used, e.g., 55 years of age. T_{55} would then be estimated as $0.5(T_{50-54} + T_{55-59})$, giving in this case an average number of first marriages per head of 0.90811.

[33]This is a typical problem, in period analysis, of interactions of two populations; it is therefore rather similar to problems encountered in migration analysis.

therefore to take into account *both* the number of eligible males and females.

Consider, for example, the number of female or male reduced first marriages at age x, respectively, denoted by M_x^f and M_x^m. These can be written as

$$M_x^f = \left(\sum_j m_{xj} \right) \Big/ F_x$$

i.e., the ratio, to women aged x, of first marriages concluded between females aged x and males aged j. A similar relation holds for males;

$$M_x^m = \left(\sum_j m_{jx} \right) \Big/ H_x$$

i.e., the ratio, to men aged x, of first marriages concluded between females aged j and males aged x.

These two expressions can be developed as an inner product of vectors of frequencies and structures:

$$M_x^f = (M_{x15}^m \quad M_{x16}^m \quad \cdots \quad M_{x50}^m) \begin{vmatrix} H_{15}/F_x \\ H_{16}/F_x \\ \cdot \\ \cdot \\ \cdot \\ H_{50}/F_x \end{vmatrix}$$

and

$$M_x^m = (M_{15x}^f \quad M_{16x}^f \quad \cdots \quad M_{50x}^f) \begin{vmatrix} F_{15}/H_x \\ F_{16}/H_x \\ \cdot \\ \cdot \\ \cdot \\ H_{50}/H_x \end{vmatrix}$$

Row vectors represent, respectively, *male* reduced first marriages aged 15, 16, . . . , 50 with females aged x, and *female* reduced first marriages aged 15, 16, . . . , 50 with males aged x. Column vectors comprise sex ratios of males aged j to females aged x, and of females aged j to males aged x.

Temporal or spatial changes in reduced first marriages[34] at age x can be due either to changes in the row *or* column vectors, or to both. In other words, male or female marriages may vary solely according to what has been

---

[34]The same holds true for first marriage *rates*.

called the "*marriage squeeze*," i.e., disproportions between the sexes at prime ages of marriage.[35]

When data on marriages by ages of spouses are available, it is therefore recommended to supplement the study of period reduced first marriages M_x^f or M_x^m with the row vectors $\langle M_{xj}^m \rangle$ or $\langle M_{jx}^f \rangle$ of reduced marriages by ages of spouses. These can then be directly standardized by the usual procedures in view of deriving summary indexes (Section 2.2.1). If cross-tabulations of marriages by ages of spouses are not available, one could choose a standard set of vectors $\langle M_{xj}^m \rangle$ and $\langle M_{jx}^f \rangle$ for every x and have recourse to *indirect* standardization procedures (Section 2.2.4), column vectors $\langle H_j/F_x \rangle$ and $\langle F_j/H_x \rangle$ being considered as the related population structures. Demographers have also tried to develop various indexes taking both female and male populations into account.[36] For example, one could use such simple indexes as

$$\frac{m_{xj}}{\frac{1}{2}(F_x + H_j)}, \qquad \frac{m_{xj}}{(F_x H_j)^{1/2}}, \qquad \text{or} \qquad \frac{m_{xj}/2H_j F_x}{H_j + F_x}$$

depending on whether one selects the arithmetic, geometric, or harmonic mean of male and female populations.[37]

All these measures, unfortunately, are based on no fundamental principles of analysis; for this to be true, "marriage market" theory should be at a more advanced stage than it is at present. The most significant advances in this field have been the nuptiality models developed by L. Henry; this topic is, however, quite outside the scope of this book.[38]

To conclude this chapter, detailed analysis of marriage and marriage dissolution must generally be based on census-type data with retrospective questions. Cohort or period analysis of first marriage can also often be performed by having recourse to reduced first marriages. Study of first marriage can also be based on the sole use of proportions single observed at census. Analysis of marriage dissolution and remarriage can sometimes be approximately performed with statistics of population change; sole data on population structures by marital status are of no great help in this field.

---

[35]The problem is complicated further by the fact that the row vectors may change under the influence of the marriage squeeze.

[36]For a detailed discussion of the problems involved, see Brackel (1970), Pollard (1971), and Keyfitz (1971).

[37]Pollard (1971) has shown that, in a marriage model, there is a good case for taking marriages proportional to the *harmonic* mean of male and female populations, in theory at least (see also Keyfitz, 1971).

[38]A good English-language introduction to these models can be found in Henry (1972).

Finally, all current measures of marriage do not fully take into account the "marriage market" problem; one should therefore always at least study the trends in the number of eligible males and females as a complement to period analysis of male or female first marriage.

4.4. REFERENCES AND SUPPLEMENTARY BIBLIOGRAPHY

Agarwala, S. N. *Age at Marriage in India.* Allahabad: Kitab-Mahal Private Ltd., 1962.

Akers, D. S. On measuring the marriage squeeze. *Demography,* 1967, *4*(2), 907–924.

Brackel, P. O. *Huwelijkskans en Partnerkeuze.* Ph.D. thesis, Nijmegen, 1970,

Carlsson, G. *Marriage rates as social indicators.* In The Second Scandinavian Demographic Symposium (Vol. 2). Stockholm: Scandinavian Population Studies, 1970, pp. 49–64.

Carter, H., & Glick, P. C. *Marriage and Divorce: a Social and Economic Study* (Rev. ed.). Cambridge, Massachusetts: Harvard University Press, 1976.

Chasteland, J. C., & Pressat, R. La nuptialité des générations françaises depuis un siècle. *Population,* 1962, *17*(2), 215–240.

Coale, A. Age patterns of marriage. *Population Studies,* 1971, *25*(2), 193–214.

Hajnal, J. Age at marriage and proportions marrying. *Population Studies,* 1953, 7(2), 111–136.

Henry, L. Mesure de la fréquence des divorces. *Population,* 1952, *7*(2), 267–282.

Henry, L. Approximations et erreurs dans les tables de nuptialité des générations. *Population,* 1963, *18*(4), 737–776.

Henry, L. Nuptiality. *Theoretical Population Biology,* 1972, *3*(2), 135–152.

Keyfitz, N. The mathematics of sex and marriage. In L. M. Lecam, J. Neyman, and E. L. Scott (Eds.), *Proceedings of the Sixth Berkeley Symposium on Mathematical Statistics and Probability* (Vol. IV). Berkeley: Biology and Health, 1971, pp. 89–108.

Kumar, J. Method of construction of attrition life tables for the single population based on two successive censuses. *Journal of the American Statistical Association,* 1967, *62,* 1433–1451.

Monnier, A. L'observation rétrospective de la nuptialité des célibataires. *Recherches Economiques de Louvain,* 1971, *XXXVII*(4), 329–364.

Pollard, J. H. *Mathematical models of marriage.* Paper presented at the 4th annual conference on the Mathematics of Population, East–West Center, 1971.

Pressat, R. Le remariage des veufs et des veuves. *Population,* 1956, *11*(1), 47–58.

Preston, S. H. Estimating the proportion of American marriages that end in divorce. *Sociological Methods and Research,* 1975, *3*(4), 435–460.

Van Houte-Minet, M. *Analyse Longitudinale de la Nuptialité des Célibataires et du Divorce* (Vol. III). Liège: I.U.S.S.P. International Population Conference, 1969, pp. 2154–2166.

Wattelar, C. *et al.* Un exemple de distorsion en analyse transversale: L'âge moyen au mariage par la méthode de Hajnal. *Recherches Economiques de Louvain,* 1970, *36*(4), 417–426.

Wunsch, G. L'utilisation des mariages réduits. *Population et Famille,* 1970, *21,* 1–15.

THE ANALYSIS OF NATALITY

5.1. CRUDE MEASURES OF NATALITY

5.1.1. Natality and Fertility

The term *natality* is used in this chapter in the general context of the contribution of births to population change, i.e., one of the three phenomena (the other two being mortality and migration) inducing population change in time and space. The term *fertility*[1] will be restricted, on the other hand, to the intensity and tempo of births actually observed in a female and/or male population subjected to the "risk" of childbearing.

Infertility, therefore, has a double cause: voluntary infertility due to antinatalist practices, and physiological infertility, also called *infecundity*[2] or *sterility*. A fecund woman is thus not necessarily fertile, e.g., if she has recourse to contraception.

5.1.2. Period Crude Birth "Rate"

Taking into account the impact of total population numbers on births during a certain period of time, the *crude birth "rate"* can be computed by dividing the number of births[3] recorded by the midperiod population (Section 2.2.4). Though widely used, the crude birth "rate" presents several disadvantages in temporal or spatial comparisons: it does not eliminate the impact of differential population structures[4] (by sex, age, marital status, etc.), and remains influenced for quite a number of years by "accidents"

---

[1]In French, fertility is translated as *fécondité*.
[2]In French, fecundity (i.e., the capacity to give birth to a live child) is translated as *fertilité*. This translation is unfortunately confusing.
[3]Most measures of natality are based on *live* births only.
[4]In some cases, one wishes to take the impact of structures into account; in these circumstances, the crude birth rate is a perfectly valid measure of the number of babies a population is producing.

experienced formerly by the various cohorts under observation.[5] Further-more, the crude "rate" evidently neither measures the intensity nor the tempo of fertility as defined in Section 1.2.1.2.

On the other hand, if used over short periods of time, crude "rates" still retain some advantages since structures usually change rather slowly over time, requiring only elementary data on births and population numbers. Furthermore, by subtracting the crude death "rate" from the birth "rate," one obtains a measure of natural increase over the time period considered.

Crude birth "rates," as well as crude death "rates," are usually com-puted on an annual basis, and are expressed as the annual number of births per 1000 persons, the latter figure being commonly used but perfectly arbitrary.

5.1.3. Period General Fertility "Rate"

Instead of dividing the number of annual births by the total midyear population one can also compute the ratio of the number of annual births to the midyear population of females in reproductive ages (e.g., from age 15 to 50). This ratio is called the *female general fertility "rate."* One can also compute legitimate and illegitimate fertility "rates" by dividing the number of legitimate or illegitimate births, respectively, by the midyear married female population in reproductive ages or by the female nonmarried popu-lation (single, widowed, and divorced) in reproductive ages; examples are given in Section 5.2.6.1.

The latter measures are only slightly more refined than the crude birth "rate" and are therefore of no great interest. A detailed analysis of fertility patterns must necessarily take into account population structures by age and marital status, by duration of marriage, and by parity, since they have a major impact on the trend of births and therefore contribute to a large extent to differential natality between different periods or areas. The following will be devoted to these *structure-specific* fertility "rates."

5.2. AGE-SPECIFIC FERTILITY

5.2.1. Types of Age-Specific "Rates"

5.2.1.1. General, Legitimate, and Illegitimate "Rates." Combining population structures by age and marital status the following age-specific "rates" can be distinguished.

---

[5]For example, a "baby boom" after a war affects the trend of crude birth "rates" for several years.

General[6] *age-specific fertility "rates"* are the number of births by age of mother[7] divided by the female population at that age. No distinction is made between legitimate and illegitimate births, nor between married and non-married females.

Legitimate age-specific fertility "rates" are the number of legitimate births by age of mother (or father) divided by the female (or male) population currently married, at the age considered.

Illegitimate age-specific fertility "rates" are the number of illegitimate births by age of mother[8] divided by the female nonmarried population at that age, i.e., females single, divorced, or widowed.

Taking into account combinations of population structures and fertility "rates" gives the following useful relation at a specified age:

$$GFR = LFR\,(FM/F) + IFR\,(FNM/F)$$

where *GFR* stands for general age-specific fertility "rate," *LFR* and *IFR* stand, respectively, for age-specific legitimate and illegitimate fertility "rates," *F* denotes the total number of females at age considered, and *FM* and *FNM* stand for the total number of females married or nonmarried at given age.

5.2.1.2. "Rates" by Age and by Age Groups. As usual, various types of "rates" can be computed according to the way durations are specified. Births can be classified according to completed age and birth-cohort of mother. In this case, events and population number can be situated in the Lexis diagram as in Fig. 5.1a; the "rate" will refer to exact age $x + 0.5$ and will cover *two* calendar years, *A* and *B*. If births are classified by birth-cohort only as in Fig. 5.1b, the "rate" will refer to *one* calendar year and will be centered on exact age *x*. Finally, if only tabulations of births by completed age of mothers are available, as in Fig. 5.1c, a *hybrid* fertility "rate" covering two cohorts and centered on exact age $x + 0.5$, may only be computed. In case a, the midyear population will be expressed as enumerated at the end of year *A*; for cases b and c the midyear population will usually be expressed as the average of populations at the beginning and end of year *A*. Similarly, fertility "rates" can be computed between ages *x* to $x + n$. Figures 5.2a and b present the usual cases of period fertility "rates" computed between (a) exact ages *x* to $x + 5$ (6 cohorts) or (b) between ages *x* to $x + 6$ in five cohorts. In both cases the midyear population will usually be expressed as the average of

[6]Common usage frequently omits "general."
[7]Similar measures can be derived for males.
[8]No corresponding data are available for males.

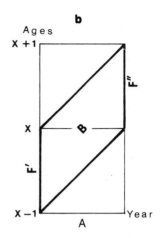

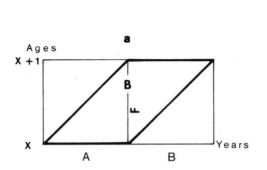

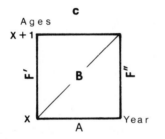

FIGURE 5.1

populations at the beginning and end of the year for the cohorts considered. Extension to other age groups is immediate.

5.2.1.3. "Rates" by Age and Birth Order. If births by age of mother are also classified by birth order, all the above "rates" (Section 5.2.1.1) can also be computed by birth order. At a given age x, one evidently has

$$f_x = \sum_j f_x^{(j)}$$

where f_x denotes the age-specific fertility rate at age x for all birth orders and $f_x^{(j)}$ stands for the age-specific fertility rate of birth order j obtained by dividing the number of births of order j at age x by the number of females at that age. Since the denominator is the same for all birth orders j (i.e., the number of females at age x) $\sum_j f_x^{(j)}$ is equal to the ratio of births of all orders to the number of females at age x, that is, to f_x.

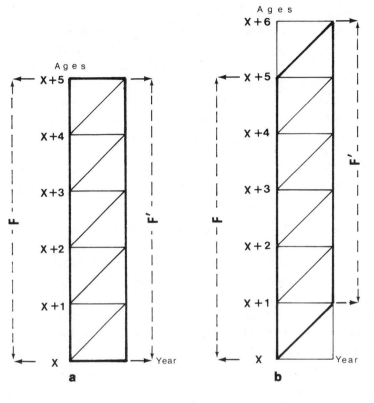

FIGURE 5.2

One can sometimes obtain data by age and *parity* for mothers, parity being the number of children born alive. In such cases age-parity-specific fertility rates can be computed by only including in the denominator the women at the risk of moving to a specified birth order. Parity-specific fertility will be examined in more detail in Sections 5.3.1.1, 5.3.2, and 5.4.

5.2.2. Age-Specific "Rates" in Cohort Analysis

5.2.2.1. Age-Specific General Fertility "Rates." Going back to the definition of an age-specific general fertility "rate" one sees that this particular measure corresponds to the number of *reduced births* in the cohort considered, as defined in Section 1.3.2.1. The number of births (all births or births by order) is indeed divided by the total population of the cohort, which has or has not experienced natality[9]; if the conditions of independence and continuity are satisfied, an age-specific fertility rate corresponds therefore to the number of reduced births in the cohort without disturbances (mortality, migration) at age x. If one computes the number of reduced births or general fertility "rates"[10] f_x at each age (or for each age group) in a male or female birth-cohort, the average number of children per head, and the average age at childbearing, will be given by the usual relations

$$\bar{e} = \sum_{\alpha}^{\beta} f_x$$

$$\bar{x} = \left(\sum_{\alpha}^{\beta} x f_x\right) \Big/ \bar{e}$$

Bounds α and β will usually be chosen as 15 and 50, respectively, for females; for males, one could choose, for example, $\alpha = 18$ and $\beta = 60$. One can also compute *partial* (or incomplete) intensities by adding up all reduced births until age $\beta - x$ for cohorts that are not observed until the end of their reproductive period. After a certain age, partial intensities often reflect the trend in final intensities. For truncated cohorts, it is also possible to use the *modal age*[11] at childbearing instead of the arithmetic weighted average of ages. The former only requires data for rates up to the mode of the fertility schedule, whereas the latter requires data for all rates between bounds α and β.[12]

If births are classified *by order j*, one similarly obtains

$$\bar{e}^{(j)} = \sum_{\alpha}^{\beta} f_x^{(j)}$$

$$\bar{x}^{(j)} = \left(\sum_{\alpha}^{\beta} x f_x^{(j)}\right) \Big/ \bar{e}^{(j)}$$

As seen in Section 1.2.2.2, the average number of children $\bar{e}$ per head (all birth orders) is then equal to

$$\bar{e} = \sum_{j} \bar{e}^{(j)}$$

[9]As seen in Sections 1.3.2.1 and 1.3.2.2, reduced events are obtained by dividing the number of events by the population of the cohort having or not having experienced the phenomenon being measured (in this case natality).

[10]Though ambiguous, the term "rate" is commonly used and will be kept here in quotation marks as specified in Section 1.2.7.

[11]That is, the age at which the fertility "rate" is the highest.

[12]General fertility is usually a unimodal function of age.

The average age at childbearing ($\bar{x}$) for all birth orders is obtained by computing a *weighted* average of mean ages for birth of order j with the weights being the mean number of children of that order (Section 1.2.2.3)

$$\bar{x} = \frac{1}{\bar{e}}[\bar{x}^{(1)}\bar{e}^{(1)} + \bar{x}^{(2)}\bar{e}^{(2)} + \cdots]$$

Finally, having computed the average number of children $\bar{e}^{(j)}$ by birth order, the proportion of females having at least $j+1$ children out of the number having at least j is equal to (Section 1.2.3)

$$a_j = \bar{e}^{(j+1)}/\bar{e}^{(j)}$$

This ratio, in the case of fertility, is called the *parity progression ratio* for the *birth-cohort* considered[13]; it indicates *ex post facto* the probability for a female having already j children ever born to ultimately having at least $j+1$.

5.2.2.2. Census-Type Data on Births by Age of Mother. As seen in Section 1.3.2.3, the same types of measures may be derived from census-type data using retrospective questions. Consider, for example, a survey of women at the end of their reproductive period, e.g., at completed age 50. These women can be classified according to their *parity* on the basis of the number of children ever born such as

Number of women	$N_0, N_1, N_2, \ldots, N_i, \ldots$
Parity	$0, \quad 1, \quad 2, \quad \ldots, \quad i, \quad \ldots$

If the conditions of independence and continuity are fulfilled, the average number of children per head, in this birth-cohort, at completed age 50 is equal to

$$\bar{e} = \frac{\sum_i iN_i}{\sum_i N_i}$$

where N_i is the number of women of parity i.

If, furthermore, one knows the date of birth of every child ever born (i.e., dead or still alive at time of survey), one can also easily derive the average age at childbearing, for the birth-cohort interviewed at the end of the reproductive period. Parity-specific measures can also be computed from this type of data; this topic will be examined in detail in Section 5.3.2.

---

[13]Parity progression ratios can also be computed for other types of cohorts; this problem will be examined later on.

Since the conditions of independence and continuity are not perfectly fulfilled, it is not recommended to interview women at old age in order to reconstruct the fertility history of their birth-cohort; due to discontinuities with respect to mortality, among others, the subcohort of women *surviving* will probably represent a selected group with respect to fertility and will not stand adequately for the experience of the whole cohort, including those women who have died or migrated prior to the interview.

5.2.2.3. Legitimate and Illegitimate Fertility. If *legitimate fertility* depends solely on age, as in the case of some high-fertility populations,[14] the mean number of legitimate children per married woman can be obtained by adding together all age-specific legitimate fertility "rates" between ages 15 and 50 in a birth-cohort of females, for women married at age 15.

In general, by summing "rates" since age $15+x$ (x positive), one obtains the average number of legitimate children per woman married at age $15+x$, always assuming that fertility depends solely upon age.

Similarly, one can obtain the mean age at childbearing for legitimate children by taking the weighted average of ages at childbearing, weights being the legitimate "rate" at each age. Once again, the fertility "rate" can be identified as the number of reduced events in a birth-cohort restricted to women married at age $15+x$ ($x \geqslant 0$).

Incidentally, these measures assume implicitly that fertility is related to *two* event-origins, birth and marriage, but that only the duration elapsed since birth (i.e., age) has an impact on fertility. This last assumption is especially incorrect for populations practicing birth control: fertility also depends on duration elapsed since marriage; the latter duration is even much more important than age. For these contracepting populations, one could even turn the assumption around: fertility depends on marriage duration but not on age,[15] and drop the reference to age when computing fertility "rates" (see Section 5.3).

Concerning *illegitimate fertility*, a similar argument does not hold: having an illegitimate child is probably a selective factor when passing from the nonmarried population (including widows and divorcées) to the married population. Analysis should be based in this case on retrospective questions asked not only to persons single at the end of the reproductive period, but also to the ever-married population.

---

[14]Even in noncontracepting populations, this is not always strictly the case, see Charbonneau (1970), for instance.

[15]At least during the reproductive period.

5.2.3. Age-Specific "Rates" in Period Analysis

5.2.3.1. Standardization. The three "rates" introduced in Section 5.2.1.1, i.e., age-specific general, legitimate, and illegitimate fertility "rates," can be used for period analysis of natality in order to eliminate the impact of population structures by age and marital status. Period "rates" are computed as above (Section 5.2.1.2) and can be condensed by the usual methods: summation, averaging, direct standardization, etc.

For standardization purposes alone, it is irrelevant whether, for example, the sum of legitimate "rates" does or does not correspond to an average intensity. All summarized indexes should only be considered for comparative purposes, in order to exclude the impact of population structures.

Double standardization (Section 2.2.5) can also be used in this field; there are no special problems involved that would require further comments.

5.2.3.2. Translation. Age-specific fertility "rates" can also be used in the translation approach, using the fictitious cohort method (Section 2.3.1). General age-specific fertility "rates" can be added up,[16] their sum being considered as the fictitious average number of children born in the synthetic cohort. Period sums of legitimate and illegitimate "rates" are restricted to the conditions specified in Section 5.2.2.3. In the translation approach, period synthetic measures are subject to all the restrictions developed in Section 2.3. Among others, distributional distortion effects due to changing intensities and tempos of fertility from cohort to cohort have a major impact on synthetic fertility measures; furthermore, period general fertility "rates" are distorted by changing intensities and tempos of *nuptiality* from one birth-cohort to the other.[17] Age-specific synthetic measures are also influenced for many years by postponements or making up in births; they thus reflect for a long time temporary accidents (economic depressions, wars, etc.) in the life of cohorts. This is due to the fact that if, for example, a woman aged 20 postpones a birth[18] for four years, this postponement will influence her eventual age-specific fertility at ages 25 to 30 or 35. It is therefore dangerous to extrapolate from age-specific synthetic measures the actual behavior of cohorts as regards their intensity and tempo of fertility.

---

[16]Multiplication by the age interval is required if age groups are used, due to differences between period "rates" by age groups and reduced events (Section 2.4.2). The sum of period general fertility rates is called the *total fertility* "*rate.*"

[17]For example, see Ryder (1969).

[18]The same argument applies to a spinster who postpones her marriage for a certain number of years; this will also have an impact, for a long time, on her eventual age-specific fertility.

5.2.4. Gross and Net Reproduction "Rates"

Instead of using the ratio of all births to the total female (or male) population at a specified age, restrict the numerator to female (or male) births only. These female (or male) age-specific general fertility "rates" can be added up, in a cohort, in order to obtain the average mean number of girls born per woman (or boys per male) in the absence of disturbances, these "rates" being considered as age–sex-specific reduced births. Writing $f_x(f)$ for such "rates" restricted to female births only, one has

$$\bar{e}(f) = \sum_{15}^{50} f_x(f)$$

or

$$\bar{e}(f) = 0.488 \sum_{15}^{50} f_x$$

where f_x represents, as above, the age-specific "rate" including male and female births, the constant 0.488 representing the proportion of female births.[19]

This completed fertility index is called the *gross reproduction "rate"* and measures the *replacement* (or reproduction) of a cohort of mothers by their daughters; a similar measure can be computed for a male birth-cohort. One can also take mortality into account and compute the product sum $\sum_{15}^{50} (l_x/l_0) f_x(f)$, where l_x/l_0 stands for the female probability of survival until age x; this index is called the *net reproduction "rate"* and measures replacement including attrition by death. Since mortality is not the only force of decrement, a true *net replacement "rate"* should also take migration as well (in- and out-migration) into account.

These gross and net reproduction "rates" have actually been widely used in the translation approach: *period* female fertility "rates" and *period* female probabilities of survival have been combined in order to obtain synthetic period measures of replacement. This approach is incorrect: the synthetic measures are usually biased by distributional distortion effects and are subject to the restrictions noted in Sections 2.3 and 5.2.3.2. True replacement measures should necessarily be computed for actual cohorts and not for fictitious period ones.

Even if computed for cohorts, however, net replacement "rates" do not measure actual replacement due to differential experiences between mothers and daughters with regard to mortality and migration. A better

---

[19]Generally, there are about 105 male births for 100 female births (*sex ratio* at birth).

approach would be to compare the number of *person-years* lived by daughters and mothers, as in the index of replacement developed by Henry (1965a).[20] It is important to note that these replacement indexes do not take into account the actual *population structures* by age; in view of the importance of the latter, it seems that *population projections* should be preferred to replacement "rates" in studying population dynamics, except in restricted theories such as the stable population model (L. Henry, 1972, pp. 260–262; N. Keyfitz, 1968, pp. 100–102).

5.2.5. Indirect Standardization of Age-Specific Fertility

In Section 5.2.3.1, it was noted that age-specific period fertility "rates" can be summarized by the usual direct standardization procedures.

If births are not classified by age of mother, direct standardization is impossible. However, as seen in Section 2.2.4, *indirect standardization* can be applied if population structures (by age, sex, and marital status) are known.

A. J. Coale (1965) has developed an interesting extension of indirect standardization procedures in view of distinguishing the impact on period fertility of nuptiality, legitimate, and illegitimate fertility. At a point of time t, the following symbols are defined: f_i as the births per woman aged i (age-specific general fertility "rate"); g_i the legitimate births per married woman aged i (age-specific legitimate fertility "rate"); h_i the illegitimate births per nonmarried woman aged i (age-specific illegitimate fertility "rate"); w_i the number of women aged i; m_i the number of married women aged i; u_i the number of nonmarried women aged i; and F_i the standard fertility schedule.[21]

The following standardized indexes can then be computed:

$$I_f = \frac{\sum f_i w_i}{\sum F_i w_i} \qquad \text{the comparative index of general fertility}$$

$$I_g = \frac{\sum g_i m_i}{\sum F_i m_i} \qquad \text{the comparative index of legitimate fertility}$$

$$I_h = \frac{\sum h_i u_i}{\sum F_i u_i} \qquad \text{the comparative index of illegitimate fertility}$$

---

[20]This measure unfortunately does not take migration into account but, if data were available, a suitable index could be devised.

[21]Coale has chosen as a standard the age-specific legitimate fertility "rates" of Hutterite women, for the period 1921–1930. See the Appendix, Table A.4.

$$I_m = \frac{\sum F_i m_i}{\sum F_i w_i} \quad \text{the comparative index of proportions married}^{22}$$

Since the sum of legitimate births $\sum g_i m_i$ and illegitimate births $\sum h_i u_i$ gives the overall number of births $\sum f_i w_i$, one can write

$$I_f = \frac{\sum f_i w_i}{\sum F_i w_i} = \frac{1}{\sum F_i w_i} (\sum g_i m_i + \sum h_i u_i)$$

Since $\sum g_i m_i = I_g \sum F_i m_i$ and $\sum h_i u_i = I_h \sum F_i u_i$, I_f can also be written as

$$I_f = \frac{1}{\sum F_i w_i} (I_g \sum F_i m_i + I_h \sum F_i u_i)$$

Since $\sum F_i m_i / \sum F_i w_i = I_m$, one derives $I_f = I_g I_m + I_h (\sum F_i u_i / \sum F_i w_i)$.

The number of nonmarried females (u_i) is obviously equal to the difference between the total number of females (w_i) and the number of married females (m_i) in the ith age interval $u_i = w_i - m_i$. Therefore,

$$\sum F_i u_i = \sum F_i (w_i - m_i)$$
$$= \sum F_i w_i - \sum F_i m_i$$

and

$$I_f = I_g I_m + I_h \left(\frac{\sum F_i w_i}{\sum F_i w_i} - \frac{\sum F_i m_i}{\sum F_i w_i} \right)$$

Finally,

$$I_f = I_g I_m + I_h (1 - I_m)$$

The comparative indexes I_g and I_m reflect the trends of legitimate fertility and of nuptiality, indirectly standardized for population structures. If illegitimate fertility can be neglected, the relation becomes

$$I_f = I_g I_m$$

In this case, the comparative index of general fertility is simply equal to the product of the comparative indexes of legitimate fertility and of nuptiality. Data required are only population structures (at census time, for example) by sex, age, and marital status, and total number of births, for the period considered, by legitimacy, plus an arbitrary standard schedule of fertility rates (see example, Section 5.2.6.2).

[22] I_m is a *weighted* index of nuptiality taking into account the impact of the proportion of married women at specified ages on natality, therefore weighting by the standard fertility schedule.

The choice of the standard schedule of Hutterite fertility (given in the Appendix, Table A.4) is sensible, as it is about the highest level of marital fertility ever observed. Therefore, the comparative index I_g of legitimate fertility will vary between 0 and 1. Since I_m evidently also varies between 0 and 1, their product I_f will also be comprised between these limits.

5.2.6. Examples

5.2.6.1. General, Legitimate, and Illegitimate "Rates." On April 1, 1960, the female population in reproductive ages (15 to 50) in the United States, and the number of births during calendar year 1960 according to legitimacy, could be classified as follows:

Female Population		*Births*	
Married	30,384,571	Legitimate	4,033,550
Not married	11,262,778	Illegitimate	224,300
Total	41,647,349	Total	4,257,850

(Source: *Demographic Yearbook 1965.* New York: United Nations 1965.)

Assuming that the midyear population is approximately equal in number to the population enumerated on April 1, the following "rates" covering the female reproductive period can be computed:

General fertility "rate"
$$4,257,850/41,647,349 = 0.10224 \qquad \text{or } 102.24\%_0$$
Legitimate fertility "rate"
$$4,033,550/30,384,571 = 0.13275 \qquad \text{or } 132.75\%_0$$
Illegitimate fertility "rate"
$$224,300/11,262,788 = 0.01992 \qquad \text{or } 19.92\%_0$$

As noted in Section 5.2.1.1, one also has the following relation:

$$0.10224 = 0.13275(30,384,571/41,647,349)$$
$$+ 0.01992(11,262,778/41,647,349)$$

5.2.6.2. Indirect Standardization of Fertility: Coale's Method. Table 5.1 presents data drawn from the 1966 census of the population of New Zealand.[23] The number of births during calendar year 1966 were the following:

All births:	60,188
Legitimate births:	53,228
Illegitimate births:	6,960

---

[23]Source: *Demographic Yearbook 1968 and 1969.* New York: United Nations, 1969.

Having recourse to the method developed in Section 5.2.5 and to the standard fertility schedule of Table A.4 in the Appendix, one obtains the following comparative indexes:

General fertility:
$$I_f = \frac{60,188}{207,943} = 0.289$$

Legitimate fertility:
$$I_g = \frac{53,228}{146,561} = 0.363$$

Illegitimate fertility:
$$I_h = \frac{6,960}{61,382} = 0.113$$

Proportions married:
$$I_m = \frac{146,561}{207,943} = 0.705$$

As a test of the results, one must have

$$I_f = I_g I_m + I_h (1 - I_m)$$

or

$$0.289 = (0.363)(0.705) + 0.113(1 - 0.705)$$

The approximation $I_f \cong I_g I_m$ yields in this case $I_f = 0.256$ instead of the true value 0.289.

As an example of the use of the various measures over time, consider Table 5.2 showing the values of the indirectly age-standardized "rates" for Belgium, between census years 1846 and 1970.

One clearly sees a substantial increase in nuptiality (I_m) and a considerable decrease in legitimate fertility (I_g). General fertility (I_f) follows the same pattern as legitimate fertility, but the trend is damped down. This is due to the fact that general fertility is influenced both by the proportions

TABLE 5.1

Age groups (in completed years)	Number of women	Number of married women	Number of unmarried women[a]
15–19	95,712	9,149	86,563
20–24	93,258	55,960	37,298
25–29	82,319	70,726	11,593
30–34	72,867	65,767	7,100
35–39	78,978	71,221	7,757
40–44	78,795	69,439	9,356
45–49	73,516	62,377	11,139

[a]Spinsters, divorcées, and widows.

TABLE 5.2[a]

Census years	General fertility I_f	Legitimate fertility I_g	Illegitimate fertility I_h	Proportions married I_m
1846	0.319	0.784	0.039	0.375
1856	0.324	0.818	0.040	0.366
1866	0.355	0.815	0.042	0.404
1880	0.355	0.751	0.049	0.436
1890	0.320	0.670	0.050	0.436
1900	0.299	0.578	0.042	0.479
1910	0.243	0.441	0.032	0.517
1920	0.199	0.370	0.026	0.501
1930	0.175	0.281	0.017	0.601
1947	0.194	0.305	0.017	0.617
1961	0.210	0.291	0.015	0.706
1970	0.179	0.247	0.016	0.703

[a] Source: Masuy-Stroobant, G. *ABC de la Démographie Belge*. Brussels: Société Belge de Démographie, 1974, p. 57.

married and by legitimate fertility; since these components have changed in opposite directions, general fertility has decreased much less than legitimate fertility. Finally, the change in illegitimate fertility (I_h) has been very slight.

5.3. MARRIAGE-DURATION-SPECIFIC FERTILITY

5.3.1. Marriage-Duration-Specific Fertility "Rates"

5.3.1.1. Cohort Analysis. In a population practicing birth control, it has been noted above (Section 5.2.2.3) that duration of marriage is at least as important as age in explaining current fertility of couples. This is because most births occur at the lower durations of marriage: women aged 30, for example, will present different eventual fertilities depending on their duration of marriage at that age.

The study of marriage-duration-specific fertility necessarily requires observation of *cohorts of marriages*, either through vital registration or by census-type material. This section will be devoted to methods based on vital statistics.

If births (all births or by birth orders) are tabulated each year by duration of marriage,[24] marriage-duration-specific fertility "rates" can be

[24] If age does not intervene, duration of marriage refers to *couples* of husband *and* wife.

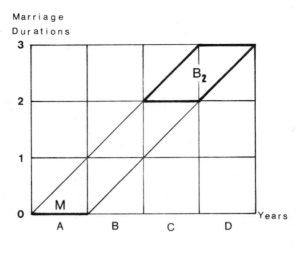

FIGURE 5.3

computed by dividing the number of births observed at a given duration by the midperiod number of couples surviving (to migration and to marriage dissolution) at this duration.[25] Except at the time of census, however, the number of surviving couples is generally unknown. An approximative "rate" can nonetheless be computed by dividing the number of births at duration x by the *initial* population of the cohort of marriages at bound α. If, for example (see Fig. 5.3), B_2 births are recorded in cohort A between exact durations of marriage 2 and 3 (during years C and D), an approximate "rate" by marriage duration is obtained by the ratio B_2/M, where M stands for the initial number of marriages concluded during year A. Let $\hat{m}_x$ stand for this approximation to the true "rate" m_x at marriage-duration x. Since the initial number of marriages is usually greater than the number surviving at duration x, except if immigration has been high, one has $\hat{m}_x < m_x$. Considering that the true "rates" are reduced events, the average number of births per marriage[26] and the average duration of marriage at birth are equal to

$$\bar{e} = \sum_{\alpha}^{\beta} m_x$$

and

$$\bar{x} = \frac{1}{\bar{e}} \sum_{\alpha}^{\beta} x m_x$$

[25] Once again, this "rate" is equivalent to *reduced births* in the cohort of marriages if the conditions of independence and of continuity are satisfied.

[26] One could also compute *partial* intensities by marriage-cohort, as in Section 5.2.2.1.

where bounds α and β are equal to $\alpha = 0$ (time of marriage) and $\beta = 20$ or 25, for example.[27] Using the approximate "rates" $\hat{m}_x$ gives

$$\hat{\bar{e}} = \sum_0^\beta \hat{m}_x < \bar{e}$$

and

$$\hat{\bar{x}} = \frac{1}{\bar{e}} \sum_0^\beta x \hat{m}_x < \bar{x}$$

since $\hat{m}_x$ increasingly underestimates m_x as duration x becomes greater.

Once again duration-specific "rates" can be computed taking birth order into account (see example, Section 5.3.3.1). Writing $m_x^{(k)}$ for the fertility rate of order k, one obtains $\bar{e}^{(k)}$ and $\bar{x}^{(k)}$ using the relations developed in Section 1.2.2. Taking the ratio $a_k = \bar{e}^{(k+1)}/\bar{e}^{(k)}$ gives the *parity progression ratio* from birth orders k to $k+1$ for the cohort of *marriages*, as seen before in the case of a birth-cohort in Section 5.2.2.1. In practice, reduced births $m_x^{(k)}$ will once again be approximated by "rates" $\hat{m}_x^{(k)}$ based on the initial number of marriages.[28]

Usually, births of high order are grouped together in an open class of order $n+$; therefore, the parity progression ratios can only be computed until $a_{n-2} = \bar{e}^{(n-1)}/\bar{e}^{(n-2)}$. Supposing that all ratios are equal to a_k above order $n-2$, one may write (Pressat, 1967, p. 196; Ryder, 1969, p. 120)

$$a_{n-1} = a_n = a_{n+1} = \cdots = a_k$$

or

$$a_k = \frac{\bar{e}^{(n)}}{\bar{e}^{(n-1)}} = \frac{\bar{e}^{(n+1)}}{\bar{e}^{(n)}} = \cdots$$

Therefore,

$$\bar{e}^{(n)} = a_k \bar{e}^{(n-1)}$$

$$\bar{e}^{(n+1)} = a_k^2 \bar{e}^{(n-1)}$$

$$\bar{e}^{(n+2)} = a_k^3 \bar{e}^{(n-1)}$$

$$\vdots$$

[27]After 20 or 25 years of marriage, fertility is usually negligible.
[28]Estimates of $\bar{e}^{(k)}$ and $\bar{x}^{(k)}$ will therefore also be biased. On the other hand, the parity progression ratios will be only slightly underestimated since biases tend to cancel out.

Since $\bar{e}^{(n+)} = \bar{e}^{(n)} + \bar{e}^{(n+1)} + \bar{e}^{(n+2)} + \cdots$, one obtains $\bar{e}^{(n+)} = \bar{e}^{(n-1)}$ $(a_k + a_k^2 + a_k + \cdots)$. The sum of the geometric progression $a_k + a_k^2 + a_k^3 + \cdots$ tends toward $a_k/(1 - a_k)$; one derives the following expression for a_k (for all $k > n - 2$):

$$a_k = \frac{\bar{e}^{(n+)}}{\bar{e}^{(n+)} + \bar{e}^{(n-1)}}$$

If births are classified by duration of marriage *and* age of mother (or father), approximate "rates" can be computed for subcohorts of marriages classified by age at marriage. Even if this classification does not exist, age can nevertheless be introduced by restricting the initial number of marriages M (the denominator of the "rate") to those for which the wife was in reproductive ages, i.e., by retaining only those marriages concluded under age 50.

5.3.1.2. Period Analysis. Period fertility "rates" by duration of marriage exclude the influence of population structures by marital duration. In the *standardization* approach, these "rates" can once again be summarized by the usual techniques (Section 2.2). Period "rates" can also be combined in the *translation* approach in view of estimating the fictitious average number of births per marriage. This synthetic measure is no longer influenced by variations in the intensity and tempo of *marriage* from cohort to cohort, but it is still subject to distributional distortion due to changing intensities and tempos of fertility by marriage-cohorts. Though better than the total fertility "rate" obtained by adding together age-specific period fertility "rates" (Section 5.2.3.2), this synthetic measure is still influenced for a number of years by postponements and making up in births in marriage-cohorts. For example, if women postpone birth from marriage-duration 5 to marriage-duration 10, all fertility rates for a long time after duration 10 will be affected by prior postponement: the whole schedule of cohort fertility is shifted toward higher durations of marriage. This problem was also noted in Section 5.2.3.2 concerning general fertility.

When legitimate births are not tabulated each year by duration of marriage, one could envisage dividing the total number of legitimate births observed during the year by a weighted average of marriages concluded during the year and during preceding years,[29] weights reflecting the schedule of births by duration of marriage. This type of measure was introduced by Gini (1933) but has never gained popularity, probably because the schedule of births has been changing over time as a result of the decrease in

---

[29]A similar method has been used in Section 4.1.1.2 in order to obtain a fictitious average number of divorces per marriage.

higher-order births.[30] A tentative schedule of weights based on recent Belgian data, is presented in the Appendix, Table A.5. Let α_i represent these weights at durations i in period differences; an estimate of the period fictitious average number of children per married couple is obtained by dividing the annual number of *legitimate* births B_0 by the weighted average of marriages[31] concluded during the year of observation (M_0) and during the preceding years ($M_{-1}, M_{-2}, \ldots, M_{-20}$):

$$\hat{\bar{e}} = \frac{B_0}{\alpha_0 M_0 + \alpha_1 M_{-1} + \alpha_2 M_{-2} + \cdots + \alpha_{20} M_{-20}}$$

5.3.2. Census-Type Data on Fertility by Marriage Duration

5.3.2.1. Children Ever-Born by Duration of Marriage. Data on children ever-born by duration of marriage can be collected by a census or survey.[32] At bound β (for example, 25 years of marriage), the number of currently married couples can be classified according to the number of legitimate children born in the current marriage, i.e., by their *parity*:

Number of married couples: $\quad N_0, N_1, N_2, \ldots, N_i, \ldots$
Parity: $\quad\quad\quad\quad\quad\quad\quad$ 0, $\quad$ 1, $\quad$ 2, $\ldots$, i, $\ldots$

As in the case of fertility by birth-cohort (Section 5.2.2.2), the average number of children per married couple[33] is obtained by

$$\bar{e} = \sum_i iN_i / \sum_i N_i$$

Let $n_0, n_1, n_2, \ldots, n_i$ represent the proportions of couples N_0/N, $N_1/N, N_2/N, \ldots, N_i/N, \ldots$ having parented exactly $0, 1, 2, \ldots, i, \ldots$ children, with $N = \sum_i N_i$. For the marriage-cohort interviewed at bound β, *parity-progression ratio* a_i can now be computed. Knowing that $a_0 = \bar{e}^{(1)}$, $a_1 = \bar{e}^{(2)}/\bar{e}^{(1)}$, $a_2 = \bar{e}^{(3)}/\bar{e}^{(2)}, \ldots, a_i = \bar{e}^{(i+1)}/\bar{e}^{(i)}$, where $\bar{e}^{(i)}$ equals the

---

[30]The schedule is also sensitive to the relative importance of *premarital conceptions*.
[31]First marriages and remarriages.
[32]It is important to note that the data may refer to all births born prior to or during current marriage, or only to the number of legitimate children born during current marriage. Marriages may also refer to first marriages only or to all marriages including remarriages.
[33]The result is a *biased* measure of marital fertility because women marrying older (usually less fertile) are underrepresented at bound β under the impact of differential mortality by age. A correction factor will be developed in Section 5.3.2.2.

average number of children of order i per married couple,[34] and noting that

$$n_0 = 1 - \bar{e}^{(1)} \qquad\qquad \bar{e}^{(1)} = 1 - n_0$$

$$n_1 = \bar{e}^{(1)} - \bar{e}^{(2)} \qquad\qquad \bar{e}^{(2)} = \bar{e}^{(1)} - n_1 = 1 - n_0 - n_1$$

$$n_2 = \bar{e}^{(2)} - \bar{e}^{(3)} \qquad\qquad \bar{e}^{(3)} = \bar{e}^{(2)} - n_2 = 1 - n_0 - n_1 - n_2$$

$$\vdots \qquad\qquad\qquad \vdots$$

$$n_i = \bar{e}^{(i)} - \bar{e}^{(i+1)} \qquad\qquad \bar{e}^{(i)} = 1 - n_0 - n_1 - n_2 - \cdots - n_{i-1}$$

The parity progression ratios will therefore be equal to

$$a_0 = \bar{e}^{(1)} = 1 - n_0$$

$$a_1 = \frac{\bar{e}^{(2)}}{\bar{e}^{(1)}} = \frac{1 - n_0 - n_1}{1 - n_0} = 1 - \frac{n_1}{1 - n_0}$$

$$a_2 = \frac{\bar{e}^{(3)}}{\bar{e}^{(2)}} = \frac{1 - n_0 - n_1 - n_2}{1 - n_0 - n_1} = 1 - \frac{n_2}{1 - n_0 - n_1}$$

$$\vdots$$

$$a_i = \frac{\bar{e}^{(i+1)}}{\bar{e}^{(i)}} = \frac{1 - n_0 - n_1 - \cdots - n_i}{1 - n_0 - n_1 - \cdots - n_{i-1}}$$

$$= 1 - \frac{n_i}{1 - n_0 - n_1 - \cdots - n_{i-1}}$$

There is, however, an equivalent method (see example, Section 5.3.3.2) of computing parity progression ratios. Since $n_0 + n_1 + n_2 + \cdots + n_i + \cdots + n_n = 1$, one has simply

$$a_0 = 1 - n_0$$

$$= n_1 + n_2 + \cdots + n_i + \cdots + n_n$$

$$a_1 = \frac{1 - n_0 - n_1}{1 - n_0}$$

$$= \frac{n_2 + n_3 + \cdots + n_i + \cdots + n_n}{n_1 + n_2 + n_3 + \cdots + n_i + \cdots + n_n}$$

[34]Note that $\bar{e}^{(i)}$ is also equal to the proportion of couples having *at least* a birth of order i.

$$a_2 = \frac{1 - n_0 - n_1 - n_2}{1 - n_0 - n_1}$$

$$= \frac{n_3 + n_4 + \cdots + n_i + \cdots + n_n}{n_2 + n_3 + \cdots + n_i + \cdots + n_n}$$

.
.
.

$$a_i = \frac{\sum\limits_{i+1}^{n} n_j}{\sum\limits_{i}^{n} n_j}$$

$$= \frac{\sum\limits_{i+1}^{n} N_j}{\sum\limits_{i}^{n} N_j}$$

the final expression on the right-hand side resulting from the fact that $n_j = N_j/N$.

The meaning of these parity progression ratios is the same as before: they state the *ex post facto* frequency, for the marriage-cohort considered, of passing from parity i to parity $i+1$.

5.3.2.2. Children Ever-Born by Duration of Marriage and Age at Marriage. The elimination of age, in the previous section, in favor of marriage duration only, is not without problems. First, among the number of marriages observed at bound β, some were concluded at post reproductive ages; since these do not contribute to fertility, one should exclude from observation all marriages concluded when the wife was over 50.

Second, as noted above, the average number of children per couple, by duration of marriage, is biased due to overrepresentation, at bound β, of women who have married at young ages: the computed mean number of children therefore *overestimates* the overall performance of the cohort with respect to fertility (as in example, Section 5.3.3.3), even if the conditions of independence and continuity are satisfied.[35] This bias is, however, easily corrected as follows. Having computed the average number of children in the subcohorts partitioned according to *age at marriage* of wives, the average number of children for the overall marriage-cohort is obtained by the weighted average

$$\bar{e} = \sum_x \bar{e}_x F_x / \sum_x F_x$$

[35]The bias is due to *differential age at marriage* between females in the marriage cohort.

where $\bar{e}_x$ stands for the average number of children (after e.g., 25 years of marriage) for females married at age x and F_x represents the number of females marrying at age x derived from *vital statistics data at the time of marriage* (e.g., 25 years before census or survey, if bound $\beta = 25$).

It is, however, advantageous to utilize more thoroughly the available data on children ever born by duration of marriage *and* age at marriage, in order to compute not only the average number of children $\bar{e}_x$ for females married at age x (or age groups x to $x+n$) but also, for this subcohort of women, the average duration of marriage at childbearing and the corresponding parity progression ratios.[36] In temporal or spatial comparisons, this approach has the advantage of distinguishing variations in the "marriage-mix," i.e., variations from cohort to cohort in the relative proportions of females marrying at specified ages. Since partitioning the marriage-cohort according to age at marriage reduces the size of the subsamples, one may extend the observation to all persons *ever-married* at bound β, i.e., also to women currently divorced or widowed. If conditions of independence and continuity are fulfilled, fertility "rates" (i.e., reduced births) can be reconstructed[37] for each subcohort of marriages if one knows the date of marriage dissolution and the date of birth of children: the number of children born during a specified duration is divided by the midperiod population still married at the duration considered. The "rates" obtained can thereafter be combined, following the usual procedure applicable to reduced events, in order to derive the average intensity[38] and tempo of fertility for each subcohort of marriages.

5.3.3. Examples

5.3.3.1. Parity Progression Ratios in a Marriage-Cohort, Computed from Vital Statistics. Consider in Table 5.3 the reduced births (marriage-duration-specific fertility "rates") computed for the Belgian marriage-cohort of 1947, by birth orders.[39]

---

[36] Another useful measure is the average age at *last* confinement in the subcohorts of marriages according to age at marriage.

[37] "Rates" evidently refer only to the population surviving (to death, to emigration) at time of census; the condition of independence must therefore be satisfied.

[38] *Partial* intensities may also be computed in studying the proportion of children already born at each duration of marriage.

[39] Approximate "rates" were computed by dividing births by the initial population of the marriage-cohort, as seen in Section 5.3.1.1.

TABLE 5.3. Reduced Births per 10,000 Marriages of 1947

Duration of marriage (completed years)	Birth orders					
	1	2	3	4	5+	Total
0	3,485	31	1	0	0	3,517
1	2,078	564	32	2	0	2,676
2	813	1,138	132	14	1	2,098
3	460	825	395	51	8	1,739
4	307	614	419	149	24	1,513
5	208	456	375	201	73	1,313
6	151	359	316	207	134	1,167
7	111	262	282	200	169	1,024
8	73	193	221	194	202	883
9	57	138	181	155	221	752
10	42	117	153	138	237	687
11	30	87	111	108	227	563
12	22	64	89	90	199	464
13	17	48	74	77	199	415
14	11	36	59	62	182	350
Total	7,865	4,932	2,840	1,648	1,876	19,161

[a]Source: Wunsch, G. *Les mesures de la natalité*. Louvain, 1967, Appendix tables.

The number of births per marriage by birth order can easily be derived, assuming that fertility after 15 years of marriage is negligible,[40] and that independence and continuity are satisfied:

$$\bar{e}^{(1)} = 0.7865, \qquad \bar{e}^{(2)} = 0.4932, \qquad \bar{e}^{(3)} = 0.2840$$

$$\bar{e}^{(4)} = 0.1648, \qquad \bar{e}^{(5+)} = 0.1876$$

Parity progression ratios can then be computed (Section 5.3.1.1):

$$a_0 = \bar{e}^{(1)} = 0.7865, \qquad a_1 = \bar{e}^{(2)}/\bar{e}^{(1)} = 0.6271$$

$$a_2 = \bar{e}^{(3)}/\bar{e}^{(2)} = 0.5758, \qquad a_3 = \bar{e}^{(4)}/\bar{e}^{(3)} = 0.5803$$

Finally, a_k ($k \geqslant 4$) can be estimated by the approximation $a_k = \bar{e}^{(5+)}/(\bar{e}^{(5+)} + \bar{e}^{(4)}) = 0.5323$ in the present case.

5.3.3.2. Parity Progression Ratios in a Marriage-Cohort, Computed from Census Data. Table 5.4 gives the distribution of Belgian couples, by number of children born, at marriage durations 20 to 24 in completed years

[40]An upper limit of 20 or 25 years would, however, be preferable.

TABLE 5.4. Distribution of Couples by Number of Children Born[a]

	Birth orders								
	0	1	2	3	4	5	6	7	8+
Number of couples	34,895	49,450	45,883	27,897	17,440	10,273	6,268	3,718	5,738
Cumulated[b]	201,562	166,667	117,217	71,334	43,437	25,997	15,724	9,456	5,738
Total	201,562								

[a]Source: *Recensement général de la population belge au 31-12-1961*. Brussels, 1961, Table 35 ff.
[b]See text.

on December 31, 1961. The second line in Table 5.4 gives the cumulated number of couples having had a birth of order k or higher. As seen in Section 5.3.2.1, the following parity progression ratios can then be easily derived:

$$a_0 = \frac{166,667}{201,562} = 0.827, \qquad a_1 = \frac{117,217}{166,667} = 0.703$$

$$a_2 = \frac{71,334}{117,217} = 0.609, \qquad a_3 = \frac{43,437}{71,334} = 0.609$$

$$a_4 = \frac{25,997}{43,437} = 0.598, \qquad a_5 = \frac{15,724}{25,997} = 0.605$$

$$a_6 = \frac{9,456}{15,724} = 0.601$$

Moreover, since 5,738 couples have had at least a child of order 8, a_7 is equal to 5,738/9,456, i.e., 0.607.

5.3.3.3. Average Number of Children per Couple. It was noted above, in Section 5.3.2.2, that the average number of children per couple, derived from census data on children ever-born by duration of marriage, is biased due to overrepresentation of women who have married at young ages.

Table 5.5 distributes the number of couples given in Section 5.3.3.2, according to age of the mother, at marriage duration 20 to 24 years. Dividing the total number of children by the number of couples gives an average

TABLE 5.5. Total Number of Children by Age of Mother[a]

Age of mother (years) (on December 31, 1961)	Total number of couples	Total number of children
35–39	7,676	22,461
40–44	67,451	172,153
45–49	75,415	180,184
50–54	30,248	63,189
55–59	11,283	14,202
60–64	5,350	2,736
65–69	2,816	476
70–74	1,323	169
Total	201,562	455,570

[a]Source: *Recensement général de la population belge au 31-12-1961.* Brussels, 1961, Table 35 ff.

TABLE 5.6

Age of mother at census (years)	Average number of children
35–39	2.926
40–44	2.552
45–49	2.389
50–54	2.089
55–59	1.259
60–64	0.511
65–69	0.169
70–74	0.128

number of children per couple of 2.26 where women marrying young are overrepresented. One can, however, compute the number of children, at census time, by age of the mother[41]; from the above data, one obtains the numbers in Table 5.6.

Weighting the averages in Table 5.6 by the number of marriages *at time of marriage* drawn from vital statistics data[42] relating to the birth-cohorts enumerated in 1961 gives an average of 2.13 children per couple, instead of 2.26.

[41]Age at marriage equals age at census minus duration of marriage at census.
[42]That is, for the years 1937 to 1941; for brevity, the latter data are not given here.

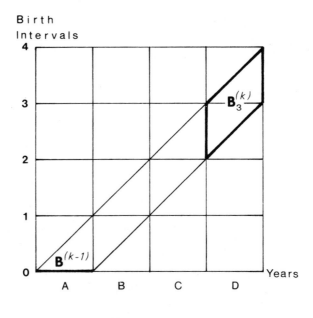

FIGURE 5.4

5.4. BIRTH-INTERVAL-SPECIFIC FERTILITY

5.4.1. Birth-Interval-Specific Fertility "Rates"

5.4.1.1. Cohort Analysis. Suppose that birth $B^{(k)}$ by birth order[43] k is registered by year of birth of the preceding child $B^{(k-1)}$. If this is the case, it is possible to study the trend in fertility by birth order and the interval elapsed since the preceding birth from vital statistics published yearly. In Fig. 5.4, for example, $B_3^{(k)}$ represents the number of live births of order k, recorded during year D at average duration 3 (in exact years) elapsed since birth $B^{(k-1)}$ of order $k-1$ (born to women during year A). The number of births $B^{(k-1)}$ during year A correspond to $B^{(k-1)}$ women attaining parity[44] $k-1$ during year A. Therefore, the *interval-specific* fertility "rate" (or reduced births) computed for this *parity-cohort*[45] at average exact duration 3 is obtained by dividing the number of births $B^{(k)}$ observed at this duration by

---

[43]Order may refer to all children born to a woman, or to births in the current marriage only (first marriage and/or remarriage). This distinction must be kept in mind when comparing fertility data by birth order.

[44]For birth order $k = 1$, parity 0 will be defined as the event-origin of the birth-cohort or marriage-cohort.

[45]A *parity-cohort* is thus the cohort formed by women attaining a given parity during a specified period (e.g., during a calendar year), i.e., giving birth to a child of birth order $k-1$.

the survivors of the parity-cohort. The number of survivors being unknown, one divides once more the number of births of order k by the *initial* population of the cohort, in this case by $B^{(k-1)}$:

$$\hat{r}_x = B_x^{(k)}/B^{(k-1)}$$

As in the case of marital fertility "rates" (Section 5.3.1.1), this approximate "rate" usually underestimates true reduced births r_x. Therefore, one has

$$\hat{\bar{e}} = \sum_0^\beta \hat{r}_x^{(k)} < \bar{e} = \sum_0^\beta r_x^{(k)}$$

and

$$\hat{\bar{x}} = \frac{1}{\hat{\bar{e}}} \sum_0^\beta x\hat{r}_x^{(k)} < \bar{x} = \frac{1}{\bar{e}} \sum_0^\beta xr_x^{(k)}$$

Bound β can usually be chosen as 10 years.[46] The average intensity $\bar{e}$ (or its approximate value $\hat{\bar{e}}$ represents the average number of births of order k to a woman of parity $k-1$; it is therefore equal to a *parity progression ratio* for each particular *parity-cohort*, i.e., the frequency of passing from parity $k-1$ to k, and will therefore be denoted by the usual expression a_{k-1}. It is important to note, however, that these parity progression ratios do not refer to a particular birth-cohort or marriage-cohort[47]: they may not, therefore, be combined in view of deriving the average number of children per head for a particular birth-cohort or marriage-cohort.

The average duration $\bar{x}$ (or $\hat{\bar{x}}$) represents the *average birth interval* elapsed in the parity-cohort between births of order $k-1$ and k. Once again this measure cannot be related to a particular birth-cohort or marriage-cohort.[48]

As with all reduced events, *partial* intensities can also be computed for segmented parity-cohorts, indicating the number of births of order k born up to given duration $\beta - x$.

Birth intervals should be derived from vital registration of births by order and duration elapsed since previous births. Frequently, this tabulation

---

[46]Birth intervals greater than 10 are scarce. Since the time period is short, underestimation of $\bar{e}$ and $\bar{x}$ is therefore restricted, in most cases.

[47]Except for parity progression ratio a_0 which denotes, as noted above, the probability of passing from parity 0 to parity 1, and is computed in a birth-cohort or a marriage-cohort as a birth-order specific fertility "rate" by age or marriage-duration (Sections 5.2.2.1 and 5.3.1.1).

[48]Except for interval 0 to 1, which represents the average age or marriage duration at *first* birth in a birth-cohort or a marriage-cohort.

is unfortunately not available. However, Ryder (1969, p. 120) has devised an approximate method based on average marriage-durations or ages at childbearing (see example, Section 5.4.3.1). Write $\bar{x}^{(1)}, \bar{x}^{(2)}, \ldots, \bar{x}^{(i)}, \ldots$ for the average duration (by birth- or marriage-cohort) at childbearing, having recourse to reduced births by birth order, as in Section 5.2.2.1 or 5.3.1.1. The mean birth interval between orders $i+1$ and i is not equal to the difference $\bar{x}^{(i+1)} - \bar{x}^{(i)}$ since some women of parity i will not have a birth of order $i+1$. Women of parity i may, however, be distinguished by the fact that they do or do not move to parity $i+1$; let $\bar{x}^{(i)}(1)$ and $\bar{x}^{(i)}(2)$, respectively, be the average duration (age or duration of marriage) at the ith birth for women who will or will not move to parity $i+1$. The overall duration $\bar{x}^{(i)}$ may be written as:

$$\bar{x}^{(i)} = a_i\bar{x}^{(i)}(1) + (1-a_i)\bar{x}^{(i)}(2)$$

where a_i represents the parity progression ratio from i to $i+1$. Adding $\bar{x}^{(i+1)} - \bar{x}^{(i)}(1)$ to both members of the equation, and redistributing terms, gives

$$\bar{x}^{(i+1)} - \bar{x}^{(i)}(1) = \bar{x}^{(i+1)} - \bar{x}^{(i)} + (1-a_i)[\bar{x}^{(i)}(2) - \bar{x}^{(i)}(1)]$$

Assuming[49] that $\bar{x}^{(i)}(2) \cong \bar{x}^{(i+1)}$, the birth *interval* $\bar{x}^{(i+1)} - \bar{x}^{(i)}(1)$ can be expressed as $\bar{x}^{(i+1)} - \bar{x}^{(i)}(1) = (\bar{x}^{(i+1)} - \bar{x}^{(i)})/a_i$.

The absolute error, equal to $(1-a_i)[\bar{x}^{(i)}(2) - \bar{x}^{(i+1)}]$, is probably rather small, especially for high values of a_i. If $\bar{x}^{(i+1)} > x^{(i)}(2)$, the real birth interval is overestimated; the converse is true if $\bar{x}^{(i+1)} < \bar{x}^{(i)}(2)$.

The same argument can be turned around in order to compute the average duration at last birth of order $i[\bar{x}^{(i)}(2)]$ knowing birth intervals and parity progression ratios (Henry, 1972, pp. 153–154).

5.4.1.2. Period Analysis. Birth-interval-specific "rates," computed for a given calendar year, can be combined either in the *standardization* approach or in the *translation* approach. The sequence of birth-interval "rates," computed as above, can be condensed into a comparative index of fertility excluding the impact of population structures by interval elapsed since last birth. The period "rates" can also be added up, in the fictitious cohort approach, in estimating synthetic parity progression ratios.

These fictitious parity progression ratios can then be combined in deriving the *synthetic average number of children per head* in a fictitious

---

[49]As one can assume the inequality $\bar{x}^{(i)}(2) > \bar{x}^{(i)} > \bar{x}^{(i)}(1)$.

birth- or marriage-cohort.[50] As seen in Section 5.3.2.1, one has

$$a_0 = \bar{e}^{(1)}$$

$$a_1 = \bar{e}^{(2)}/\bar{e}^{(1)}$$

$$\vdots$$

$$a_i = \bar{e}^{(i+1)}/\bar{e}^{(i)}$$

Therefore, the synthetic average numbers of children *by birth order* are obtained by:

$$\bar{e}^{(1)} = a_0$$

$$\bar{e}^{(2)} = a_1\bar{e}^{(1)} = a_1 a_0$$

$$\vdots$$

$$\bar{e}^{(i+1)} = a_i\bar{e}^{(i)} = a_i a_{i-1} a_{i-2} \cdots a_1 a_0$$

and generally

$$\bar{e}^{(n)} = \prod_0^{n-1} a_j$$

The fictitious proportions of couples having exactly $0, 1, 2, \ldots, i$ children ever-born are given by

$$n_0 = 1 - \bar{e}^{(1)} = 1 - a_0$$

$$n_1 = \bar{e}^{(1)} - \bar{e}^{(2)} = (1 - a_1)a_0$$

$$\vdots$$

$$n_i = \bar{e}^{(i)} - \bar{e}^{(i+1)} = (1 - a_i) \prod_0^{i-1} a_j$$

Finally, the synthetic average number of children per head (all **birth orders**) is defined by

$$\bar{e} = \bar{e}^{(1)} + \bar{e}^{(2)} + \bar{e}^{(3)} + \cdots + \bar{e}^{(i)} + \cdots$$

or

$$\bar{e} = a_0 + a_0 a_1 + a_0 a_1 a_2 + \cdots + \prod_0^{i-1} a_j + \cdots$$

[50]Depending on the fact that data relate to overall birth orders, or to birth orders in current marriage only.

Period parity progression ratios and related indexes, such as the synthetic average number of children, are influenced (as all period measures in the translation approach) by the biases noted in Section 2.3. Among others, distributional distortion due to changing birth intervals from one parity-cohort to the other are reflected in the period parity progression ratios.[51] Period ratios, and the synthetic index $\bar{e}$, are, however, excellent standardized measures of period fertility because they do not remain influenced for very long by accidents in the reproductive histories of the cohorts concerned, as was the case with age-specific or even with marriage-duration-specific fertility "rates." This is due to the fact that, once a postponed birth is made up, parity-specific fertility behaves as if no postponement had occurred, except for changes in behavior dependent on increased age or duration of marriage.[52] In periods of short-term changes in fertility patterns, synthetic measures based on period parity progression ratios are therefore highly recommended.

In most countries, births by order are not tabulated according to year of birth of the preceding child. Direct computation of birth interval-specific fertility "rates" is therefore impossible. One may, however, have recourse once more to the *weighted average method* (as in example, Section 5.4.3.2) already introduced in the study of divorce (Section 4.1.1.2) and of fertility by duration of marriage (Section 5.3.1.2).

The period parity progression ratio can be written as

$$a_i = \frac{B_0^{(i+1)}}{\sum_j \alpha_j^{(i+1)} B_{-j}^{(i)}}$$

where $B_0^{(i+1)}$ stands for the number of births of order $i+1$ born during a given calendar year 0; $B_{-j}^{(i)}$ represents the number of births of order i born during year 0 and preceding years; and $\alpha_j^{(i+1)}$ is a standard schedule of interval-specific fertility for births of order $i+1$.

L. Henry (1953, 1954) has derived standard schedules $\alpha_j^{(i+1)}$ for computation of period parity progression ratios a_1 to a_7. Usually a_0 can be computed directly from data on first births by age of mother or duration of marriage. Table A.6 in the Appendix presents a set of standard fertility schedules for low-fertility (LF) and high-fertility (HF) countries,[53] for ratios

---

[51]If birth intervals are decreasing, the period parity progression ratio can even sometimes become greater than unity, an impossibility in a true parity-cohort.

[52]For an interesting discussion of this problem, see Henry (1953, pp.15–18).

[53]LF standards are Henry's French schedules for 1907; HF standards are Henry's schedule for Slovakia for 1925–1926. Differences between both schedules are very slight.

a_1 to a_7, and two tentative schedules for deriving a_0 in a marriage-cohort derived from recent European data.[54] All durations are in period differences.

Once ratios a_i are obtained up to a_7, these period estimates can be combined as above into a synthetic average number of children per head. One may choose all a_k $(k > 7)$ equal to a_7; then, having recourse to the relation[55] developed in Section 5.3.1.1, one may write

$$\bar{e}^{(8+)} = \frac{a_7 \bar{e}^{(7)}}{1 - a_7}$$

Finally, the synthetic average number of children per head is equal to

$$\bar{e} = \sum_1^7 \bar{e}^{(i)} + \bar{e}^{(8+)}$$

or

$$\bar{e} = (a_0 + a_0 a_1 + \cdots + a_0 a_1 a_2 \cdots a_6) + [a_7/(1 - a_7)](a_0 a_1 a_2 \cdots a_6)$$

Variants of the above formulas can easily be developed if parity progression ratios are computed up to a_5 or a_6 only.

5.4.2. Census-Type Data on Birth Intervals

Birth intervals computed as in Section 5.4.1.1, from birth-interval-specific fertility "rates," are rather crude measures of birth timing as births are classified by year of occurrence only and not by date. More refined measures of birth intervals must therefore be obtained from censuses or surveys.

Birth intervals derived from census-type data should be computed for marriages of *completed* fertility, at the end of the reproductive period. Since high-parity families usually have shorter birth intervals than low-parity families, birth intervals should be computed only for families of the *same parity*,[56] i.e., the same number of children ever born.

An alternative method, avoiding the problem of reducing population

---

[54] Schedules for a_0 may differ rather widely from one population to the other; direct computation of a_0 should therefore be preferred whenever possible. Schedule (A) corresponds to populations with a high incidence of premarital pregnancies, and schedule (B) to populations with a low incidence of premarital pregnancies.

[55] $a_k = \bar{e}^{(n+)}/[\bar{e}^{(n+)} + \bar{e}^{(n-1)}]$.

[56] If one does not observe this rule, birth intervals tend to decrease with order of birth; this erroneous conclusion derives from the fact that birth intervals of high order are obviously computed for high-parity families only, i.e., families with short overall birth intervals.

TABLE 5.7

Average number of children per couple	Parity progression ratios	Duration of marriage at birth of order i
$\bar{e}(1) = 0.7865$	$a_0 = 0.7865$	$\bar{x}(1) = 1.96$
$\bar{e}(2) = 0.4932$	$a_1 = 0.6271$	$\bar{x}(2) = 4.73$
$\bar{e}(3) = 0.2840$	$a_2 = 0.5758$	$\bar{x}(3) = 6.80$
$\bar{e}(4) = 0.1648$	$a_3 = 0.5803$	$\bar{x}(4) = 8.32$
$\bar{e}(5+) = 0.1876$	$a_k = 0.5323^a$	$\bar{x}(5+) = 10.34$

$^a k \geqslant 4.$

sizes as in the above method, is to compute average birth intervals (last intervals excluded) at orders for which all families are represented. The *last intervals* will be computed separately for each category and averaged. For example, intervals 1–2, 2–3, 3–4 will be computed separately for couples having parented 5 children *or more*. The two or three *last* intervals are then computed separately for women of parity 5 (intervals 3–4 and 4–5), of parity 6 (intervals 4–5 and 5–6), etc.; these measures are then averaged in order to give the mean last intervals by weighting the duration of a specific interval (last interval, for example) in each category by the number of women in the category. As each parity is always represented this method avoids the selection of higher-parity women when computing birth intervals of higher order.[57]

A final problem remains when computing the average interval between marriage and *first birth*: this interval is often influenced by the impact of premarital conceptions. An approximate solution is to retain only births born after eight months of marriage, i.e., to eliminate from computation births born during completed months 0 to 7 included.

5.4.3. Examples

5.4.3.1. Birth Intervals and Duration of Marriage. Consider the data

in Table 5.7 for the Belgian marriage-cohort of 1947. Data on $\bar{e}^{(i)}$ and a_i are taken from the example, Section 5.3.3.1; the same data yield values of duration of marriage $\bar{x}^{(i)}$ at birth of order i, using the formula

$$\bar{x}^{(i)} = \frac{\sum (x + 0.5) N_x(i)}{\sum N_x(i)}$$

[57] One usually notices, when the adequate method is used, that the last birth intervals tend to increase, instead of decreasing as for the simple average of birth intervals does.

where $N_x(i)$ represents the number of reduced births of order i at marriage duration x in completed years.

Having recourse to Ryder's method, developed in Section 5.4.1.1, estimates of birth intervals can then be derived using the approximation $(\bar{x}^{(i+1)} - \bar{x}^{(i)})(1/a_i)$:

$$\text{Birth interval (1) to (2)} = (4.73 - 1.96)/0.6271 = 4.42$$
$$\text{Birth interval (2) to (3)} = (6.80 - 4.73)/0.5758 = 3.59$$
$$\text{Birth interval (3) to (4)} = (8.32 - 6.80)/0.5803 = 2.62$$

5.4.3.2. Period Parity Progression Ratios. Table 5.8 (on pages 176 and 177) gives the number of births by birth order for the USA, for calendar years 1958–1968.[58]

Estimates of period parity progression ratios, using the method developed in Section 5.4.1.2, can be computed for orders 1 to 6, for calendar year 1968. With standard weights taken from the Appendix, Table A.6 (LF), one obtains, for example,

$$a_1 = 917{,}928/[0.02(1{,}311{,}460)$$

$$+ 0.22(1{,}228{,}274) + \cdots + 0.1(1{,}099{,}462)] = 0.772$$

Similarly, one obtains

$$a_2 = 0.581$$

$$a_3 = 0.481$$

$$a_4 = 0.426$$

$$a_5 = 0.425$$

$$a_6 = 0.440$$

5.5. MEASURES OF NATURAL FERTILITY AND CONTRACEPTIVE EFFECTIVENESS

5.5.1. Measures of Natural Fertility

5.5.1.1. Natural Fertility. L. Henry has coined the term *natural*[59] *fertility* for the fertility of a population that does not *voluntarily* practice birth control. Though this distinction is rather theoretical, one may say that, in these populations, marital fertility is mainly dependent upon biological

---

[58]Source: *Demographic Yearbook*. New York: United Nations, 1965, 1969, and 1970.

[59]One sometimes also finds the equivalent terms: "non-Malthusian" fertility or the fertility of "noncontracepting" couples.

TABLE 5.8

Birth order	Year				
	1968	1967	1966	1965	1964
1	1,311,460	1,228,274	1,224,786	1,157,386	1,164,548
2	917,928	900,474	887,954	909,822	962,896
3	539,138	556,032	584,790	646,022	719,068
4	307,626	331,143	362,670	415,802	469,364
5	171,020	190,815	215,034	248,474	280,182
6	99,332	112,273	127,854	147,232	165,976
7	58,782	67,327	76,544	87,604	99,052
8+	93,888	107,786	124,604	142,284	158,252

variables[60]; even here social norms intervene in such fields as the duration of lactation or taboos on intercourse during lactation.

The study of natural fertility presents considerable difficulties of observation: studies relate either to present noncontracepting populations sampled by surveys, or to noncontracepting populations of the 18th and 19th centuries reconstructed from parish registration data or genealogies.

The first distinction to be drawn is between fecund and sterile couples. The first few sections will be devoted to *fecund* couples only; the number of fecund couples is in practice estimated by the number of couples *eventually fertile*, i.e., those that bear at least one child. After each ovulation period, only a certain proportion of these fecund women will usually become pregnant; conception may therefore be considered as a stochastic phenomenon: the probability of conceiving during a menstrual cycle (or one month) is called *fecundability*.[61]

Since in a noncontracepting population the risk of bearing a child is not influenced by duration of marriage,[62] fecundability will be considered as a function of age solely, providing that *nonsusceptible periods* are excluded, i.e., duration of gestation and a period of temporary sterility after confinement.

Finally, since the study of fertility is restricted to live births and not to conceptions, one must take into account the proportion of conceptions producing a live birth or its complement, the *proportion of fetal deaths*.

[60]For an excellent overview, see Léridon (1973).
[61]Fecundability is a statistical measure, not an individual one.
[62]It has been noted above (Section 5.2.2.3) that this assumption is not always valid.

TABLE 5.8 (*continued*)

Year					
1963	1962	1961	1960	1959	1958
1,122,138	1,086,312	1,099,688	1,090,152	1,093,496	1,099,462
979,944	974,378	1,002,556	1,022,356	1,036,484	1,043,172
746,080	759,576	789,852	797,402	798,432	793,018
490,448	497,988	515,250	511,308	504,758	489,866
293,342	295,984	301,166	292,610	284,258	272,492
171,412	172,356	174,406	168,210	163,420	154,188
102,096	101,594	103,218	99,882	96,436	90,792
161,338	161,292	161,056	154,532	149,520	141,044

5.5.1.2. Fecundability. The concept of fecundability stems from the work of the Italian demographer C. Gini (1924).[63] Let F represent a set of fecund females (i.e., eventually fertile) observed *since marriage* in order to eliminate the influence of nonsusceptible periods on the measure of fecundability. Let f represent the monthly fecundability of these females, and assume that f is constant during the period prior to first conception. If C_0 and C_1 denote the number of conceptions observed during the first two months of marriage, one may write

$$C_0 = Ff$$
$$C_1 = F(1-f)f$$

Therefore $f = 1 - C_1/C_0 = (C_0 - C_1)/C_0$.

The same argument holds for succeeding pairs of months, and for *differential fecundabilities* between women: $1 - C_{x+1}/C_x$ then represents the average fecundability (Léridon, 1973, pp. 27–28) of women conceiving during month x. To avoid an estimate based on a small number of cases (conceptions during months x and $x + 1$), Gini recommends computing an average overall fecundability for the first n months of marriage by weighting the bimonthly estimates C_{x+1}/C_x by C_x and subtracting this average from one:

$$1 - \frac{1}{\sum\limits_{0}^{n-1} C_x} \left(\sum\limits_{0}^{n-1} C_x \frac{C_{x+1}}{C_x} \right)$$

[63]For a recent discussion and an extensive bibliography, see Bongaarts (1975).

This expression is equal to

$$\frac{1}{\sum\limits_0^{n-1} C_x}\left(\sum\limits_0^{n-1} C_x f_x\right)$$

with $f_x = 1 - C_{x+1}/C_x$, i.e., to the weighted average of fecundabilities f_x.

The main problem consists obviously in estimating the number of conceptions C_i. If one does not have recourse to clinical observations, conceptions C_i will be estimated by the number of children born nine months afterwards. If the number of births are used instead of conceptions, one obtains a measure of "*effective*" *fecundability*, as it is sometimes called.

As a measure of the fecundability of newly married women, L. Henry (1953, p. 95) has proposed determining the average fecundability f_0 during the first month of marriage (0 in completed months) by dividing the number of first births N_9 born during the tenth month of marriage (9 in completed months) by the number of fecund women at time of marriage, premarital conceptions excluded. The latter population is expressed as the eventual number of females bearing a first child[64]; therefore, the average fecundability is equal to $f_0 = N_9/\sum_i N_i$ (for $i \geq 8$), where N_i represents the number of first births per month i. Here again, since births and not conceptions are used, a measure of "effective" fecundability is obtained.

An important selection effect must be noted here. If one computes monthly *probabilities of conception* (or fecundabilities) by dividing the number of conceptions observed during a given month by the number of fecund women not yet pregnant, at the beginning of the month, one observes a decrease in the monthly probabilities of conception over time (Henripin, 1954, p. 80). This is because the population is heterogeneous with respect to fecundability[65]: the more fecund women tend to conceive rapidly and are therefore excluded from observation; since the observation period increases, the population "surviving" to conception is therefore composed of less and less fecund women.

Consider now a situation where the population is *homogeneous* with respect to fecundability (or probability of conception); assume also that this probability f is constant over time.[66] The probability of conceiving during

---

[64]Excluding premarital conceptions, i.e., births occurring before eight months of marriage (0–7 in completed months).

[65]Also, with respect to fetal mortality, if births are used in place of conceptions, see Henry (1964a, 1972, Chap. 13).

[66]This model was developed by Vincent (1961). See also Henry (1972, Chap. 12), for a thorough discussion of these models.

the first month of marriage is equal to f; during the second month, the probability of conception is $(1-f)f$; during the third month $(1-f)^2f$, etc. Since conception is preceded by ovulation, the *average number of ovulations before conception* will be equal to the weighted average

$$i = \frac{[f + 2(1-f)f + 3(1-f)^2f + \cdots)]}{[f + (1-f)f + (1-f)^2f + \cdots]}$$

The sum of weights $f[(1 + (1-f) + (1-f)^2 + \cdots)]$ tends toward $f(1/f)$, i.e., unity, being the sum of a geometric progression.

Therefore $i = f[1 + 2(1-f) + 3(1-f)^2 \cdots]$. The factor of f is equal to the expansion of $[1 - (1-f)]^{-2}$ and therefore tends toward $1/f^2$. Finally, $i = 1/f$, i.e., fecundability is equal to the *reciprocal* of the average number of ovulations before conception. As to the *average interval between marriage and first conception*, it is equal to $1/f$ only if marriage takes place immediately after ovulation; generally, it will be slightly shorter and approximately equal to $1/f - 1/2$, assuming that half of the marriages are concluded in the pre-ovulation period of the menstrual cycle.

When fecundability is heterogeneous and variable over time, the above conclusions are not valid. In the case of a heterogeneous population, as regards fecundability, Vincent has shown that the average interval is approximately equal to $1/\psi - 1/2$, where ψ stands for the *harmonic* mean of fecundabilities of subgroups composing the heterogeneous population.

Another approach has been attempted recently by J. Bongaarts (1975). His procedure is based on a model for the distribution of intervals from marriage to first birth, from which he has derived the relation between mean fecundability and the ratio of the births occurring during the 9th, 10th, and 11th completed months after marriage to all first births in month 9 or later (i.e., excluding births in months 0 through 8, in order to eliminate premarital conceptions). The reference table is given in Table 5.9.

The relationship between both variables depends on the model's parameter values, but the method probably does yield the magnitude of average fecundability as derived from first births distributed according to marriage duration.

The above methods are all based on the observation of first pregnancies (or births) in a group of newly married women; measures of fecundabilities relate therefore only to a short fraction of the reproductive period, a fraction usually characterized by a high fecundability. In order to compute fecundabilities over the whole reproductive period, one should necessarily extend the observation to higher-order births. It is then difficult to disentangle

TABLE 5.9

Fecundability mean	Ratio of births in months 9, 10, and 11 after marriage to all first births—excluding births before month 9	Fecundability mean	Ratio of births in months 9, 10, and 11 after marriage to all first births—excluding births before month 9
0.10	0.211	0.23	0.406
0.11	0.229	0.24	0.418
0.12	0.247	0.25	0.429
0.13	0.264	0.26	0.440
0.14	0.281	0.27	0.451
0.15	0.297	0.28	0.461
0.16	0.312	0.29	0.471
0.17	0.327	0.30	0.480
0.18	0.341	0.31	0.489
0.19	0.355	0.32	0.498
0.20	0.369	0.33	0.506
0.21	0.382	0.34	0.513
0.22	0.394	0.35	0.520

[a]Source: Bongaarts (1975, p. 654).

fecundability from the influence of postpartum infecundity, i.e., the nonsusceptible period following the outcome of pregnancy.

5.5.1.3. Nonsusceptible Period. The nonsusceptible period is composed of the duration of pregnancy plus the postpartum infecundable period. When the outcome of pregnancy is a live birth, the average duration of pregnancy varies little and is equal to about 9 months. The average duration of pregnancy leading to a fetal death is not well known; it seems to be more or less equal to 3 months.

The postpartum infecundable period for fecund women depends, among others, on the duration of breast feeding and on the resumption of sexual intercourse. A method of measuring the duration of this period consists in distinguishing confinements according to the outcome of pregnancy, i.e., a stillbirth (or a live child dying shortly after birth) or a live child surviving at least one year. If probabilities of conception are computed for a group of women having had a stillbirth, there is evidently no bias due to breast feeding. From Vincent's data (1961, p. 256), one concludes that these probabilities of conception are negligible during the first months compared to probabilities of conception *after marriage*: the postpartum infecundity period *excluding breast feeding* would therefore be equal to about 3 months.

Furthermore, comparison of birth intervals after stillbirth and without stillbirth, for women of the same ultimate parity, yields the increase in the postpartum infecundity period due to *breast feeding*.[67]

5.5.1.4. Fetal Mortality. Fetal mortality data are scarce. In many countries, data on stillbirths are, however, collected by the vital registration system. In theory, the *probability of stillbirth* should be computed by dividing the number of stillbirths observed by the initial number of conceptions. The latter is usually unknown and one divides instead the number of stillbirths observed during a given period by the number of live[68] births recorded during that period; this ratio is called a *stillbirth "rate."* This "rate" varies with age and parity of the mother; it is also higher for multiple births.

Data on spontaneous abortions, on the other hand, are scarce or of dubious quality; they are obtained usually from medical statistics and relate to small sample sizes. One can compute *probabilities of intrauterine mortality* by dividing, if available, the number of fetal deaths observed by duration of pregnancy, by the number of women still pregnant at the beginning of each duration, correcting the probability for possible occurrence of live births.[69] An *intrauterine attrition table* can then be derived by the usual methods[70] (Section 1.2.5).

5.5.1.5. Sterility. In a noncontracepting population, contrary to a population practicing birth control, infertile couples are usually sterile. In this case, let a_0 represent the parity progression ratio for couples without children, i.e., the probability of passing from parity 0 to parity 1. The complement $1 - a_0$ will then represent the *proportion of sterile couples* at time of marriage, i.e., *primary sterility*.

One must also take into account women initially fecund, who bear children and eventually become sterile; in this case, one speaks instead of *secondary sterility*. The latter can be measured by the *average age at final sterility* approximated by the mean age at birth of *last* child.[71]

The increase in the *proportion of sterile women by age* can be analyzed starting from the fertility "rates" of *fecund* women (i.e., eventually fertile). Let g_x denote the overall fertility "rate" (for fecund and infecund women)

---

[67]From Vincent's data, one finds an increase of about 4 months due to breast-feeding; it can be even higher on the average with prolonged breast-feeding.

[68]Sometimes one uses all births instead, i.e., live births *and* stillbirths.

[69]Birth acts as a disturbance in the study of fetal mortality. Other disturbances are in- and out-migration from the groups observed.

[70]An example can be found in Henry (1972, pp. 186–189), and a thorough analysis of existing data in Léridon (1973, Chap. IV).

[71]Women should therefore be observed until the end of their reproductive period.

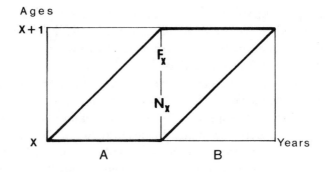

FIGURE 5.5

and f_x the fertility "rate" for fecund women only. One may write

$$g_x = N_x/F_x$$

where N_x and F_x represent the number of births and the number of women (fecund or not) at age x (see Fig. 5.5). The fertility "rate" for fecund women only[72] (obtained by retrospective data on women who eventually become fertile) is equal to $f_x = N_x/(F_x - S_x)$, where S_x stands for the number of sterile women at age x. Using the ratio of both "rates" gives $g_x/f_x = (F_x - S_x)/F_x$, i.e., the proportion of fecund women at age x. The proportion of sterile women at age x is therefore equal to $1 - g_x/f_x$. An example is given in Section 5.5.3.2.

It is important to note that these measures are slightly biased because women who eventually become fertile are used in place of fecund women; this bias is unavoidable, even if one has recourse to sophisticated clinical observations.

5.5.2. Measures of Contraceptive Effectiveness

5.5.2.1. Malthusian Fertility. "Malthusian" fertility, as opposed to "natural" fertility, relates to a population having recourse to voluntary[73] birth control practices. These behaviors can be detected by sample surveys, but there are also some indirect means (useful in retrospective analysis, for example, as in Section 5.5.3.3) enabling detection of Malthusian fertility.

---

[72]Henry (1961) has shown that this "rate" is approximately also equal to the reciprocal of the average of intervals (in years) between births of all orders, for marriages of sufficient duration, intervals that start and/or end during the age groups considered. Intervals starting *and* ending in this age group are counted twice.

[73]As opposed to, e.g., breast-feeding.

A first sign of gradual recourse to birth control can be derived from fertility *"rates"* specific for age and age at marriage. In a non-Malthusian population, legitimate fertility "rates" at a given age are only slightly affected, as already noted, by duration of marriage or its equivalent, by age at marriage.[74] When the population resorts to birth control, these "rates" become highly dependent upon age at marriage: at a given age, the higher the duration of marriage, the lower the fertility "rate" will be.

Another indication of Malthusianism can be drawn from the *pattern* of legitimate fertility schedules by age (see Fig. 5.6).[75] In the case of natural fertility (NF), the fertility schedule is convex; a malthusian fertility schedule (MF) tends, on the other hand, to become concave.

Another sign of birth-control practices is the gradual lowering of the *age at last birth* and the corresponding increase in the proportion of women having their last child before a given age, 35 years, for example.

One should note that none of these methods, used separately, gives a definite indication of gradual use of birth control. The convergence of various indicators, however, would be a clear sign of Malthusian fertility.

5.5.2.2. Use-Effectiveness of Contraception. Measurement of contraceptive effectiveness was first introduced, before the second world war, by R. Pearl. Pearl devised a widely used measure, now known as the *Pearl pregnancy rate*, obtained by dividing the number of conceptions during a given period, observed in a group of contracepting women, by the number of person-years of exposure to risk.[76] The Pearl index is therefore an exposure rate, as defined in Section 1.2.7, and is usually expressed as the number of contraceptive failures per 100 person-years[77] of exposure to risk of pregnancy (see example, Section 5.5.3.4).

Adequate measurement of contraceptive effectiveness should, however, consider the following periods:

(a) the interval between marriage and outset of contraception: the pregnancy rate in this case measures the incidence of natural fertility;

[74]The relation between legitimate fertility at a given age and age at marriage, in a non-Malthusian population, is partly due to the relation between sterility and age at marriage; see Henry and Houdaille (1973).
[75]Figure 5.6 is based on data relating to Geneva, for cohorts born in the 17th century (NF) and during the 19th century (MF); see Henry (1956, p. 77).
[76]Pearl has later used the ratio of numbers of pregnancies to *ovulations*.
[77]If the rate is expressed as a number of pregnancies per month of exposure to risk, the result is therefore multiplied by $12 \times 100 = 1200$.

Legitimate
fertility "rates"

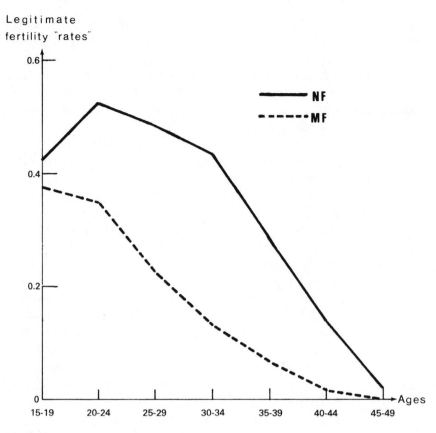

FIGURE 5.6

(b) the period of time during which contraceptive practices are used: a pregnancy rate in this case measures contraceptive failure; and

(c) the interval between interruption of contraception and possible conception: the conception rate, in this case, measures the result of pregnancy planning.[78]

Contraceptive effectiveness can now be obtained by comparing pregnancy rates computed for periods (b) and (c). Rate (c) measures the *natural fecundability of contracepting couples* (f_n) interrupting contraception in order to conceive; rate (b), on the other hand, measures *residual fecundabil-*

[78]Discontinuation of contraception may also be due to other reasons (e.g., separation from husband).

ity (f_r) for couples actually resorting to contraception. The use-effectiveness of contraception can therefore be measured by the ratio f_r/f_n, or better by the difference

$$1 - f_r/f_n$$

which has the practical advantage of increasing with higher contraceptive effectiveness (i.e., with lower residual fecundability). For example, a contraceptive effectiveness of 95% means that residual fecundability equals only 5% of natural fecundability of contracepting couples. Henry (1968, p. 271) has derived the following relation between contraceptive effectiveness $(1 - f_r/f_n)$ and the Pearl rate R_{12} computed over a period of 12 months for contracepting couples (see example, Section 5.5.3.4):

R_{12} (per 100 person-years)	1.5–2	3–4	6–8	12–21	Around 30
Contraceptive effectiveness (%)	99.5	99	98	95	90

An inadequate comparison would be between residual fecundability of contraceptors and fecundability of noncontraceptors, since natural fecundability is related to contraceptive practice: the more fecund women will tend to be rapidly fertile and will therefore usually resort sooner (or more effectively) than the less fecund to contraception. Noncontracepting couples will, on average, be less fecund than contraceptors, and the comparison will lead to a biased measure of contraceptive effectiveness.

Another important selection effect can be noted when one computes the monthly probabilities of conception by using the ratio of the number of conceptions observed during a given month to the number of women not yet having conceived at the beginning of the month. These probabilities will tend to decrease as the period of observation increases because women with high natural fecundity and/or low contraceptive effectiveness will conceive sooner than the others and will therefore rapidly be excluded from observation.[79] A Pearl contraceptive failure rate will therefore be highly dependent upon the length of the observation period, as pregnancy leaves behind an increasingly subfecond group (Tietze, 1959; Potter *et al.*, 1970). Therefore, Pearl pregnancy rates relating to different populations should be compared if computed for the *same length* of observation period. At present, the Pearl pregnancy rate computed on the basis of an observation length of *12 months* has become standard practice.

[79] A similar effect was already noted in Section 5.5.1.2.

Instead of using the Pearl pregnancy rate, a better single index of contraceptive effectiveness can be derived from the monthly probabilities of conception: *the cumulative failure "rate"* (Potter, 1966) (an example is given in Section 5.5.3.4). This measure is obtained by the attrition table technique (Section 1.2.5). Let $f_0, f_1, f_2, \ldots, f_n$ denote the monthly probabilities of conception for a group of contraceptors followed since marriage or birth of a child. Probabilities of nonconception will be equal to $(1 - f_i)$ for each month i; therefore, the proportion of couples not yet having conceived at the end of the nth month of observation is equal to $\prod_0^{n-1} (1 - f_i)$. The cumulative failure rate at the end of the n-month period is therefore $1 - \prod_0^{n-1} (1 - f_i)$. In spatial or temporal comparisons, the cumulative failure rate must also refer to the same observation length, as pregnancy rates tend to decrease with increasing observation length. However, the cumulative failure "rate" can exclude disturbances due to discontinuation of contraception, loss to follow-up, etc., if *corrected* probabilities of conception are used. The latter are obtained by the usual formula (Section 1.3.2.2) for nonrenewable events:

$$f_x = \frac{C_x}{F_x - D_x/2}$$

where C_x stands for the number of conceptions observed during month x; F_x denotes the number of women not yet pregnant, at the beginning of month x; and D_x represents the number of disturbances observed during month x.

For example, using corrected probabilities of conception, one can compute a cumulative failure rate for contraceptive method X, excluding discontinuation of method X, change to method Y, loss to follow-up, etc. The method is therefore a straightforward application of attrition table techniques. The major problem, however, resides in collecting the adequate data from surveys or clinical studies.[80]

The cumulative failure rate yields a measure of the *intensity* of contraceptive failure, i.e., the percentage of women becoming pregnant during the observation period. This intensity can be achieved through different tempos of risks of childbearing, i.e., different time schedules of probabilities of conception. One should therefore supplement the cumulative failure rate computed over a period of n months with a measure of the *tempo* of contraceptive failure, such as the average number of ovulations before conception or the average time required to conceive. Writing $k_i = 1 - f_i$,

---

[80]For practical applications, see, for example, Potter (1966), Tietze (1967), Balakrishnan *et al.* (1970), and Chandrasekaran and Karkal (1972).

TABLE 5.10[a]

Month of birth since marriage	Number of first births	Number of fecund women
9	138	544
10	86	406
11	58	320
12	42	262
13	32	220
14	25	188
15	20	163
16	17	143

[a]Source: Henripin, J. *La Population Canadienne au Début du XVIIIè Siècle*. Paris: I.N.E.D., P.U.F., 1954, p.80.

where f_i stands as above for the monthly probability of conception, the *average number of ovulations before conception* can be written as[81]

$$\frac{f_0 + 2f_1 k_0 + 3f_2 k_0 k_1 + \cdots + n f_{n-1} \prod_0^{n-2} k_i}{f_0 + f_1 k_0 + \cdots + f_{n-1} \prod_0^{n-2} k_i}$$

This measure plus the cumulative failure rate are two useful summary indexes of the sequence of monthly probabilities of conception (see example, Section 5.5.3.4).

If all women conceive, over a sufficiently long observation period, the average number of ovulations before pregnancy can be written as (Henry, 1972, p. 275)[82]

$$1 + k_0 + k_0 k_1 + \cdots + \prod_0^n k_i + \cdots$$

5.5.3. Examples

5.5.3.1. Monthly "Effective" Fecundabilities. Table 5.10 gives the distribution of 418 first births by duration of marriage in a noncontracepting population.

---

[81]If f_i is constant over time, the formula is similar to that derived in Section 5.5.1.2.

[82]This is easily derived from the above formula by writing $f_0 = 1 - k_0$, $f_1 = 1 - k_1$, etc., with the sum of the weights being equal to 1.

TABLE 5.11

Month of conception	"Effective" fecundability	Month of conception	"Effective" fecundability
0	0.254	4	0.145
1	0.212	5	0.133
2	0.181	6	0.123
3	0.160	7	0.119

TABLE 5.12[a]

Age of women (completed years)	Fertility "rate" for all women	Fertility "rate" for fecund women
Less than 20	0.493	0.512
20–24	0.509	0.522
25–29	0.496	0.522
30–34	0.484	0.512
35–39	0.410	0.495
40–44	0.231	0.328

[a] Source: Henripin, J. *La Population Canadienne au Début du XVIIIè Siècle*. Paris: I.N.E.D., P.U.F., 1954, pp. 60 and 62.

Using first births instead of pregnancies gives the "effective" fecundabilities by month since marriage, obtained by dividing first births by the number of women still fecund at the beginning of each month (Table 5.11). One notices the decrease in monthly probabilities of conception due to the selection effect described in Section 5.5.1.2.

5.5.3.2. Proportion of Sterile Couples. Fertility "rates" for the 18th-century Canadian population are given in Table 5.12, by age of women, for all married women and for fecund (i.e., eventually fertile) women only.

As seen in Section 5.5.1.5, an estimate of the proportion of sterile women by age groups can be derived from these data by using the complement to one of the ratios of the overall fertility rate to that of fecund women only (Table 5.13).

5.5.3.3. Malthusian and Non-Malthusian Fertility. The following data on the French town of Meulan[83] between 1660 and 1860 offer a good example of a population evolving from a noncontracepting state to a

[83] Source: Henry, L. Evolution de la fécondité légitime à Meulan de 1660 à 1860. *Population*, 1970, *25*(4), 875–885.

TABLE 5.13

Age of women (in completed years)	Proportion of fertile women	Proportion of sterile women
Less than 20	0.963	0.037
20–24	0.975	0.025
25–29	0.950	0.050
30–34	0.945	0.055
35–39	0.828	0.172
40–44	0.704	0.296

TABLE 5.14

Calendar year of marriage	Proportion of women	Age at last birth (year)
1660–1739	0.08	40.7
1740–1789	0.24	38.4
1790–1839	0.53	34.3

contracepting one. Table 5.14 gives the proportion of married women having their last child before age 35, for various marriage-cohorts, and their age at last birth (see Section 5.5.2.1).

Another indication of gradual resort to birth control is given by the differential pattern of age-specific legitimate fertility "rates" between cohorts 1660–1709 and cohorts 1815–1839, for women marrying at ages 20–24 (Fig. 5.7).

A final indication as to the extent of contraception can be obtained upon analysis of fertility "rates" by duration of marriage (or age at marriage) and age (Table 5.15).

The "rates" in Table 5.15 are actually influenced by small population numbers, but it is nevertheless obvious that, for a given age, the "rates" for marriage-cohorts 1815–1839 were much more influenced by duration of marriage than those for marriage-cohorts 1660–1709. Higher fertility "rates" for the latter are also quite apparent.

5.5.3.4. Measures of Contraceptive Effectiveness. As an example of computation of the Pearl pregnancy rate, consider the data (by month) in Table 5.16 on the number of women wearing an IUD [intrauterine (contraceptive) device] after first insertion, and on "relevant closures" defined as including accidental pregnancies, expulsions, and removals for medical and

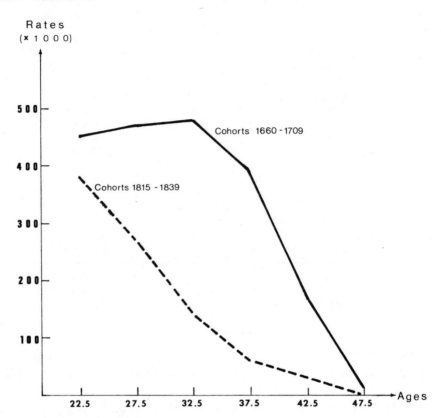

FIGURE 5.7   Age-specific legitimate fertility rates for Meulan.

TABLE 5.15. "Rates" by Age Groups

Age at marriage (years)	Age Groups					
	20–24	25–29	30–34	35–39	40–44	45–49
	Marriage cohorts 1660–1709					
20–24	0.453	0.471	0.481	0.388	0.171	0.015
25–29		0.473	0.484	0.431	0.165	0.015
30–34			0.530	0.350	0.143	0.000
	Marriage cohorts 1815–1839					
20–24	0.379	0.273	0.136	0.059	0.029	0.000
25–29		0.388	0.272	0.148	0.056	0.014
30–34			0.456	0.277	0.145	0.000

TABLE 5.16

Month	Wearers at beginning of month	Woman-months of exposure to risk	Relevant closures
0	250	232.0	12
1	214	206.5	4
2	199	187.5	6
3	176	165.0	5
4	154	146.5	1
5	139	133.0	1
6	127	117.5	2
7	108	103.0	3
8	98	88.0	3
9	78	71.5	1
10	65	57.5	0
11	50	43.0	1
12	36		
Total		1551.0	39

personal reasons.[84] The term "closure" is used here as defining an event (e.g., accidental pregnancy, expulsion of IUD, etc.) not followed by a reinsertion of an IUD.

Attrition of IUD wearers is due not only to "relevant closures" but also to loss of "follow-up," i.e., women for whom no information has been obtained following first IUD insertion. The latter event acts therefore as a disturbance on the study of "relevant closures."

With data on wearers of IUDs at the beginning of each month since first insertion, woman-months of exposure to risk can be computed as the arithmetic average of the number of wearers at the beginning of two consecutive months.

The *Pearl rate* R_{12} covering the twelve-month period is obtained by the relation (Section 5.5.2.2) $(39/1551) 1200 = 30.17$ relevant closures per 100 woman-years of exposure to risk, i.e., a *contraceptive effectiveness*[85] of around 90% following the relation given in Section 5.5.2.2.

The *cumulative failure "rate"* (as defined in Section 5.5.2.2) can also be computed from the above data. In order to exclude disturbances due to loss

[84]Source: Adapted from Tietze, C. Intra-uterine contraception: Recommended procedures for data analysis. *Studies in Family Planning*, No. 18 (Supplement), April, 1967.

[85]Note that this rate includes, in this example, IUD expulsions and removals, in addition to accidental pregnancies. For the latter alone, the Pearl rate is only 5.41.

TABLE 5.17

Month x	Probability of relevant closure c_x	Probability of nonclosure $1 - c_x$
0	0.05042	0.94958
1	0.01918	0.98082
2	0.03150	0.96850
3	0.02985	0.97015
4	0.00680	0.99320
5	0.00749	0.99251
6	0.01688	0.98312
7	0.02871	0.97129
8	0.03352	0.96648
9	0.01389	0.98611
10	0.00000	1.00000
11	0.02299	0.97701

of follow-ups, "relevant closure" exposure rates can be transformed into probabilities, as seen in Section 1.3.3. For example, for the first month one obtains rate r_x, $12/232 = 0.051724$, and probability c_x, $[2(0.051724)]/(2 + 0.051724) = 0.05042$, using the transformation formula

$$c_x = \frac{2r_x}{(2 + r_x)}$$

The latter probability can be derived immediately, as seen in Section 1.2.8, by the relation

$$c_x = \frac{C_x}{(W_x + 0.5C_x)}$$

where C_x denotes the number of "relevant closures" during completed month x, and W_x represents woman-months of exposure during completed month x. In this example, one obtains

$$c_x = \frac{12}{232 + 0.5(12)} = 0.05042$$

For the twelve-month period, one obtains Table 5.17. The cumulative failure rate, over the twelve-month period, is equal to

$$1 - \prod_{0}^{11} (1 - c_x) = 1 - 0.76701 = 23.3\%$$

The corresponding average number of ovulations[86] before conception, for this twelve-month period, is equal to 5.25, i.e., an average "waiting time" to conceive of about 4.75 months for women who have conceived during the year.

5.6. REFERENCES AND SUPPLEMENTARY BIBLIOGRAPHY

Balakrishnan, T. R., Allingham, J. D., & Kantner, J. F. Analysis of oral contraceptive use through multiple decrement life table techniques. *Demography*, 1970, *7*(4), 459–465.

Barrett, J. C., & Marshall, J. The risk of conception on different days of the menstrual cycle. *Population Studies*, 1969, *XIII*(3), 455–461.

Bongaarts, J. A method for the estimation of fecundability. *Demography*, 1975, *12*(4), 645–660.

Bourgeois-Pichat, J. Les facteurs de la fécondité non dirigée. *Population*, 1965, *20*(3), 383–424.

Chandrasekaran, C., & Karkal, M. "Continuation rate," "Use-Effectiveness," and their assessment for the diaphragm and jelly method. *Population Studies*, 1972, *26*(3), 487–494.

Charbonneau, H. *Tourouvre-au-Perche aux XVIIe et XVIIIe Siècles.* Paris: Presses Universitaires de France, Cahier No. 55, I.N.E.D., 1970.

Coale, A. J. *Factors Associated with the Development of Low Fertility: An Historic Summary,* Vol. II. Belgrade: World Population Conference, United Nations, 1965, pp. 205–209.

Gini, C. Premières recherches sur la fécondabilité de la femme. In *Proceedings of the International Mathematical Congress, Toronto 1924*, Vol. II. University of Toronto Press, 1928, pp. 889–892.

Gini, C. Sur une méthode pour déterminer le nombre moyen d'enfants légitimes par mariage. *Revue de l'Institut International de Statistique*, 1933, *1*(I), 56–60.

Hajnal, J. The study of fertility and reproduction—a survey of thirty years. In *Thirty Years of Research in Human Fertility: Retrospect and Prospect.* New York: Millbank Memorial Fund, 1959, pp. 11–37.

Henripin, J. *La Population Canadienne au Début du XVIIIe Siècle.* Paris: Presses Universitaires de France, Cahier No. 22, I.N.E.D., 1954.

Henry, L. *Fécondité des Mariages. Nouvelle Méthode de Mesure.* Paris: Presses Universitaires de France, Cahier No. 16, I.N.E.D., 1953.

Henry, L. La fécondité des ménages suivant le nombre d'enfants déjà nés: Application à l'Australie. In *Bulletin Démographique*, ST/SOA/Ser. N/4. New York: Nations Unies, 1954, pp. 9–21.

Henry, L. *Anciennes Familles Genevoises.* Paris: Presses Universitaires de France, Cahier No. 26, I.N.E.D., 1956.

Henry, L. Fécondité et Famille. Modèles mathématiques. *Population*, 1961, *16*(1), 27–48.

Henry, L. Mortalité intra-utérine et fécondabilité. *Population*, 1964a, *19*(5), 899–940.

Henry, L. Mesure du temps mort en fécondité naturelle. *Population*, 1964b, *19*(3), 485–514.

Henry, L. Réflexions sur les taux de reproduction. *Population*, 1965a, *20*(1), 53–69.

Henry, L. French statistical research in natural fertility. In M. C. Sheps and J. C. Ridley (Eds.) *Public Health and Population Change. Current Research Issues.* University of Pittsburgh Press, 1965b, pp. 333–350.

---

[86]If the contraceptive method suppresses ovulation, the average time it takes to conceive should be used instead.

Henry, L. Essai de calcul de l'efficacité de la contraception. *Population*, 1968, *23*(2), 265–278.

Henry, L. *Démographie. Analyse et Modèles*. Paris: Larousse, 1972.

Henry, L., & Houdaille, J. Fécondité des mariages dans le quart nord-ouest de la France de 1670 à 1829. *Population*, 1973, *28*(4–5), 873–924.

Holmberg, I. *Fecundity, Fertility and Family Planning*. Demographic Institute, University of Gothenburg, 1970.

James, W. H. The incidence of spontaneous abortion. *Population Studies*, 1970, *XXIV*(2), 241–245.

Keyfitz, N. *Introduction to the Mathematics of Population*. Reading: Addison-Wesley Publishing Co., 1968.

Léridon, H. *Aspects Biométriques de la Fécondité Humaine*. Paris: Presses Universitaires de France, Cahier No. 65, I.N.E.D., 1973.

National Center for Health Statistics. *Fertility Measurement—a Report of the United States National Committee on Vital and Health Statistics*. Washington D.C., Series 4, No. 1, 1965.

Pearl, R. Contraception and fertility in 2,000 women. *Human Biology*, 1932, *IV*, 363–407.

Potter, R. G. Application of life table techniques to measurement of contraceptive effectiveness. *Demography*, 1966, *3*(2), 297–304.

Potter, R. G., McCann, B., & Sakoda, J. M. Selective fecundability and contraceptive effectiveness. *Milbank Memorial Fund Quarterly*, 1970, *XLVIII*(1), 91–102.

Pressat, R. *Pratique de la Démographie*. Paris: Dunod, 1967.

Pressat, R. Interprétation des variations à court terme du taux de natalité. *Population*, 1969, *24*(1), 47–56.

Ryder, N. B. La mesure des variations de la fécondité au cours du temps. *Population*, 1956, *11*(1), 29–46.

Ryder, N. B. The measurement of fertility patterns. In M. C. Sheps, and J. C. Ridley (Eds.), *Public Health and Population Change. Current Research Issues*. University of Pittsburgh Press, 1965, pp. 287–306.

Ryder, N. B. The emergence of a modern fertility pattern: United States 1917–66. In S. J. Behrmann, *et al.* (Eds.), *Fertility and Family Planning*. University of Michigan Press, 1969, pp. 99–123.

Ryder, N. B. Notes on fertility measurement. In *Forty years of research in human fertility. Retrospect and Prospect. Milbank Memorial Fund Quarterly*, 1971, *XLIX*(4), Part 2, 109–127.

Seklani, M. Efficacité de la contraception: Méthodes et résultats. *Population*, 1963, *18*(2), 329–348.

Tietze, C. Differential fecundity and effectiveness of contraception. *The Eugenics Review*, 1959, *50*, 231–237.

Tietze, C. Intra-uterine contraception: recommended procedures for data analysis. *Studies in Family Planning*, 1967, *18*(Suppl.), 1–6.

Tietze, C., & Lewit, S. Statistical evaluation of contraceptive methods: Use-effectiveness and extended use-effectiveness. *Demography*, 1968, *5*(2), 931–940.

Tietze, C. Prevalence and effectiveness of family planning. In *Forty years of research in human fertility. Retrospect and Prospect. Milbank Memorial Fund Quarterly*, 1971, *XLIX*(4), Part 2, 132–142.

Vincent, P. La stérilité physiologique des populations. *Population*, 1950, *5*(1), 45–64.

Vincent, P. *Recherches sur la Fécondité Biologique*. Paris: Presses Universitaires de France, I.N.E.D., Cahier No. 37, 1961.

Whelpton, P. K. Cohort analysis of fertility. *American Sociological Review*, 1959, *XIV*(6), 735–749.

Wunsch, G. *Les mesures de la natalité*. Louvain: Département de Démographie, Université Catholique de Louvain, 1967.

THE ANALYSIS OF MIGRATION

6

6.1. TIME AND SPACE IN MIGRATION ANALYSIS

6.1.1. Introduction

In all the demographic processes covered up to now, space has never been considered *per se*. Population change through natural increase has been viewed independently from the area in which the population lives.[1] In the study of migration, this approach is obviously no longer valid, since migration implies moving from one area to another. Migration analysis is therefore fundamentally different from that of natality or mortality, as one takes both time and space into account.

One should not, however, push this difference too far. First, migration depends upon the definition of the area itself: a move from New York to New Jersey will be considered as a migration if states are the areas under study; if nations are the areal units being considered, this move will be disregarded. A major problem of migration analysis consists therefore in defining what one considers to be a migration. Second, various measures of migration do not take space directly into account. Having defined migration as a change in the place of residence, for example, one can consider the number of changes of residence a person has made before a specified age; this approach is identical to determining a woman's parity at a given age, and can be studied through retrospective questions based on similar assumptions. Similarly, migration by rank can be studied by procedures analogous to those used in fertility analysis.

A second major difference between migration and the other components of population change exists in the field of data collection. For administrative purposes mainly, most developed countries have set up a permanent system of recording births and deaths, as well as marriages and

---

[1] If one, however, takes into consideration changes of areal borders over time.

marriage dissolutions. These events are recorded in registers, such as the registers of births and deaths. In the case of migration, specific registers usually do not exist, though changes of residence are recorded in some countries having population registers. One of the major tasks confronting the demographer in the study of migration is therefore evaluating the number of moves itself.[2] Various alternatives to permanent registration procedures have therefore been developed, as well as indirect methods of evaluating the number of moves in the absence of such sources.

The following sections deal with the various aspects of migration which have been briefly touched upon here: the definition of migration (Section 6.1.2), direct and indirect estimation of migration (Sections 6.2–6.4), the study of migration without specifically taking space into account (Sections 6.5 and 6.7), and finally some spatial aspects of migration analysis (Section 6.6).

6.1.2. Definitions

Spatial mobility is defined as the ability to move in space. This phenomenon is revealed either by *migration*, which involves a change in the place of residence,[3] or by *commuting* between a given place of residence and some other point in space. Since commuting does not directly affect the level and the structure of the population of a given territory,[4] it is not, strictly speaking, a demographic phenomenon and will not be considered further in this chapter.[5]

Shifting from this conceptual definition of migration to an operational one usually implies a division of space in administrative units. Migration is then operationally defined as a change of residence from one administrative

---

[2]This is also one of the major problems in studying natural increase in less developed countries having no permanent registration of vital events.

[3]Migration is sometimes distinguished from moving, both involving a change in residence but the former over a "greater" distance. Because of the arbitrariness of this spatial criterion, this distinction has not been retained here: any change in the place of residence is considered as a migration, which does not exclude that some migrations (over a small distance) will not be recorded (for instance, because of the high cost of recording).

[4]Commuting involves the daytime population (for instance, the population at its place of work) whereas the nighttime population (i.e., the population at its place of residence) is the one commonly recorded as the *de jure* population and the one to which demographic analysis refers. As long as there is no migration (no change in the place of residence), the level and the structure of the nighttime population do not change, by definition.

[5]For a study on the role of commuting in demographic analysis, see, for instance, Termote (1975).

spatial unit to another, made during some given migration interval (i.e., between two points in time). This leads to the definition of a *migration stream* or *migration flow*, which represents the total number of migrations that have a common area of origin and a common area of destination. When the area of origin and the area of destination are located within the same country, the change of residence between them is called an *internal migration*. This implies that an *out-migrant* has left an area of origin (not necessarily his birthplace, since migration is a renewable phenomenon) and has become an *in-migrant* in another area within the same country.

When the area of origin and the area of destination are not located within the same country, the change of residence between them is called an *international migration*, which implies that an *emigrant* has left his country of origin and has become an *immigrant* by entering another country.

When we refer to all migrants leaving or entering an area (whether the area of destination or origin is specified or not), the term *gross migration* will be used. The term *net migration* refers to the balance of migrants in one area, i.e., the difference between the number of migrants entering the area and the number of migrants leaving the area. By definition, the sum of the net internal migration over all areas within the same country, and the sum of net international migration over all countries, are equal to zero.

6.2. SPATIAL DEMOGRAPHIC ACCOUNTING

Let us consider two areas only in space (regions i and j) and two points in time (t and $t+n$). As long as no population exchange between i and j is allowed for, there are only three "states": birth (B), survival (S), and death (D), these two last states being mutually exclusive at the same moment in time. Combining these three states two by two gives only four possible pairs (transitions): $B \to S$, $B \to D$, $S \to S$, and $S \to D$, the five other pairs not being acceptable in our present world: no multiple births ($B \to B$), no rebirth ($S \to B$), no reincarnation ($D \to B$), no resurrection ($D \to S$), and no multiple deaths ($D \to D$).

Once we introduce migration, however, the number of relevant combinations (two by two and three by three) increases remarkably: there are now 12 of them.

Let us indeed take the cohort of residents in region i at time $t+n$; four different combinations are possible if we consider only those who were alive at the beginning of the period:

1. born in i before t, surviving in i at t, and still surviving[6] in i at $t+n (S_{ii}^i)$;
2. born in j before t, surviving in i at t, and still surviving in i at $t+n (S_{ii}^j)$;
3. born in j before t, surviving in j at t and surviving in i at $t+n (S_{ji}^j)$;
4. born in i before t, surviving in j at t and surviving in i at $t+n (S_{ji}^i)$.

Categories 3 and 4 imply a migration from j to i during the migration interval $(t, t+n)$, the *total number of surviving in-migrants* in i who were *alive at t* being equal to $S_{ji}^j + S_{ji}^i$.

During the migration interval, there were, however, deaths in region i; this again gives rise to four possible combinations:

5. born in i before t, surviving in i at t and dead in i between t and $t+n$ (D_{ii}^i);
6. born in j before t, surviving in i at t and dead in i between t and $t+n$ (D_{ii}^j);
7. born in j before t, surviving in j at t and dead in i between t and $t+n$ (D_{ji}^j);
8. born in i before t, surviving in j at t and dead in i between t and $t+n$ (D_{ji}^i).

Categories 7 and 8 imply a migration from j to i during the migration interval $(t, t+n)$, the number of in-migrants in i who were alive at t but did not survive in i at $t+n$ being equal to $D_{ji}^j + D_{ji}^i$.

The same 8 combinations are valid for the population of residents in the other region (j) at $t+n$, which gives a total of 16 combinations, when only two regions and two points in time are considered.

The total number of in-migrants in i alive at t is thus equal to the sum of categories 3, 4, 7, and 8, and in a two-region system, the sum of the corresponding categories for region j represents the total number of out-migrants from i who were alive at t.

In order to obtain the total number of in-migrants in i, we have, however, to take into account births during the migration interval, more precisely the following:

9. those born in i between t and $t+n$ and surviving in i at $t+n$ (B_i^i);

[6]In our notation, the superscript refers to the place of birth, the subscripts indicate the successive places of residence; if there is only one subscript, it implies that birth took place during the migration interval.

10. those born in j between t and $t+n$ and surviving in i at $t+n$ (B_i^j);
11. those born in i between t and $t+n$ and dead in i at $t+n$ or before (D_i^i);
12. those born in j between t and $t+n$ and dead in i at $t+n$ or before (D_i^j).

The total number of in-migrants in i *from* j (M_{ji}) during the migration interval $(t, t+n)$ is thus given by the sum

$$M_{ji} = S_{ji}^j + S_{ji}^i + D_{ji}^j + D_{ji}^i + B_i^j + D_i^j \qquad (6.1)$$

if we add the restriction that nobody can in-migrate into i and out-migrate from i later, during the same migration interval. The last expression, however, does not represent the *total number of migrations in* i from j, unless we introduce the additional restriction that nobody can successively in-migrate into region i, out-migrate from i and migrate again into i during the same migration interval $(t, t+n)$.

It thus appears, from this simple accounting exercise, that by introducing migration, the complexity of the demographic problem has exponentially increased: by considering only one migration interval and two regions, we obtain 24 relevant categories of demographic events (12 for each region), and even when we disregard the two restrictions on multiple migrations during the same migration interval, we are still left with the necessity to know six migration components if we wish to correctly estimate each migration flow. This illustrates the difficulty of the problem of migration statistics and explains why such an important part of migration analysis has been devoted only to the task of "getting the data." [7] In most cases indeed, there is no *direct* information on those migration components, and the main task of migration analysis has been to develop *indirect* ways of estimating the migration phenomenon. We will now discuss those direct and indirect ways of estimating migration, by referring to our accounting presentation in order to show what migration components are actually estimated.

6.3. DIRECT ESTIMATION OF MIGRATION

There are two main methods of obtaining direct information on migration (see example, Section 6.8.1): (1) either by an act of the public

---

[7] A very useful presentation of regional demographic accounting is to be found in Rees and Wilson (1973, 1974). These authors consider, however, only 8 categories of demographic events for each region: our categories 1 and 2 are grouped into one category, as well as our categories 3 and 4, 5 and 6, and 7 and 8.

authorities who more or less periodically try to reach all those residing in their territory, in order to ask them (among other questions) a set of questions concerning their spatial mobility (this is the *census*); or (2) by imposing upon each resident of the territory to declare, upon their own initiative, each change of residence: this usually implies the existence of a *population register*, wherein these declarations are recorded.

Despite the fact that only in a dozen countries is one able to obtain migration data from a population register, it seems worthwhile to present a brief critical analysis of migration data based on this method, not only because of its future potentialities, but also because it will help to interpret the meaning of migration data based on the census.

6.3.1. The Population Register

In those countries where a population register does exist, this register is usually kept in the smallest administrative unit, the municipality. Before each change of residence (even within this municipality), every individual residing in the municipality has to declare, besides a set of other informations, for instance, on his personal characteristics (age, profession, status, number, and age of children, etc.), the date of his departure and the place of destination; this statement is then recorded in the population register of the municipality. When the new residence is located in another municipality, the migrant will usually have to declare to the administration of his municipality of in-migration where he comes from and the date he arrived; this statement on the municipality of out-migration and on the date of migration will then be recorded (with some information on the personal characteristics of the migrant) in the population register of the municipality of in-migration.

All those individual declarations are then either classified and totalized in the municipalities themselves, with the central institute for statistics playing only a role of collecting the data prepared by the municipalities; or they are centralized, classified, and summed by the central institute itself. The latter system seems preferable, because it allows for a check of the out-migration statements against the corresponding in-migration statements, and for a deeper, a more disaggregated, and a more global analysis of the data. Migration data obtained from a population register present the following characteristics:

1. The population register records the act of migration, and therefore the migration figures obtained from such a register usually refer to the *number of migrations* and not to the number of migrants. Of course, the

difference between both figures will be small when the migration interval
$(t, t+n)$ is short and the spatial units large: for instance, if n equals one year,
not many individuals will migrate twice over a one-year period. This means
that except, of course, for errors and omissions in declaration and recording,
the population register will provide a figure equal to or (slightly) larger than
the total number of in- (out-) migrants in (from) each area i, as given in
expression (6.1) (Section 6.2): all migrations, whether they are made by
surviving migrants $(S_{ji}^{j}+S_{ji}^{i})$ or by dead migrants $(D_{ji}^{j}+D_{ji}^{i})$, or by migrants
born during the migration interval who are still alive (B_i^{j}) or who are dead
(D_i^{j}), will be accounted for.

2. *International* emigration and immigration as well as *internal* migration are recorded [when, in expression (6.1), (Section 6.2), i represents a
region of the country and j the rest of the world, excluding the country, then
M_{ji} represents the flow of international immigration in area i]. But in the
case of internal migration, as opposed to international migration, because
the places of origin and destination are, by definition, submitted to the same
jurisdiction, it is possible to check each statement of out-migration against
its corresponding statement of in-migration, while in the case of international migration, this check is almost impossible. In the case of internal
migration, the number and the content of the statements at the area of origin
are theoretically identical to those at the area of destination; however, in
practice, it appears preferable to use only the declarations at the place of
in-migration, because as experience shows[8] it is likely that a nonnegligible
percentage of migrants neglects to declare their departure, while it is much
more difficult to hide their arrival. Of course, choosing to use the statements
at the place of destination, instead of the statements at the place of origin,
makes sense only for internal migration; for international migration, only
immigration data could be obtained this way, while data on emigration could
obviously only be obtained by using the information recorded in the
population register at the place of departure.

3. Usually, *all individuals* residing in the country are obliged to declare
their change of residence, regardless of their nationality. In some countries,

---

[8]Belgium is one of the rare countries where a yearly comparison between the number of
declarations at the place of in-migration and the number of declarations at the place of
out-migration is possible. For each year since 1948, the latter is inferior to the former, an
annual average of 0.7 of one percent of the migrations between municipalities being recorded
in the municipality of in-migration but not in the municipality of out-migration. While on an
annual basis the difference is small, over a longer period the error may become quite
important, since it is cumulative over time.

however, migration of aliens are not recorded in the population register, but in a special register.

4. Migration is a phenomenon over space, necessarily involving two areas. One has thus to be particularly careful for temporal variations in the *administrative limits* of either one of these areas. This is, of course, particularly important for migration streams between small spatial units, the limits of which are much more frequently modified. This condition holds of course for all migration data, regardless of its source. But in the case of migration data obtained from the census, the areal homogeneity is even much more difficult to preserve, because the migration interval is usually much longer.

6.3.2. The Census

The census is for most countries the only way to obtain, either directly or indirectly, some information on migration. Direct information is obtained by including some specific questions on migration. The most commonly used approach is to introduce a question on the place of residence at a fixed prior date; another approach is to inquire about the place of last residence, and possibly to add a second question on the duration of residence at the present place (i.e., the residence where one is recorded at census time).

The main characteristics of migration data obtained from these direct questions are the following:

1. Migration data obtained from the census refer to the number of migrants and not to the number of migrations, contrary to the case of migration data obtained from the population register. For a given migration interval, the migration figures obtained from the census will thus necessarily be smaller than those derived from the register, the difference being the larger the longer the migration interval. As explained above, the source of this difference resides in the fact that multiple migrations made by the same individual are not accounted for: each individual is given a maximum of only one migration during the migration interval.

2. Not all migrants are recorded: only those migrants who *survive* at the moment the census is taken, and who did not emigrate to another country, will be accounted for. It is clear that international emigration cannot be directly estimated from the census: only data on international immigration can be obtained. By asking the place of residence at a fixed prior date, one excludes, moreover, two other categories of migrants: first, the return migrants, i.e., those who moved out of an area during the time interval (between the fixed prior date and the date of the census) and returned to it before the end of the interval; and second, the migrants who

were born during the time interval. Compared to the accounting formula [Eq. (6.1), Section 6.2] this means that, when the census question refers to the previous residence (with or without a second question on duration of residence in present residence), we obtain

$$\hat{M}_{ji} = S_{ji}^j + S_{ji}^i + B_i^j$$

disregarding the migration components D_i^j, D_{ji}^j, and D_{ji}^i. When the migration question refers to the residence at a fixed prior date, one disregards B_i^j, i.e., those migrants born between the fixed prior date and the census date.

3. One important drawback of the census, when the migration question refers only to the last previous residence, is that there is no definite *time reference*: centenarians who migrated only once in their life, just after birth, will be mixed with people who made multiple moves and whose last migration was made only a few days before the census date. The best, but also the most costly solution, is undoubtedly to ask simultaneously for the place of last previous residence and for the duration of residence in the present residence.

4. Migration is a *renewable* phenomenon; this implies that the intensity of the phenomenon for members of a cohort be considered, i.e., the number of migrations per head. The census, being concerned with the migrant more than with the act of migration, is particularly apt to produce the retrospective view necessary to estimate this frequency. The obvious way would be to ask for the list of all previous residences, with the duration of residence in each residence, but this would be a rather costly and burdensome information, and would probably be affected by recall lapses. The simplest way to obtain a (very partial) estimate of the frequency of migration is to use data on place of birth, cross-classified by place of last previous residence and duration of residence at the present residence: this could give an idea of the frequency of migration for a given cohort and of the migration path of this cohort. Since observations are now available for three moments in time, the following meaningful categories of migrants can be analyzed (Eldridge, 1965): (a) *primary migrants*, i.e., those whose previous residence was identical to their place of birth, but different from their residence at the date of the census; (b) *secondary migrants*, i.e., those whose place of residence at the census date is different from their previous residence which itself was not their place of birth; and (c) *return migrants*, i.e., those whose place of residence at the census date is different from their previous residence but identical to their place of birth.

Referring again to the accounting formula [Eq. (6.1), Section 6.2] the migration components S_{ji}^{j} and B_{i}^{j} are recorded by the census and classified as primary migrants (if the last previous residence was taken at a fixed prior date, then primary migrants B_{i}^{j} would not be accounted for); component S_{ji}^{i} would be classified as return migrants. Finally, in order to account for secondary migrants, we should, by definition, consider a third region (the accounting system presented above was a two-region system), thus introducing component S_{ji}^{k}.

By combining, whenever possible, migration data based on the population register with migration data derived from the census, it is possible to obtain another measure of the frequency of migration. For instance, by comparing the number of persons who declare at the census that they arrived in a given area in year t, with an estimate of the survivors among the cohort of persons who were recorded in the register as in-migrants (or immigrants) during that same year, one obtains an indication of the degree of retention of migrants in that area.

5. The census provides, more easily than the register, data on the *personal characteristics* of the migrants. It should, however, be emphasized that these personal attributes are those of the migrant at the moment the census is taken, and not at the moment of the migration. Of course, for attributes that evolve in a constant way (age), this problem could be solved by using data on year of birth and by asking a question on the duration of residence. But for most characteristics (income level, profession, marital status, number of children, educational level, etc.), it is not possible to know to what extent the personal attributes recorded at the census are a cause or a consequence of migration.

6.3.3. Other Sources

In many cases, neither the census nor the population register are useful as a source of migration data, and therefore secondary sources have been used. We will only mention a few of them: the election register, school records, social security data, and sample surveys; the latter seem to have a large potential development in migration analysis, but offer the same limits as the census.

6.4. INDIRECT ESTIMATION OF MIGRATION

Demographic analysis is closely related to the availability of data. Data on migration are, however, seldom provided directly from a population register or a census: most countries have no population register, and even when there is one, it is rarely used as a means for collecting migration data; and not many countries include a specific question on migration in their census questionnaire. It is thus not surprising that the main effort of demographers in the field of migration has been devoted to the development of indirect ways of estimating the migration phenomenon.

As far as migration flows are concerned, one solution is to compare census data on *place of birth* with census data on the present residence. Estimates of net migration, however, are sometimes sufficient. They may be obtained residually by comparing the total increase of population with the natural increase; when this natural increase has been directly observed, the method is called the *vital statistics method*, while when natural growth is estimated, one may use *survival ratio* ("rate") *methods* in order to estimate an expected population, i.e., the population that would be present in the area in the absence of migration.

6.4.1. The Place of Birth Method

Almost every recent census includes a question on the place of birth, and the degree of accuracy in answer to this question is usually high, at least when areas are large enough to make identical the area where birth took place and the area where the residence of the parents at the moment of birth was located. By comparing place of birth and place of residence at the census, one obtains the following information:

1. The number of persons born in a given area i and who are enumerated in the same area at the census: these persons are called *lifetime nonmigrants*;

2. the number of persons who reside in area i but who were born in area j: these persons are called *lifetime in-migrants from j to i*;

3. the number of persons who were born in area i but who reside in area j at the census; these persons are called *lifetime out-migrants from i to j*;

4. *the migration balance between areas i and j* is obtained by subtracting the number of persons born in area i but residing in area j, from the number of persons residing in i but born in j; this is commonly referred to as "net lifetime migration";

5. the *total number of lifetime out-migrants* from i is obtained by summing all those born in area i who reside outside i (in any area j);

6. the *total number of lifetime in-migrants* in i is obtained by summing all those residing in area i who were born outside the area (i.e., born in any area j);

7. the total migration balance of area i is obtained by subtracting (5) from (6); the standard, but erroneous, terminology for this migration balance is the *"birth-residence index."*[9]

8. When data on place of birth are available for the same set of areas at two censuses, an estimation of *intercensal net migration* for each area is obtained by taking the difference between the two birth residence indexes.

The main characteristics and problems of migration data obtained by this method are the following (see example, Section 6.8.2):

1. Migration data obtained by comparing place of birth and place of residence refer to the *number of migrants* and not to the number of migrations.

2. *Not all migrants* are considered: (a) *Return migrants* have made at least two migrations in their lifetime, but are excluded; by making a return migration during the intercensal period, they decrease the total number of estimated migrants (this corresponds to category S_{ji}^i in expression 6.1, Section 6.2). This means that some persons who are considered as lifetime nonmigrants are actually out-migrants from another region who came back to their birthplace.[10] In fact, only those who made only one migration in their lifetime are sure to be counted as migrants. (b) *Secondary migrants*, i.e., those who have made more than one migration between their place of birth and their residence at the census are given only one migration; this makes any study on migration distances and on the causes of migration highly hazardous. (c) *Deceased migrants* are excluded: persons born in area i and residing in area j at the previous census, who die during the intercensal period, represent a decrease in the number of in-migrants in area j. This is an important drawback of the method since it implies that mortality among migrants from *previous* intercensal periods will affect the estimated number of migrants for the current intercensal period. Of course, people born outside area i who migrate into area i *during* the intercensal period and die before the census is taken, will not be counted as in-migrants, even if they spent most of the period in the area; the same is true for people born in i who out-migrate during the period, but die before the census. This category of disregarded migrants corresponds to components D_j^j, D_{ji}^j, and D_{ji}^i in expression (6.1), Section 6.2, so that the estimated number of in-migrants is

---

[9]This terminology was suggested by Thornthwaite (1934).

[10]This bias could be important for the age groups of 60 and over in those countries where retirement and widowhood induce a return to the place of birth. In other countries however (in the United States, for example), recent data show a trend for retirement migration to be strongly influenced by climate, away from the place of birth.

reduced to

$$\hat{M}^j_{ji} = S^j_{ji} + B^j_i$$

(d) *International emigrants* (i.e., people who left the country) are not accounted for, and the departure during the intercensal period for a foreign country of people who were previously internal migrants will reduce the estimated number of internal migrants. These "omissions" and "errors" affect obviously both out- and in-migration and the biases are necessarily of opposite sign for in- and for out-migration. By computing net migration over an intercensal period, some of these errors will be completely neutralized; this is the case for return migrants and secondary migrants. The problem of identifying this kind of migrant is obviously not solved by computing net migration, but the estimate of net migration is at least not biased by the omission of these migrants. Indeed, persons born in area i and residing in area j at the previous census will not be recorded as in-migrants (S^i_{ji}) in area i if they return to i during the intercensal period, but by returning to their place of birth, they decrease the number of out-migrants from i, so that the net migration figure will not be affected. Similarly, persons born outside area i and living in i at the previous census will induce a decrease in the number of in-migrants in area i when they leave area i during the intercensal period for another area of the country, but they will not be recorded as out-migrants from i, as area i is not their place of birth: again, the errors are completely neutralized.

This is, however, not the case for the two remaining sources of errors, mortality and international migration, which lead to four error terms in the estimation of net internal migration during the intercensal period:

1. For a given intercensal period, the number of deaths among those who migrated in area i *before* the beginning of the period is not necessarily equal to the number of deaths among those who left area i before the beginning of the same period (our previous notation $D^j_{ii} \neq D^i_{jj}$).

2. The number of deaths among those who migrated in area i *during* the intercensal period will not necessarily be equal to the number of deaths among those who left area i during the intercensal period (in our previous notation $D^i_{ij} \neq D^j_{ji}$).

3. The number of international emigrants (over the intercensal period) among previous internal in-migrants in area i is not necessarily equal to the number of international emigrants (over the same intercensal period) among previous internal out-migrants from area i (in our notation, $S^j_{ir} \neq S^i_{jr}$, where r is a third area, comprising all other countries).

4. The number of false internal in-migrants in area i, i.e., those born in the country in another area than i, who were in a foreign country at the previous census but resided in area i at the last census, is not necessarily equal to the number of "false" internal out-migrants from i, i.e., those born in area i, who were in a foreign country at the previous census but back in their native country at the last census, in an area different from i (in our previous notation, $S_{rj}^i \neq S_{ri}^j$, where r is a third area, comprising all other countries).

The first three error terms introduce a negative bias for in-migration and a positive bias for out-migration; the reverse is true for the fourth error term, which is probably the less important.

It is possible to correct for mortality among migrants, first for those who have migrated before the previous census (i.e., the first error term), by applying intercensal survival probabilities to those who at the previous census were counted as in-migrants and out-migrants. Net intercensal migration (m) in a given area is then obtained according to the following formula:

$$m = (I_{t+n} - O_{t+n}) - (p_I I_t - p_O O_t) \tag{6.2}$$

$$= (I_{t+n} - O_{t+n}) - [(1 - q_I)I_t - (1 - q_O)O_t]$$

$$= [(I_{t+n} - O_{t+n}) - (I_t - O_t)] + q_I I_t - q_O O_t \tag{6.3}$$

where I_t, I_{t+n} are the number of in-migrants, i.e., the number of persons born outside the area but residing in the area, respectively, at the first and the second census (n years later); O_t, O_{t+n} are the number of out-migrants, i.e., the number of persons born in the area but residing outside the area, respectively, at the first and second census; p_I, p_O are the (age-specific, and whenever possible, area-specific) probabilities of surviving during n years (the intercensal period) for in-migrants and out-migrants, respectively; q_I, q_O are the (age-specific, area-specific) probabilities of dying during the intercensal period[11] for in-migrants (q_I) and out-migrants (q_O).

The expression containing the first two terms (square brackets) in formula (6.3) represents net intercensal migration without correction, while the last two terms clearly represent estimates of deaths among the in-migrants and the out-migrants, respectively, as counted in the first census, and thus correspond to a correction for the first error term as specified above.

---

[11]On the estimation of p_I, p_O, q_I, and q_O, see Section 6.4.2, and United Nations (1970, pp. 8–12). Ages refer to completed years.

Formula (6.2) may also be written as

$$m = (I_{t+n} - p_I I_t) + (p_O O_t - O_{t+n}) = m_1 + m_2 \qquad (6.4)$$

which decomposes net intercensal migration into two components: net migration among persons born outside the area and net migration among persons born inside the area.[12]

It now becomes necessary to correct also for the second error term. Indeed, formula (6.2) still represents only surviving net migrants. Some people, however, could have in-migrated, for example, one day after the beginning of the intercensal period and died one day before the end of the period. If one is allowed to assume that the flow of in- and out-migration is uniform over the intercensal period, so that the average in-migrant and out-migrant has spent one-half of the period in the area, then one could "revive" the cohort of which those net migrants are the survivors, by applying the reverse of the probability of survival:

$$m = \frac{1}{1 - 0.5 q_I}(I_{t+n} - p_I I_t) + \frac{1}{1 - 0.5 q_O}(p_O O_t - O_{t+n}) \qquad (6.5)$$

It is, however, not possible to correct for the two remaining error terms since the census does not record the international emigrants, nor the "false" internal migrants; the latter could, however, be estimated if the census questionnaire had a question on the place of residence at the first census (but in this case, one does not need an indirect way to estimate migration).

6.4.2. The Vital Statistics Method

The simplest way to obtain an estimate of region i's net migration, is to subtract the natural increase from the total population change

$$m_i = (P_{i(t+n)} - P_{i(t)}) - (B_i - D_i) \qquad (6.6)$$

where $P_{i(t)}$, $P_{i(t+n)}$ are the enumerated population at time t and $t+n$, respectively; B_i is the number of births that occurred to residents of the area during the period; and D_i is the number of deaths that occurred to residents of the area during the period. The main characteristics and problems of migration data obtained by this method are the following (see example, Section 6.8.3):

1. Only net migration is estimated.

[12]See United Nations (1970, p. 7).

2. This estimate of net migration is the sum of net internal migration and net international migration. One way to partially exclude external migration would be to use Eq. (6.6) only on the population in the country. But, besides the fact that regional data on population, birth, and death are rarely available separately for the native and the foreign born, this procedure requires the strong assumption that natives have not left the country during the period.

3. This estimate reflects the number of surviving in-migrants and immigrants $(S_{ji}^{j} + S_{ji}^{i} + B_{i}^{j})$ who did not leave the region before the end of the period: in-migrants who left the region before $(t+n)$ are excluded, while out-migrants and emigrants who did not return to their region before $(t+n)$ are accounted for, whether they are surviving or not at $t+n$.

4. The method contains a logical weakness because the estimate of natural increase does not exactly correspond to the natural increase which would have been experienced in the region in the absence of migration: the births and deaths $(D_{ji}^{i} + D_{ji}^{j} + D_{i}^{j})$ among in-migrants and immigrants are accounted for, while the births and deaths among out-migrants and emigrants are not.

5. The net migration estimate being obtained as a residual, it is clear that any error in the enumeration of population and recording of births and deaths will be reflected in the estimate. This could be an important problem when the method is applied in developing countries.

6. The method can of course also yield estimates of net migration by age; in this case, Eq. (6.6) becomes

$$m_i(x) = P_{i(t+n)}(x+n) - P_{i(t)}(x) + D_i(x) \tag{6.7}$$

where age (x) refers to the age at the beginning of the migration interval (i.e., at time t), and where, according to our previous accounting system,

$$D_i(x) = D_{ii}^{i}(x) + D_{ii}^{j}(x) + D_{ji}^{j}(x) + D_{ji}^{i}(x) + D_{ii}^{r}(x) + D_{ri}^{r}(x) + D_{ri}^{i}(x)$$

This obviously requires that data on death are available both by age and by time of death for each area, which unfortunately is quite unlikely to be the case in most countries.

6.4.3. The Probability of Survival or "Survival Ratio" Method

Instead of obtaining the death component of formula (6.7) directly from vital statistics, which, as mentioned, is difficult if not impossible in most cases (particularly for an analysis by age), one could indirectly estimate those deaths by applying a probability of survival[13] to a base population, in order to obtain an expected population $\hat{P}$ (i.e., the population figure which should have been obtained in the absence of migration); the difference between the enumerated population P_i and the expected population $\hat{P}_i$ represents an estimate of net migration for region i.

Formula (6.7) could indeed be rewritten as

$$m_i(x) = P_{i(t+n)}(x+n) - [P_{i(t)}(x) - D_i(x)]$$
$$= P_{i(t+n)}(x+n) - [P_{i(t)}(x) - {}_nq_i(x)P_{i(t)}(x)] \qquad (6.8)$$

where ${}_nq_i(x)$ is the probability of dying in the next n years for those having age x in region i at time t (age, once again, is given in completed years), or

$$m_i(x) = P_{i(t+n)}(x+n) - [1 - {}_nq_i(x)]P_{i(t)}(x)$$
$$= P_{i(t+n)}(x+n) - {}_np_i(x)P_{i(t)}(x) \qquad (6.9)$$
$$= P_{i(t+n)}(x+n) - \hat{P}_{i(t+n)}(x+n)$$

where ${}_np_i(x)$ is the probability of surviving during the next n years for those of age x in region i at time t. This method thus requires the knowledge of the number of persons classified by age (and sex) in each area at two successive moments of time (usually, two successive censuses) and of the probabilities of survival by age (and sex) for the (intercensal) period, and implies that an answer be given to two main questions:

a. Assuming the probabilities of survival are known, how do we apply them in order to obtain the "expected population"?

b. How do we obtain, for each area, the age–sex-specific probabilities of surviving (or dying) during the n years of the (intercensal) period?

6.4.3.1. Forward, Reverse, and Average Methods. The most used (and, as we will show, usually the most adequate) method is to apply the probability of surviving (during n years for those having age x at the first census, at time t) to the population of age x at time t, in order to obtain an expected population of age $x+n$ at time $t+n$, as was done in formula (6.9). This is called the "*forward method.*"

But an alternative would be to apply the reverse of the probability of survival to the population of age $x+n$ at time $t+n$, in order to obtain an "expected" population of age x at time t, i.e., an estimate of the population (cohort) which should have been present in area i at the beginning of the

---

[13]In the literature on migration, this probability is often called a "*survival ratio.*" Examples are given in Section 6.8.3.

period if there had not been any migration, and of which the population at the end of the period are the survivors. In other words, instead of taking the initial population and letting it survive to the end of the period, one takes the final population and let it "revive." This approach is called the *"reverse"* method, where

$$m_i(x)^{\text{rev}} = P_{i(t+n)}(x+n)[1/{_np_i(x)}] - P_{i(t)}(x) \qquad (6.10)$$

Both methods are obviously related. Dividing formulation (6.9) by the probability of survival, one indeed obtains formula (6.10)

$$m^{\text{rev}} = m^f/p \qquad (6.11)$$

This simple relation leads to three important remarks.

1. Since the probability of survival (p) is positive, the two methods always give the same sign for the estimate of net migration; i.e., one could never obtain net out-migration by using one method and net in-migration by using the other method.

2. Since the probability p of surviving is different from unity, the two methods always give different estimates of net migration; the closer p is to unity (i.e., the higher the probability of surviving), the smaller the difference in the estimates will be; thus, differences will usually be relatively larger for older ages than for younger ages, and for past intercensal periods than for more recent periods.

3. Since the probability of survival is less than unity, the reverse method always gives an estimate of net migration superior to the estimate obtained by the forward method.

The difference in the estimate of net migration obtained by each method is thus related to the estimation of deaths, more precisely to the fact that the biases introduced in the estimation of deaths are different in both methods.

As shown by Eq. (6.8), in the forward method, only deaths among those persons present at the beginning of the period are accounted for, but deaths among in-migrants (and immigrants) are excluded. In our accounting notation, the number of deaths estimated by the forward method is the sum of $D_{ii}^i + D_{ii}^j$, but D_{ji}^j and D_{ji}^i are not accounted for. Moreover, out-migrants (and emigrants) who died during the migration interval are counted twice: once as dead [being present at the beginning of the period, they are included in $P_{i(t)}(x)$ of formula (6.8)], and once more as out-migrant (or emigrant). Net migration is therefore overestimated by these deaths among out-migrants (and emigrants) just as it is underestimated by the unaccounted deaths among in-migrants (and immigrants). The error term introduced by the forward method is thus equal to $(D^i_{ij} + D^j_{ij}) - (D^i_{ji} + D^j_{ji})$; there is no reason to believe that this difference is equal to zero. If deaths are overestimated, i.e., if $(D^i_{ij} + D^j_{ij}) > (D^i_{ji} + D^j_{ji})$, then net migration will be overestimated, as demonstrated by Eq. (6.7). This means that the forward method implicitly assumes that all out- and in-migration occurred at the end of the period; only in this case will the method produce a correct estimate of net migration.

The reverse method also introduces some biases as far as death estimates is concerned. Here, deaths among in-migrants (and immigrants) are overestimated because one "revives" these in-migrants during the whole period, as if they had been in the region during the whole period. But, on the other side, deaths among out-migrants (and emigrants) who spent some part of the period in the region before leaving and who would have been dead in the region had they not migrated, are not accounted for. Net migration is thus overestimated by the overestimation of deaths among in-migrants and underestimated by the underestimation of deaths among out-migrants, the error term being $(D^i_{ji} + D^j_{ji}) - (D^i_{ij} + D^j_{ij})$. The reverse method thus implicitly assumes that all migration flows (in as well as out of the region) occurred at the beginning of the period: only in this case will the method produce a correct estimate of net migration.

Because one method is correct if all migration flows are concentrated at the beginning of the period, and the other method is correct if all migration is concentrated at the end, it seems tempting to use, as a third approach, the *average method*:

$$m_i(x)^{av} = \frac{[P_{i(t+n)}(x+n) - {_np_i}(x)P_{i(t)}(x)] + [P_{i(t+n)}(x+n)(1/{_np_i}(x) - P_{i(t)}(x)]}{2}$$

which relates to the forward method (m^f) in the following way:

$$m_i(x)^{av} = \frac{{_np_i}(x)[P_{i(t+n)}(x+n) - {_np_i}(x)P_{i(t)}(x)] + [P_{i(t+n)}(x+n) - {_np_i}(x)P_{i(t)}(x)]}{2{_np_i}(x)}$$

$$= \frac{[P_{i(t+n)}(x+n) - {_np_i}(x)P_{i(t)}(x)][1 + {_np_i}(x)]}{2{_np_i}(x)}$$

so that $m^{av} = m^f[(1+p)/2p]$.

It will be shown later on that, contrary to what is often proposed, the average method does not imply that all migration is evenly distributed over the period or that all migration occurred at the middle of the period. The main criteria in the choice among those three methods, is indeed the distribution over time of the flows of in- and out-migration; but, by hypothesis, this distribution is unknown.[14]

6.4.3.2. The Problem of the Temporal Distribution of Migration Flows.[15] Not knowing, by assumption, the temporal distribution of the migration flows over the time interval considered, it is impossible to obtain, except by chance, a correct estimate of net migration by any of the three methods presented in the previous section (i.e., the forward, reverse, and average methods). But it is at least possible to choose the method that is the most likely to produce the smallest error, and, the choice having been made, to know in what direction the bias will be. The purpose of this section is to provide a justification for this choice.

In the absence of any knowledge of migration flows, let us first assume that in-migration (I) and out-migration (O) are evenly distributed over the period t to $t+n$. In this case, we may say that at midperiod, net migration is $0.5(I-O)$. In order to take into account deaths among migrants, and assuming, for the time being, that there is no differential mortality between migrants and nonmigrants, we thus add $0.5(I-O)q(x)$ or $0.5[m(x)]q(x)$ to Eq. (6.8):

$$m_i(x) = P_{i(t+n)}(x+n) - P_{i(t)}(x) + {}_nq_i(x)P_{i(t)}(x) + 0.5[m_i(x)]_nq_i(x) \quad (6.12)$$

so that the true figure of net migration $[m_i(x)^*]$ is

$$m_i(x)^* = [P_{i(t+n)}(x+n) - P_{i(t)}(x) + {}_nq_i(x)P_{i(t)}(x)]\left[\frac{1}{1-0.5{}_nq_i(x)}\right] \quad (6.13)$$

But the number of migrants increases as we approach the end of the period, so that we should give more weight to the mortality conditions of the end of the period, instead of giving an equal weight to the two half-periods. By using $0.5{}_nq_i(x)$, one actually assumes that the risk of dying for a given cohort of age x at the beginning of the period decreases as one progresses in the period, an assumption that is rather unrealistic for most ages.

To illustrate this problem, let us divide the period into two equal subperiods (see Fig. 6.1), and assume that we know the probability of dying for each of these two subperiods (q_I and q_{II}). In this case, the migrants of the first half-period are exposed to a risk of dying during the first half-period, which is equal to $0.5q_I$ and they are fully exposed to q_{II} during the second half-period, except for those who died through $0.5q_I$. The migrants of the

---

[14]If the distribution over time of migration flows was known, we should not need to try to estimate net migration!

[15]This section draws heavily upon Wunsch (1969) and Dionne (1970).

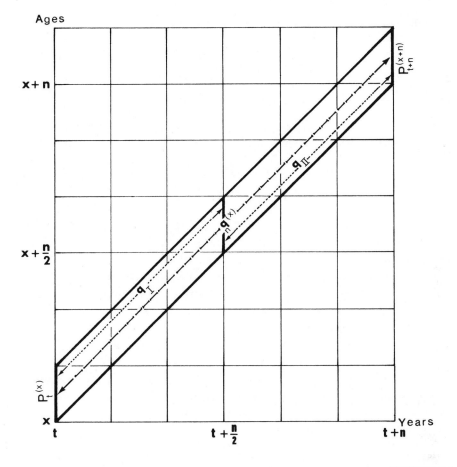

FIGURE 6.1

second half-period are exposed to $0.5q_{II}$. The total number of deaths among migrants[16] is thus equal to

$$0.5\left[\frac{m_i(x)}{2}\right]q_{Ii}+\left[\frac{m_i(x)}{2}-0.5\left(\frac{m_i(x)}{2}\right)q_{Ii}\right]q_{IIi}+0.5\left[\frac{m_i(x)}{2}\right]q_{IIi}$$

or

$$\frac{m_i(x)}{2}[0.5q_{Ii}+0.5q_{IIi}+(1-0.5q_{Ii})q_{IIi}] \qquad (6.14)$$

[16]Of course, the problem just mentioned arises also for each quotient q_I and q_{II}, but the error term so introduced is obviously smaller because the periods are not so long.

The correct probability of dying to be applied to migrants is thus

$$_nq_i'(x) = 0.5q_{Ii} + 1.5q_{IIi} - 0.5q_{Ii}q_{IIi}$$

instead of

$$_nq_i(x) = q_{Ii} + q_{IIi} - q_{Ii}q_{IIi} \qquad (6.15)$$

In order to have $_nq_i'(x) = {}_nq_i(x)$, i.e., in order to be allowed to use $0.5_nq_i(x)$ in Eq. (6.12), one has to assume that

$$q_{II} = q_I/(1 + q_I)$$

or

$$q_I = q_{II}/(1 - q_{II}) \qquad (6.16)$$

which obviously implies $q_{II} < q_I$: the risk of dying is assumed to decrease for a given cohort despite the aging of the cohort![17]

Having made explicit the assumptions underlying the use of $[0.5_nq(x)]$ in formula (6.12), we now look for a way of correcting the bias introduced by each method (forward, reverse, and average) in different cases of temporal distribution of migrants.

Let us assume, as before, that the (unknown) migration flows were evenly distributed over the period and that we have used the forward method in estimating net migration. In this case, it is easy to compute the correction factor, i.e., the coefficient by which to multiply the net migration figure estimated by the forward method (m^f), in order to obtain the correct figure. Indeed, Eq. (6.13) shows that

$$m^*(x) = m^f(x)\left[\frac{1}{1 - 0.5_nq(x)}\right] \qquad \text{if } _nq(x) = {}_nq'(x) \qquad (6.17)$$

If $_nq(x) \neq {}_nq'(x)$, the correction factor is $1/[1 - 0.5_nq'(x)]$.

We may follow a similar line of reasoning for the other methods and with other assumptions on the temporal distribution of migration flows. Besides the assumption on an even distribution of in- and out-migration flows over the period, let us, for instance, consider concentration of all migrations at the beginning (first quarter) of the period, and concentration at the end (third quarter) of the period. Results are summarized in Table 6.1, for the case where $_nq(x) = {}_nq'(x)$ (thus implying $q_{II} < q_I$). This table leads to some important results:

[17]Of course, the problem just mentioned arises also for each quotient q_I and q_{II}, but the error term so introduced is obviously smaller because the periods are not so long.

TABLE 6.1. Table of Correction Factors[a,b]

Hypothesis on temporal distribution of migration flows	Method used		
	Forward	Reverse	Average
Concentration at the beginning of the period (1st quarter)	$\dfrac{1}{1-\frac{3}{4}q}$	$\dfrac{1-q}{1-\frac{3}{4}q}$	$\dfrac{1-q}{1-\frac{5}{4}q+\frac{3}{8}q^{2}}$
Even distribution over the period	$\dfrac{1}{1-\frac{1}{2}q}$	$\dfrac{1-q}{1-\frac{1}{2}q}$	$\dfrac{1-q}{1-q+\frac{1}{4}q^{2}}$
Concentration at the end of the period (3rd quarter)	$\dfrac{1}{1-\frac{1}{4}q}$	$\dfrac{1-q}{1-\frac{1}{4}q}$	$\dfrac{1-q}{1-\frac{3}{4}q+\frac{1}{8}q^{2}}$

[a]The correction factor is the coefficient by which we multiply the estimated net migration figure in order to obtain the correct figure.
[b]In order to use this table in the more realistic case where $_{n}q'(x) \neq _{n}q(x)$ (i.e., where $q_{II} \gtrless q_{I}$), one needs only to substitute in the denominators $_{n}q'(x)$ for $_{n}q(x)$ and $_{n}q'(x)\,q(x)$ for $_{n}q^{2}(x)$.

1. The forward method always underestimates the net migration figure (the correction factor is indeed always >1), while the reverse method always overestimates the net migration figure (the correction factor is always <1).

2. The average method sometimes overestimates, sometimes underestimates the net migration figure, depending on the value of $_{n}q(x)$ and on the hypothesis made on the temporal distribution of migration flows; if migration flows are evenly distributed or concentrated at the end of the period, the average method overestimates the true value of net migration; if migration flows are concentrated at the beginning of the period (first quarter), then the average method produces a correct estimate if $_{n}q(x)=\frac{2}{3}$, overestimates if $_{n}q(x)>\frac{2}{3}$ and underestimates if $_{n}q(x)<\frac{2}{3}$.[18]

3. If one has decided *a priori* to apply the forward method, then the more the migration flows are concentrated at the end of the period the better the results will be; the reverse is true for the reverse method and for the average method.

4. In some cases, one has some exogenous information on the probable temporal distribution of migration flows.[19] Reading the table of correction

[18]In order to have no bias (i.e., correction factor equals 1), one should have $\{(1-q)/[1-q-(\frac{1}{4}q-\frac{3}{8}q^{2})]\}=1$, implying $(\frac{1}{4}q-\frac{3}{8}q^{2})=0$. The roots of this last expression are zero (which is absurd) and $\frac{2}{3}$.

[19]For instance, if one knows that at the end of the period the region experienced an important structural crisis in its economic activities, or was particularly hit by a recession in the business cycle, then one could assume that net out-migration was concentrated mainly at the end of the period.

factors line by line enables us to learn what the best method is in each of the three main cases of temporal distribution of migration flows:

If these flows are concentrated in the beginning of the period, the best method is the *average method*; indeed

$$1-\frac{1-q}{1-\frac{3}{4}q}=\frac{\frac{1}{4}q}{1-\frac{3}{4}q}<\frac{1}{1-\frac{3}{4}q}-1=\frac{\frac{3}{4}q}{1-\frac{3}{4}q}$$

and

$$\left|1-\frac{1-q}{1-\frac{5}{4}q+\frac{3}{8}q^2}\right|<\frac{\frac{1}{4}q}{1-\frac{3}{4}q}\qquad\text{for all }q<1$$

If the migration flows are evenly distributed over the period, the best method is again the *average method*[20]; indeed

$$\frac{1}{1-\frac{1}{2}q}-1=\frac{\frac{1}{2}q}{1-\frac{1}{2}q}=1-\frac{1-q}{1-\frac{1}{2}q}$$

and

$$1-\frac{1-q}{1-q+\frac{1}{4}q^2}=\frac{\frac{1}{4}q^2}{1-q+\frac{1}{4}q^2}<\frac{\frac{1}{2}q}{1-\frac{1}{2}q}$$

If the migration flows are concentrated at the end of the period, the best method is the *forward method*; indeed

$$1-\frac{1-q}{1-\frac{3}{4}q+\frac{1}{8}q^2}=\frac{\frac{3}{4}q(1+\frac{1}{2}q)}{(1-\frac{1}{4}q)(3-\frac{3}{2}q)}<1-\frac{1-q}{1-\frac{1}{4}q}=\frac{\frac{3}{4}q}{1-\frac{1}{4}q}$$

and

$$\frac{1}{1-\frac{1}{4}q}-1=\frac{\frac{1}{4}q}{1-\frac{1}{4}q}<1-\frac{1-q}{1-\frac{3}{4}q+\frac{1}{8}q^2}=\frac{\frac{1}{4}q(1+\frac{1}{2}q)}{(1-\frac{1}{4}q)(1-\frac{1}{2}q)}$$

Thus, the main conclusion of this section is that, depending on the assumption made on the distribution of migration flows over the period, and depending on the probability of dying, and thus on the age for which net migration is estimated, a different method of estimation would have to be used. The usual result of this is that different methods would have to be applied for different regions and age, because mortality conditions and the distribution of migrants over time may vary significantly from one region to

[20]Note that when q is small, $\frac{1}{4}q^2$ is negligible, so that the average method produces a quasi-correct estimate of net migration when migration flows are evenly distributed and for all age groups with a small probability of dying during the period.

another and from one age to another. This is obviously not an advisable approach, because it would produce net migration estimates having a different bias from one region to another.

Moreover, the various methods will yield net migration estimates that are very close as long as the probability of dying is small, i.e., as long as one limits the analysis to young ages (except for infantile mortality) and to working ages. For old ages, it should be considered that any bias introduced by these indirect methods will have a large impact, because these ages usually have small net migration figures; except for some particular cases, it thus seems preferable to refrain from any estimation of net migration for old ages.

These considerations lead to the conclusion that only one method should be applied to all regions and ages. As we have shown above, we have to disregard the reverse method anyway, so that we have to choose between the forward method and the average method. The *forward method* seems preferable, because of two important characteristics. First, the net migration figure obtained by applying the forward method has a logical meaning: it represents the balance between surviving in-migrants and surviving out-migrants, all deaths among migrants being disregarded in this method. Second, and correlatively, estimates of net migration obtained by the forward method are comparable to those obtained by the place of birth method, which also disregards deceased migrants.

Indeed, comparing Eqs. (6.2) and (6.9) shows that if the probability of survival is correctly estimated (and of course, if the census figures are accurate[21]), the two equations will yield the same estimate of net migration for a given age x to $x+n$. But, if the probability of survival is not correct, then, for a given percentage of error in the estimate of the probability of survival, the error (in absolute terms) in the estimate of net migration obtained by the forward method will be larger than the error in the estimate obtained by the place of birth method, because P_t and P_{t+n} are much larger than $(I_t - O_t)$ and $(I_{t+n} - O_{t+n})$.

Of course, in order to compare estimates of total net migration (over all ages) obtained by the place of birth method, and estimates produced by the use of the forward method, one has to add to the latter estimates an estimate of net migration for the individuals born during the intercensal period [Section 6.4.3.4b (point 5)].

---

[21]Note, however, that even if census figures are not correct, a self-correcting procedure may be used by selecting the appropriate type of survival ratios. See Section 6.4.3.4b (point 2).

6.4.3.3. The Problem of Differential Mortality between Migrants and Nonmigrants. Until now, we have implicitly assumed that migrants and nonmigrants have, for a given age x, the same probability of dying. Let us now estimate the bias introduced by this hypothesis. We will only consider the case where migration flows are evenly distributed over the period, with in-migrants (I) in region i being subject to risk of dying k and out-migrants (O) from region i having the same probability of dying q as the nonmigrants of the region, which seems a reasonable assumption.[22]

Equation (6.8) now becomes

$$m_i(x) = P_{i(t+n)}(x+n) - P_{i(t)}(x) + {}_nq_i(x)P_{i(t)}(x) - 0.5\,{}_nq_i(x)O + 0.5\,{}_nk_i(x)I$$

Using ${}_nk_i(x)/{}_nq_i(x) = {}_nz_i(x)$ we obtain

$$m_i(x) = P_{i(t+n)}(x+n) - P_{i(t)}(x) + {}_nq_i(x)P_{i(t)}(x) + 0.5[{}_nz_i(x)I - O]{}_nq_i(x) \tag{6.18}$$

In order to measure the bias introduced by assuming equal mortality between migrants and nonmigrants, i.e., by assuming ${}_nz_i(x) = 1$, we subtract Eq. (6.12), representing the net migration figure $(\widehat{I-O})$ estimated with the equal mortality hypothesis, from Eq. (6.18), which represents the true net migration figure $(I-O)$:

$$(I-O) - (\widehat{I-O}) = 0.5[{}_nz_i(x)I - O]\,{}_nq_i(x) - 0.5(I-O)\,{}_nq_i(x)$$

$$= 0.5\,{}_nq_i(x)I({}_nz_i(x)-1)$$

so that

$$(\widehat{I-O}) = I[1 - 0.5\,{}_nq_i(x)({}_nz_i(x)-1)] - O$$

In most cases, the value of $0.5\,{}_nq_i(x)\,[{}_nz_i(x)-1]$ will be very small, so that the hypothesis of equal mortality conditions between migrants and nonmigrants seems usually to have a negligible influence on the estimate of net migration. Obviously, if ${}_nz_i(x) > 1$, i.e., if in-migrants have a higher probability of dying than out-migrants and nonmigrants, then net migration will be underestimated, while if ${}_nz_i(x) < 1$, i.e., if in-migrants have a lower probability of dying, net migration will be overestimated.

6.4.3.4. Estimation of the Probabilities of Survival. Another implicit assumption we have made thus far is that we have perfect knowledge of the probabilities of survival over the period. We now will consider two sources for estimating these probabilities: the life table and the census.

[22]This case has been analyzed by Wunsch (1969).

a. Life-Table Survival Probabilities. In most cases, the life table will not reflect the mortality conditions for the whole migration interval, which is often quite long (over the whole intercensal period). Usually, the informations provided by two or more life tables will have to be combined.

Let us, for instance, assume that life table No. I correctly reflects mortality conditions during the first half of the intercensal period t to $t + n/2$, and that life table No. II is valid for the second half of the period, $t + n/2$ to $t + n$. The probability of surviving for n years, for individuals of age x at the beginning of the period, may then be written as (see Section 3.2.2.1)

$$_n p(x) = \left(\frac{L_{x+n/2}}{L_x}\right)^{(I)} \left(\frac{L_{x+n}}{L_{x+n/2}}\right)^{(II)}$$

using L_x as the number of persons of age x in the stationary population of the life table, superscripts (I) and (II) designating the first and second life tables, respectively.

Usually, net migration is estimated by age group and not by age. As a shortcut, we may then want to use probabilities of survival for age groups. If, for instance, we want to estimate the probability of surviving during an intercensal period of ten years for those having between 10 and 15 years of age at the beginning of the period, we may use the following formula:

$$_{10} p(10-15) = \left(\frac{_5L_{15}}{_5L_{10}}\right)^{(I)} \left(\frac{_5L_{20}}{_5L_{15}}\right)^{(II)}$$

b. Census Survival Probabilities. The *census survival probability* for age x is defined as the ratio of the total population of the country aged $x + n$ at a given census to the total population of the country of age x at the census taken n years earlier

$$_n p(x) = P_{t+n}(x + n)/P_t(x)$$

or when five-year age groups are used

$$_n p_{(x,x+5)} = \frac{\begin{aligned}P_{t+n}(x+n)+P_{t+n}(x+1+n)+P_{t+n}(x+2+n)+P_{t+n}(x+3+n)\\ + P_{t+n}(x+4+n)\end{aligned}}{P_t(x)+P_t(x+1)+P_t(x+2)+P_t(x+3)+P_t(x+4)}$$

As in most countries, the sex differences in mortality are sharp, separate survival ratios by sex are obviously required.

The life-table approach and the census approach are based on different assumptions and have different characteristics, which should be kept in mind when choosing between them:

1. The use of census survival probabilities implies that the population of the country for which regional net migration estimates are made is a closed population, i.e., without international migration. Of course, if data on international migration are available by age (for instance, through a population register; but even in this case, as was already mentioned, data on emigration are usually poor), then the necessary adjustments could be made. The existence of international migration could lead to census survival "probabilities" greater than 1. This is why census survival ratios should not be calculated for the total population; for instance, if a country is not affected by international emigration, the native population could be used.

2. When computing the census survival probabilities, one has to assume that, in each region and in any age–sex group, the ratio between the enumerated population and the real population is the same from one census to the next one, for the same cohort.

If, for instance, the percentage of underenumeration is smaller at the second census than at the first, then the census survival probability will be biased upward, so that net migration will be underestimated. Indeed, if e_t and e_{t+n} represent the percentages of enumeration at the first and second census, respectively, while p^* stands for the true value of the survival probability, then the census survival probability is

$$_np = \frac{e_{t+n}P_{t+n}}{e_tP_t} = \frac{e_{t+n}(_np^*P_t)}{e_tP_t} = \frac{e_{t+n}}{e_t}{_np^*}$$

so that net migration estimated by the forward method is given by

$$\hat{m} = e_{t+n}P_{t+n} - \frac{e_{t+n}}{e_t}{_np^*}e_tP_t$$

$$= e_{t+n}P_{t+n} - e_{t+n}\,_np^*P_t$$

$$= e_{t+n}(P_{t+n} - {_np^*}P_t) \qquad (6.19)$$

With $e_{t+n} > e_t$, we have $p > p^*$, and therefore $\hat{m} < m^*$: net migration is underestimated and the degree of underestimation is directly proportional to the degree of completeness in the enumeration at the *second* census (the percentage of underestimation of net migration is equal to $1 - e_{t+n}$).

However, even if the degree of completeness of enumeration is different in both censuses, so that net migration estimates are biased, we may obtain correct estimates of net migration "*rates,*" depending on the way these rates are computed. This is obvious from Eq. (6.19). Indeed, if one estimates the "rate" of net migration (R_{nm}) by dividing the net migration estimate by the population figure enumerated at the second census,[23] we obtain

$$R_{nm} = \frac{e_{t+n}(P_{t+n} - {}_np^*P_t)}{e_{t+n}P_{t+n}} = \frac{P_{t+n} - {}_np^*P_t}{P_{t+n}}$$

The "rate" of net migration, obtained by the forward method and by applying census survival probabilities to uncorrectly enumerated populations, is equal to the "rate" of net migration we should have obtained with populations correctly enumerated and with a correct estimate of the survival probabilities, if the "rate" is computed by expressing the final population as the denominator. The same reasoning may be applied to the reverse method; in this case, the initial population should be expressed as denominator.

The use of census survival probabilities thus presents the important advantage of having a built-in correction mechanism, when net migration "rates" are computed.

3. However, even if the use of census survival probabilities allows for a built-in correction of enumeration errors, there still remains a difficulty: we indeed have to make the assumption that the distribution (by age and sex) and the importance of the enumeration errors is the same in each region. This kind of hypothesis is obviously not to be realized: there are too many regional differences in the education level, in the urban–rural structure, in the proportion of pseudo- or quasi-households, in the percentage of people without fixed residence, for this assumption to be verified. But these regional disparities in the degree of completeness of enumeration actually represent a further reason for using census survival probabilities instead of life-table survival probabilities. Indeed the percentage of error in the enumeration of the national population is a weighted average of the regional percentages of error, so that the errors in the enumeration of the regional populations are centered around a national average, and not around zero as in the case of the life table, which assumes perfect enumeration. The regional disparities in the percentage of error of enumeration are thus relatively larger with life tables than with census survival probabilities.

4. The same idea, that it is sometimes better to apply an error term to another error term than to a correct term, is valid not only in the estimation of net migration rates, but also in estimating net migration itself. Indeed, life-table survival probabilities are often smoothed by graduation methods

---

[23] As will be mentioned later (Section 6.5.1), there is, however, usually no logical basis for using the final population as the denominator in computing net migration "rates."

(see Section 3.2.2.1), and by applying smoothed survival probabilities to an age distribution distorted by underenumeration, one necessarily obtains distorted net migration estimates. This distortion will manifest itself through an irregular pattern of net migration by age and in the fact that the net migration figures for a given age do not add to zero when summed over all regions, as it should be.

5. Census survival probabilities cannot be used for estimating net migration of those persons who were born during the intercensal period, unless a reliable birth registration system exists in each region. If this is the case, the survival probability of persons born, for instance, at time $t+k$ ($k<n$), is obtained by dividing the national population of age $n-k$ as enumerated at the second census by the national figure of births in year $t+k$. This probability of survival (or the life-table survival probability, if available) is then applied to the regional figure of births in year $t+k$, in order to obtain the regional net migration estimate for this age.

6. Another problem relates to the regional disparities of the survival probabilities. Life tables are indeed usually constructed for the nation as a whole (only a few countries, the United States and Canada among them, have regional life tables), and the census survival probabilities, as obtained above, are (by definition) valid only at the national level. By applying national survival probabilities to regional populations, which in reality are subjected to above or below average mortality conditions, one obtains, respectively, an underestimation or an overestimation of net migration.

One way to solve this problem is to use the census data by place of birth. By considering at two subsequent censuses the age-cohorts of all persons born in a same region, one obtains regional census survival probabilities.[24] In other words, to the previous hypothesis where national survival probabilities are assumed valid for the whole population disregarding its region of birth or residence, is substituted a new hypothesis, where census survival probabilities obtained for each region of birth are assumed valid for all those who were born in the region, disregarding their region of residence at the moment of the census. It is as if one assumed that migrants carry with them the mortality conditions of their region of birth. It is thus hypothesized that there is less regional heterogeneity in mortality conditions within the cohort of all people having a common region of birth, than within the national population considered as a whole; but of course, by using this approach one

[24]Of course, this implies that international emigration of the natives of the region considered is negligible.

introduces a new source of error—namely, in the enumeration of the population by place of birth.

The census survival probabilities for region i are thus given by

$$_np_i(x) = \sum_{\substack{j \\ j=i}} P^i_{j(t+n)}(x+n) \Big/ \sum_{\substack{j \\ j=i}} P^i_{j(t)}(x)$$

where $P^i_{j(t)}(x)$ designates the population of age x born in region i and residing at time t in region j, and $\sum_{j,j=i}$ represents the sum over j *including i*.

Using the expression

$$\hat{P}_{j(t+n)}(x+n) = {}_np_i(x)P^i_{j(t)}(x)$$

we may state the following characteristics of the method:

(a)

$$\sum_j \hat{P}^i_{j\,(t+n)}(x+n) = \sum_j P^i_{j(t+n)}(x+n) \tag{6.20}$$

i.e., the sum (over all regions of residence, including region i) of all expected survivors in the cohort of those born in region i, equals the sum (over all regions) of the persons really surviving.

(b)

$$m^i_j(x) = P^i_{j(t+n)}(x+n) - \hat{P}^i_{j(t+n)}(x+n)$$

i.e., in the cohort of all individuals having age x at time t, the net migration for region i from migrations between i and j is equal to the difference between observed survivors in j among those born in i, and expected survivors.

(c)

$$\sum_j m^i_j = 0$$

i.e., the sum over all regions of the gains and losses resulting from the migrations of people born in a same region i, is equal to zero for that region.

(d) Total net internal migration for region j is equal to

$$\sum_i m^i_j \gtreqless 0$$

(e)

$$\sum_j \sum_i m^i_j = 0$$

i.e., total net internal migration for the whole nation is necessarily equal to zero.

(f) For those individuals born during the intercensal period (i.e., having an age $x < n$ at time $t + n$), we have directly

$$m_j^i(x) = P_{j(t+n)}^i(x)$$

6.5. INTENSITY OF MIGRATION

Migration may be considered as a flow affecting a stock (of population). It is clear that the intensity of the migration process in a region cannot be measured by merely considering the absolute number of migrations or migrants (estimated either directly or indirectly, by applying the methods developed in·the previous section). At first and obvious method of measuring the intensity of migration is to compute a *migration rate*, i.e., to divide the flow of migrants (or migrations) observed or estimated for a given period, by the population affected by this flow. Our first problem will thus be to define this base population. Next, we consider the interdependence between migration and mortality, and proceed to develop a multiregional life table integrating both phenomena.

In analyzing the intensity of migration, however, we also have to take into account the fact that migration is a renewable phenomenon, which leads us to the problem of the average intensity and tempo of migration in the framework of *cohort analysis*. In the absence of longitudinal data on migration (except for some rare surveys), some methods have been devised where period data are used in order to obtain some estimates of the average intensity and tempo of migration for a given cohort.

6.5.1. The Migration Rate

Let us consider again the basic identity

$$P_{t+n} - P_t = B - D + I - O \tag{6.21}$$

If we want to express Eq. (6.21) in terms of rates, i.e.,

$$R = R_B - R_D + R_I - R_O \tag{6.22}$$

we need a common denominator for each of these rates. The best common denominator is the number of person-years lived in the region:

$$Y = \int_0^n P_{t+i} \, di$$

$$= \int_0^n P_t e^{ri} \, di \tag{6.23}$$

where n is the number of units of time (years) of the period and r is the yearly rate of population growth in continuous time, i.e., $\ln(1+j)$ with j representing the yearly growth rate if time is considered as discontinuous. From (6.23), we have

$$Y = P_t \left[\frac{e^{ri}}{r} \right]_0^n$$

$$= P_t \frac{e^{rn}}{r} - P_t \frac{e^0}{r}$$

$$= \frac{P_t}{r}(e^{rn} - 1) \qquad \text{as } e^0 = 1$$

Remembering that $e^{rn} = P_{t+n}/P_t$ and $r = [\ln(P_{t+n}/P_t)/n]$ where $\ln$ denotes the natural logarithm, we obtain

$$Y = \frac{P_t}{\ln(P_{t+n}/P_t)} \left(\frac{P_{t+n} - P_t}{P_t} \right) n$$

$$= \frac{(P_{t+n} - P_t)}{\ln(P_{t+n}/P_t)}(n) \tag{6.24}$$

It may be shown that a very good approximation of the number of person-years lived in a region, as expressed by formula (6.24), is obtained by the arithmetic mean of the initial and final populations, as long as the total growth rate (R) of the population in the region is not greater than $\pm 35\%$. Indeed

$$\frac{(P_{t+n} - P_t)}{\ln(P_{t+n}/P_t)}(n) \cong \frac{(P_{t+n} + P_t)}{2}(n)$$

$$2\frac{(P_{t+n} - P_t)}{(P_{t+n} + P_t)} \cong \ln\left(\frac{P_{t+n}}{P_t}\right)$$

$$2\frac{P_{t+n}/P_t - 1}{P_{t+n}/P_t + 1} \cong \ln\frac{P_{t+n}}{P_t}$$

which gives us, for $P_{t+n}/P_t = 1.35$,

$$2(0.35/2.35) = 0.29787234 \cong \ln(1.35) = 0.300104593$$

and for $P_{t+n}/P_t = 0.65$,

$$2(-0.35/1.65) = -0.42424242 \cong \ln(0.65) = -0.430782916$$

Thus, as long as the total rate of growth (or decline) of the population in the region does not exceed 35% over the time interval for which the migration rate is estimated, then one is justified to use the arithmetic mean of the initial and final populations as the denominator in the computation of the migration rate (see example, Section 6.8.4).

In other words, when in region i, one has $1.35 \geqslant P_{t+n}/P_t \geqslant 0.65$; then the rate of out-migration of region i can be written as

$$R_{O(i)} = \frac{\sum_j M_{ij}}{(P_{i(t)} + P_{i(t+n)})/2}$$

Similarly the "rate" of in-migration is

$$R_{I(i)} = \frac{\sum_j M_{ji}}{(P_{i(t)} + P_{i(t+n)})/2}$$

and the "rate" of net migration is

$$R_{m(i)} = \frac{\sum_j M_{ji} - \sum_j M_{ij}}{(P_{i(t)} + P_{i(t+n)})/2}$$

The main exceptions where one does not use the arithmetic mean of the initial and final populations are for underdeveloped countries and for cities and metropolitan areas in some developed countries. In these cases where the demographic growth rate over the period appears to be very large (i.e., superior to 35%), it seems preferable (Hamilton, 1965) to use as a base population the following:

For the "rate" of out-migration

$$P_t + \frac{P_t}{(P_t + P_{t+n})}(B_{(t,t+n)} + I_{(t,t+n)} - D_{(t,t+n)})$$

For the "rate" of in-migration

$$P_{t+n} - \frac{P_{t+n}}{(P_t + P_{t+n})}(B_{(t,t+n)} - O_{(t,t+n)} - D_{(t,t+n)})$$

For the "rate" of net migration when negative $[(I - O) < 0]$

$$P_t + \frac{P_t}{(P_t + P_{t+n})}(B_{(t,t+n)} - D_{(t,t+n)})$$

For the "rate" of net migration when positive $[(I - O) > 0]$

$$P_{t+n} - \frac{P_{t+n}}{(P_t + P_{t+n})}(B_{(t,t+n)} - D_{(t,t+n)})$$

Even in the cases where the arithmetic mean of P_t and P_{t+n} represents a good approximation of the number of person-years lived in the region, we are no longer allowed to interpret it as a measure of the *population at risk*, as in the case of natality and mortality. This interpretation would be meaningful only in the case of births, deaths, and out-migrations, but not in the case of in-migrations, where the population at risk is the population of the rest of the country (or the rest of the world, in the case of international immigration) and not the population of the region. The integration of migration obliges us therefore to abandon a traditional concept of demographic analysis, and to reduce the meaning of a rate to a mere standardization process (see Section 2.4.1), which makes possible the comparison of the different components of the demographic growth for a given region [as in Eq. (6.21)] and of the same component for different regions. And even in those cases where an interpretation in terms of risk is justified (i.e., for births, deaths, and out-migrations), one still has to assume that all individuals encounter a constant and identical risk, an assumption that is not valid any longer by the mere fact that people enter or leave the region during the period. It should, moreover, be emphasized that by using the arithmetic mean of the initial and final populations, we actually assume a linear demographic growth, i.e., that the increase of population over the period has been constant.

There are certain cases where a justification could be found for choosing either the initial population or the final population. For instance, if the number of surviving in-migrants (for a given period) is expressed as the numerator, then by using the final population as a base in computing the in-migration "rate," one actually obtains the percentage of in-migrants in the population of the region, or the probability to find an in-migrant of the period if one randomly chooses a member of this population. It will also be remembered that when the forward method has been used for estimating net migration by applying a census survival probability, it is advisable to divide by the final population if one wants to eliminate census errors in the enumeration of population [see Section 6.4.3.4b].

When the migration interval is short, it is probably more meaningful to use the *initial population* instead of the average population for computing the rate of out-migration. If for instance, we have out-migration data for a one-year period, it may be assumed that only those who have stayed at least six months in the region are subject to the risk of out-migration. This is not an unreasonable assumption considering the importance of the decision to migrate and the delay which is often necessary for preparing the move once the decision has been made. One may also consider the fact that most migrations actually occur in the first half of the period (more precisely, in spring). These two considerations would lead to the choice of the initial population as the denominator in computing the rate of out-migration.

As long as we work with total figures, i.e., total out-migration $(\sum_j M_{ij})$, total in-migration $(\sum_j M_{ji})$, or total net migration, in other words, as long as we do not disaggregate by region of origin or destination, it is obviously the population of only one region (region i in this case) that will have to appear in the denominator of the migration rate. But when we want to compute the rate of migration from region i to region j, one has to standardize by using the populations of i and j simultaneously. The problem is then one of combining the populations. The three most used combinations of P_i and P_j are their average mean, their product, and the square root of their product. Applying by analogy the law of gravitation, where the interaction between two masses is a function of the volume of the masses, it seems preferable to use the product of P_i and P_j as the denominator (and to multiply the resulting ratio by k, a large constant, in order to avoid very small rates). The rate of migration from i to j would thus be

$$R_{ij} = \frac{M_{ij(t,t+n)}}{[(P_{i(t)}+P_{i(t+n)})/2][(P_{j(t)}+P_{j(t+n)})/2]}k \qquad (6.25)$$

Of course, if we want only to compare migration flows to various regions of destination j for a given region of origin i, then it is not necessary to introduce P_i in the denominator of Eq. (6.25).

But standardizing by the affected populations still does not assure the rigorous interregional comparability of the migration flows. One indeed has to take also into account the interregional differences in the area and the configuration of the regions, and in the spatial dispersion of the population within these regions. Other things being equal, a small elongated region where the population is dispersed at the periphery will have a larger rate of migration than a large circular region where the population is concentrated in the geographical center of the area.[25] It is very rare that the researcher has the possibility to choose the areal subdivision; most often, the data will be available only for one type of areal subdivision. In the rare cases where one has the opportunity to choose the level of spatial disaggregation (for instance, when data are available for small spatial units so that any combination of them, i.e., any degree of areal subdivision, is possible), one should consider the ultimate use of the migration rates one intends to compute. If the regional migration rates are to be used later on in an explanatory study analyzing the determinants of migration, then one has to maximize the probability that these explanatory variables could reveal themselves, which implies maximizing the variance (with respect to these variables) among the spatial units. This is obviously obtained by minimizing the variance within the spatial units, in other words, by choosing the smallest possible areal subdivision. But migration is a bipolar phenomenon, and its intensity is a function of the opportunities existing outside of the area of departure. In an explanatory analysis of the regional differences in the migration rate, these external opportunities should be as comparable as possible. It is obvious that the comparability of the external opportunities increases when the size of the spatial units increases, so that we are faced with a dilemma: on the one hand, we have to maximize the variance among the spatial observations, which leads to an areal subdivision in small spatial units, and on the other hand, we have to maximize the comparability of the external opportunities, which leads to an areal subdivision in large spatial units. The demographer should thus be careful in choosing the degree of areal subdivision, because his choice will affect the possibilities and the meaning of a subsequent explanatory analysis, and therefore the efficiency of forecasting.

6.5.2. The Multiregional Multiple-Decrement Life Table

Let us consider the cohort of those surviving at age x in region i at some moment t $[S_{i(t)}(x)]$. One year later, at $t+1$, the members of this cohort will be in either one of the following "states": they will either be surviving in i $[S_{ii(t+1)}(x+1)]$, surviving in j $[S_{ij(t+1)}(x+1)]$, or deceased, in either region $[D_{i(t,t+1)}(x) = D_{ij(t,t+1)}(x) + D_{ii(t,t+1)}(x)]$.

Note that, according to our notation,

$$S_{ij(t+1)}(x+1) = M_{ij(t,t+1)}(x)$$

[25]On the problem of areal subdivision in migration analysis see, for instance, Thomlinson (1961) and Courgeau (1973b).

if no migrant from i to j died in j before $t+1$, i.e., if $D_{ij(t,t+1)}(x)=0$. We may thus write:

$$P_{i(t)}(x) = S_{i(t)}(x) = S_{ii(t+1)}(x+1) + S_{ij(t+1)}(x+1) + D_{ij(t,t+1)}(x) + D_{ii(t,t+1)}(x)$$

or $\hspace{8cm}$ (6.26)

$$S_{ii(t+1)}(x+1) = P_{i(t)}(x) - S_{ij(t+1)}(x+1) - D_{ij(t,t+1)}(x) - D_{ii(t,t+1)}(x) \hspace{1cm} (6.26')$$

If we let $a_{ii}(x)$ represent the average fraction of a year lived in region i by persons who were alive at age x in region i at time t and are still surviving at age $x+1$ in region i at time $t+1$ (this fraction will be equal to 1 if there were no return migrants during the period, i.e., if no out-migrants of the period returned to i before the end of the period); $a_{ij}(x)$ the average fraction of a year lived in region i by persons who were alive at age x in region i at time t and are surviving at age $x+1$ in region j at time $t+1$; $a_{iD}(x)$ the average fraction of a year lived in i by persons who were alive at age x in region i at time t, and who died in region i before time $t+1$; and $a_{jD}(x)$ the average fraction of a year lived in i by persons who were alive at age x in region i at time t, and who died in region j before time $t+1$, then the total number of person-years, lived during the year, in region i by those having age x at time t, may be written as

$$Y_i(x) = [a_{ii}(x)]S_{ii(t+1)}(x+1) + [a_{ij}(x)]S_{ij(t+1)}(x+1) + [a_{iD}(x)]D_{ii(t,t+1)}(x)$$
$$+ [a_{jD}(x)]D_{ij(t,t+1)}(x) \hspace{5cm} (6.27)$$

$$= [a_{ii}(x)][P_{i(t)}(x) - S_{ij(t+1)}(x+1) - D_{ij(t,t+1)}(x) - D_{ii(t,t+1)}(x)]$$
$$+ [a_{ij}(x)]S_{ij(t+1)}(x+1)$$
$$+ [a_{iD}(x)]D_{ii(t,t+1)}(x) + [a_{jD}(x)]D_{ij(t,t+1)}(x) \hspace{3cm} (6.28)$$

by substituting Eq. (6.26′) into Eq. (6.27). From Eq. (6.28), we obtain

$$P_{i(t)}(x) = \frac{Y_i(x)}{a_{ii}(x)} + \left(1 - \frac{a_{ij}(x)}{a_{ii}(x)}\right)S_{ij(t+1)}(x+1) + \left(1 - \frac{a_{jD}(x)}{a_{ii}(x)}\right)D_{ij(t,t+1)}(x)$$
$$+ \left(1 - \frac{a_{iD}(x)}{a_{ii}(x)}\right)D_{ii(t,t+1)}(x) \hspace{4cm} (6.29)$$

Now, let us go back to some definitions and symbols. In order to lighten the notation, we will consider that j represents all regions other than i, and we will delete the time and age indexes whenever possible. *Multiple-decrement* measures[26] (Section 3.2.2.3) of mortality and migration can then be set up as follows:

$p_{ij}^* =$ the probability of out-migrating

$$= (S_{ij} + D_{ij})/P_{i(t)} \tag{6.30}$$

$p_{ij} =$ the probability of out-migrating and surviving

$$= S_{ij}/P_{i(t)} \tag{6.31}$$

$p_{ii} =$ the probability of surviving in the region

$$= S_{ii}/P_{i(t)} \tag{6.32}$$

$q_i =$ the probability of dying (in either region)

$$= (D_{ii} + D_{ij})/P_{i(t)} = q_{ii} + q_{ij} \qquad \text{where } p_{ij} + p_{ii} + q_i = 1 \tag{6.33}$$

$r_0^* =$ the rate of out-migration

$$= (S_{ij} + D_{ij})/Y_i \tag{6.34}$$

$r_0 =$ the rate of survival for out-migrants

$$= S_{ij}/Y_i \tag{6.35}$$

$r_{ii} =$ the rate of survival for nonmigrants

$$= S_{ii}/Y_i \tag{6.36}$$

$r_D =$ the death rate

$$= (D_{ii} + D_{ij})/Y_i = r_{iD} + r_{jD} \tag{6.37}$$

Let us assume that $a_{iD} = a_{jD} = a_D$, which would, for instance, be the case if the number of deaths in the region (D_{ii}) and the number of out-migrations from the region are evenly spread over the one-year period. Then, by substituting Eq. (6.29) into Eq. (6.33), we obtain the probability of dying:

$$q_i = \frac{r_D}{1/a_{ii} + (1 - a_{ij}/a_{ii})r_0 + (1 - a_D/a_{ii})r_D} \tag{6.38}$$

---

[26]These measures are not corrected for disturbances, as in the case of the *single-decrement* life table considered in Section 3.2.2.

In the particular case where mortality and out-migration are evenly spread over the period, and where there are no return migrants, this expression equals

$$q_i = r_D/(1+\tfrac{1}{2}r_0+\tfrac{1}{2}r_D) \tag{6.39}$$

Correspondingly, for the probability to out-migrate (and survive), we obtain, by substituting Eq. (6.29) into Eq. (6.31),

$$p_{ij} = \frac{r_0}{1/a_{ii}+(1-a_{ij}/a_{ii})r_0+(1-a_D/a_{ii})r_D} \tag{6.40}$$

and

$$p_{ij} = r_0/(1+\tfrac{1}{2}r_0+\tfrac{1}{2}r_D) \tag{6.41}$$

The corrected probability to migrate out of region i (at any time between t and $t+1$) may be obtained by adding to the numerator of Eq. (6.31) those who died after having migrated (D_{ij}) and those who would have out-migrated had they not died in region i:

$$\rho_i = \frac{S_{ij}+D_{ij}+(1-a_{iD}/a_{ii})D_{ii}(p_{ij}^*)}{P_i}$$

$$= \frac{(r_0^*)[1+q_{ii}-(a_{iD}/a_{ii})q_{ii}]}{1/a_{ii}+(1-a_{ij}/a_{ii})r_0+(1-a_D/a_{ii})r_D}$$

which, with the same hypotheses as before, reduces to

$$\rho_i = (r_0^*)(1+\tfrac{1}{2}q_{ii})/(1+\tfrac{1}{2}r_0+\tfrac{1}{2}r_D)$$

Equations (6.39) and (6.40) show, respectively, how the rate of out-migration affects the probability of dying and how the death rate affects the probability of migrating. The results obtained for q_i and p_{ij} may then be presented in the framework of a *multiregional multiple decrement* life table. A simple way to present such a multiregional life table would be as in Table 6.2 (with imaginary data and j being all regions other than region i).

From this, one can obtain the average expectation of life beyond age z $(z \geqslant x)(z=0,\dots,\omega)$ for the cohort $l_k(x)$ of those residing at age x in region k $(k=i,j,\dots,n)$, for each possible future region of residence; for $k=i$ one has

$$_{ix}e_{i(z)} = \left(\sum_{y=z}^{\omega} {_{ix}L_{ii(y)}} + \sum_{j\neq i} {_{ix}L_{ji(y)}} \right) / {_{ix}l_{i(z)}}$$

Here $_{ix}e_{i(z)}$ is the average expected number of years of residence in region i beyond age z for those of age x and residing in i; $_{ix}L_{ii(y)}$ the total number of

TABLE 6.2

Age x	$S_{ii}(x)$	$D_i(x)$	$S_{ij}(x+1)$	$q_i(x)$ (per 1000)	$p_{ij}(x)$ (per 1000)
0	100,000	3000	2000	30.0	20.0
1	95,000	500	2500	5.3	26.3
2	92,000	200	2800	2.2	30.4
3	89,000				

Age x	$S_{jj}(x)$	$D_j(x)$	$S_{ji}(x+1)$	$q_j(x)$ (per 1000)	$p_{ji}(x)$ (per 1000)
0	100,000	3500	1000	35.0	10.0
1	95,500	500	1000	5.2	10.5
2	94,000	200	1800	2.1	19.1
3	92,000				

person-years lived in region i by individuals of age y who were in region i at the beginning of the time interval (one year) and who previously were living in region i at age x, i.e., the total number of person-years lived by nonmigrants; $_{ix}L_{ji(y)}$ the total number of person-years lived in region i by individuals of age y who were in region j at the beginning of the time interval (one year), and who previously were living in region i at age x, i.e., the total number of person-years lived by return in-migrants in i; and $_{ix}l_{i(z)}$ the expected number of survivors of age z alive in region i, among the individuals of age x now alive in region i (corresponding to $S_{ii}(x)$ in the table above). Then the average expected remaining lifetime in any region of residence beyond age z ($z \geq x$), for an individual alive at age x in region i, is

$$_{ix}e_{(z)} = {_{ix}e_{i(z)}} + \sum_{j \neq i} {_{ix}e_{j(z)}}$$

By definition, when $z = 0$, one obtains the expectation of life at birth by region of possible future residence, which may be conveniently presented in the form of a matrix. For instance, using imaginary figures for boys born in 1975, we could establish the type of matrix as shown in Table 6.3. In this example, a baby boy born in region A may be expected to live a total of 70 years and 6 months, of which 40 years and 4 months will be spent in his region of birth (not necessarily 40 *subsequent* years), 5 years and 3 months in region B, and so on, while a baby boy born in region B is expected to spend a larger number of years in his region of birth despite a shorter life expectation.

TABLE 6.3

Region of birth	Region of residence					Total
	A	B	C	$\cdots$	N	
A	40.33	5.25	3.70	$\cdots$	0.4	70.5
B	7.10	45.35	1.25	$\cdots$		69.2
C	$\vdots$	$\vdots$	$\vdots$		$\vdots$	71.3
$\vdots$						$\vdots$
N						

By doing these calculations of q_j, p_{ij}, and e_i for each age $(0, \ldots, \omega)$ and for each region $(i, j = 1, \ldots, N)$, one obtains what may be called the *multiregional multiple-decrement* life table.[27]

6.5.3. Cohort Analysis: Intensity and Tempo

6.5.3.1. Direct Estimation. Migration is a renewable phenomenon: the same individual may migrate many times during his lifetime, but the duration of residence in each successive place of residence is not necessarily equal. In this respect we are faced with the same problems as in the case of births; actually, many measures of intensity and tempo used in the analysis of natality may be applied by analogy to migration. However, in most cases, a direct analysis of the intensity and the tempo of migrations by cohort is impossible, owing to a lack of data. Longitudinal data revealing the whole migration history from birth to death for different cohorts of a population are extremely rare. The optimal method of obtaining this kind of data would be to use a permanent population register, wherein each change of residence made by every person residing in the territory is registered in a personal register so that the whole sequence of migrations of this person may appear. But only a very few countries do apply or intend to apply this system so that the only other direct sources of longitudinal data are the census and the survey with their inherent limitations, particularly the nonavailability of the migration history of deceased migrants and international emigrants. In a census questionnaire, asking each resident of the country to give his complete migration history seems, however, difficult, very costly, and even

---

[27]For a more detailed presentation of the multiregional life table, see Rogers (1973a, b, 1975).

TABLE 6.4

	Yearly "rate" of migration by age group (in 0/00)			
Birth-cohorts	15–19	20–24 $\cdots$ 45–49	50–54 $\cdots$ 75 and more	
1900–1904 1905–1909	$a_k(17.5)$	$a_k(22.5) \cdots a_k(47.5)$	$a_k(52.5) \cdots a_k(75+)$	

	Average number of migrations made between the age of 15 and	
Birth-cohorts	50	death
1900–1904 1905–1909	$_{15-49}\mu_k = 5 \sum\limits_{x=17.5}^{47.5} a_k(x)$	$_{15-\omega}\mu_k = 5 \sum\limits_{x=17.5}^{75+} a_k(x)$

unnecessary, so that most longitudinal data used in the analysis of the intensity and the tempo of migration come from surveys.

Let us assume that we have obtained, from each individual in a representative sample of the population, correct answers concerning age (at the moment of the survey), set of successive places of residence, and duration of residence in each subsequent residence. This information allows us to compute the following measures, if the conditions of independence and continuity are satisfied (Section 1.3.2.3):

1. The age-specific yearly migration "rate" for migrations of the first order (i.e., the first migration in the life of the individual[28]) for each birth-cohort; this is obtained by relating the number of first-order migrations at each age, to the number of persons observed in the cohort.

2. By summing for a given cohort these age-specific yearly "rates" of first-order migration over all ages, one obtains the average number of first-order migrations per head.

3. The same calculations may be made for migrations of the 2nd order, 3rd order, . . . , nth order, so that by summing from age x to age z for a given cohort, the yearly "rates" of 1st-, 2nd-, . . . , nth-order migration, one obtains the average number of migrations made between ages x and z by the members of this cohort. For instance, see Table 6.4, where $a_k(x)$ is obtained

---

[28]It seems reasonable, however, to consider only the first migration after some defined age, for instance, 15 or 18 years old, because migrations made before that age usually reflect the spatial mobility of the parents.

TABLE 6.5

Birth-cohorts	Number of migrations									Total
	0	1	2	3	4	5	$\cdots$	9	10 and more	
1900–1904	200	300	150	100	80	50	$\cdots$	15	10	1000
$\vdots$	$\vdots$	$\vdots$	$\vdots$	$\vdots$	$\vdots$	$\vdots$	$\vdots$	$\vdots$	$\vdots$	$\vdots$

by summing the yearly "rates" of 1st-, 2nd-, ..., nth-order migration, for the members of cohort k of average age x. $_{\alpha\beta}\mu_k$ represents the average number of migrations made between ages α and β by members of cohort k, and is obtained by summing over age groups α to β, the yearly "rates" of migration (of any order), each of these "rates" having been multiplied by the number of years in the age group (in our case, five years).

4. The conditional probability that a member of a given cohort makes a migration of the nth order, given that he already has made $n - 1$ migrations, is obtained by relating the percentage of members of the cohort who have made at least n migrations to the total number of members of the cohort who have made at least $n - 1$ migrations (Section 1.2.3). For instance, if we have data as in Table 6.5 then the probability h_{n-1} of making a migration of order n given that one has made already $n - 1$ migrations is, for $n = 1, \ldots, 10$,

$$h_0 = 0.800 \qquad h_3 = 0.714$$

$$h_1 = 0.625 \qquad h_4 = 0.680$$

$$h_2 = 0.700 \qquad h_5 = 0.400$$

5. One way to characterize the tempo of migrations for each birth-cohort is to calculate the average age at each migration of order n. This, however, raises a problem. Indeed, contrary to births, where the end of the reproductive period of a woman is reached at the age of about 45 years, one may migrate until the last day of life, so that in order to know the final number of migrations for a given cohort one should wait until this cohort is dead; but when the cohort is dead it cannot be reached through a survey or a census! This leads to the conclusion that the mean age for each order of migration obtained by survey or census, is usually underestimated. One way to present this kind of information is shown in Table 6.6.

6.5.3.2. Indirect Estimation. As we mentioned before, longitudinal data of migration are very rare. Some methods, however, have been proposed where period data are used in order to estimate the migratory behavior of a cohort, following the "fictitious cohort" approach (Section 2.3.1); see example, Section 6.8.4.

Let us assume that we know, either by a population register or by a census, the number of migrations between municipalities made over a one-year period by the persons of age x residing in region i. The following formula allows us to estimate the expected number of migrations to be made in the n forthcoming years by an individual who is presently x years old:

$$_{x,x+n}\hat{\mu}_i = \frac{\sum\limits_{x}^{x+n} [r_{E(i)}(x)L_i(x)]}{l_i(x)} = \frac{\sum\limits_{x}^{x+n} \hat{v}_i(x)}{l_i(x)}$$

where $r_{E(i)}(x)$ is the yearly migration rate of age x (or of age group $x+h$, where h is the number of years in the age group); $L_i(x)$ the number of person-years lived in region i by those having age x in the stationary population; $l_i(x)$ the number of survivors at the beginning of the age interval x, among 100,000 life births; and $\hat{v}_i(x)$ the total expected number of migrations made during age interval x by all individuals of age x. Table 6.7 illustrates this procedure with imaginary data. It follows from this hypothetical example (see also Section 6.8.4) that, if the migration "rate" presently observed for each age group remains constant over time, the average individual of age 0 to 4 presently residing in region i may be expected to change at least 13 times his municipality of residence during the rest of his life, but, by the time he has reached the ages of 15–19, he is expected to have made already 5 of these 13 moves.

The main advantage of this approach, which was first applied by Wilber (1963, see also Long, 1973), is that it controls for mortality by standardizing through the surviving population. But, on the other hand, by using period data one actually assumes that the "behavior" (for mortality as well as for

TABLE 6.6

Final number of migrations	1	2		3			4			
Migration order	1	1	2	1	2	3	1	2	3	4
Mean age at migration for birth-cohort: 1900–1904 1905–1909 : ·										

TABLE 6.7

Age group	(1) $P_i(x)$, population (in 1000)	(2) $M_i(x)$, number of migrants over one year (in 1000)	(3) $r_i(x)$, migration rate = (2)/(1)	(4) $l_i(x)$ survivors	(5) $L_i(x)$ person–years lived	(6) $\hat{v}_i(x) = $ (3)·(5)	(7) $\sum\limits_{x}^{\omega} \hat{v}_i$	(8) $\hat{\mu}_i(x) = $ (7)/(4)
0–4	16,000	4,000	0.25	98,000	380,000	95,000	1,250,000	12.76
5–9				97,000		200,000	1,155,000	11.91
10–14				95,000		150,000	955,000	10.05
15–19				94,000		—	805,000	8.56
⋯				⋯		⋯	⋯	⋯
75 and over			0.05	56,000	450,000	22,500	22,500	0.40
Total	—	—	—	—	—	1,250,000	—	—

migration) presently observed for individuals of age $x + n$, will still be valid n years from now for those individuals who were of age x when the data were collected. Correlatively the migration "rates" at different ages are assumed to be independent from each other for the same individual: future migration does not depend on past migration (on the duration of residence in the present place of residence, for instance). In other words, the expected number of migrations to be made by the average individual will be under-estimated if, on an individual basis, there is a positive correlation between the migration "rates" at subsequent ages. This kind of limitation is obviously inherent in any method trying to estimate a longitudinal phenomenon with only the help of period data. Often, we do not even have period data on migration flows, particularly in the case of historical studies, so that we have to rely on estimates of net migration by age obtained for the various intercensal periods, for instance, by applying one of the methods analyzed in Section 6.4.3. Let us thus assume that we have successive net migration "rates" by age group for intercensal periods, these "rates" having been obtained by dividing the sum of age-specific net gains through interregional migration (over all regions that had such gains in the specified age group) by the arithmetic mean of the initial and final population residing in the whole country, i.e.,

$$r_{E(i)}(x) = \frac{\sum_i \left[\sum_j M_{ji}(x) - \sum_j M_{ij}(x) \right]}{\frac{1}{2}\left[\sum_k P_{k(t)}(x) + \sum_k P_{k(t+n)}(x+n) \right]}$$

for all i such that $\sum_j M_{ji}(x) > \sum_j M_{ij}(x)$.

Since migration "rates" are usually estimated for five-year age groups, while intercensal periods usually cover ten years, we have two five-year cohorts entering in each decade: for instance, one cohort reaching ages 10–14 at the end of each intercensal decade, and another cohort reaching ages 15–19 at the end of the same decade. In other words, some cohorts will be observed at subsequent decennal intervals when their members reach ages 10–14, 20–24, 30–34, . . . , 70–74, and other cohorts will be observed at "odd" ages, i.e., when their members reach ages 15–19, 25–29, 35–39, 75–79. This method of presenting intercensal migration "rates" by age group may provide some indications relative to the tempo of migration (here approached through temporal distribution of net migration "rates" at different ages of the cohort), and these tempos of migration may then be compared from one cohort to another.[29]

---

[29]This approach was applied by Eldridge (1964).

In interpreting the results obtained by this method, it should be remembered that the "rates" used are "rates" of *net migration*. A net migrant does not exist, he has no propensity to migrate, he does not take migration decisions, he does not defer a migration until conditions are more favorable. Net migration is a mere concept, and refers to the spatial distribution of population, not to the migration phenomenon as expression of individual behavior.

6.6. SPATIAL ORIENTATION OF MIGRATION

Migration is a bipolar phenomenon: contrary to the other components of demographic growth, it affects two populations, the population of origin and the population of destination. This implies the analysis of the *spatial relation* between the location of these two populations: distance, degree of dispersion over space, and regional preference are three of the most covered fields in this problem.

The problem of finding the mathematical function that gives the best fit for the relation between migration (rate) and distance goes beyond the scope of this chapter.[30] We also will not discuss at length the various measures of concentration or dispersion, which have been proposed in various fields and which could be applied to the problem of measuring the spatial dispersion of migrants (Biraben and Duhourcau, 1974). Only two measures will be presented here. If we want, for instance, to test the hypothesis that out-migrants residing in regions (or cities) that are at the top of the regional (urban) hierarchy, are more likely because of better information, higher income, etc., to disperse more evenly over space than out-migrants from lower-rank regions or cities, we may calculate a Gini *coefficient of concentration* for the out-migration flows of each region of the country, by using the following formula:

$$G_i = \frac{\sum_{j=1}^{n} f_j - (100/n)(1+2+\cdots+n)}{100^2 - (100/n)(1+2+\cdots+n)} \tag{6.42}$$

where G_i is the measure of concentration, which varies from 0 for total (completely uniform) dispersion (i.e., each possible region of destination

[30]On this topic, see for instance, Kulldorff (1955), Bachi (1963), Cavalli Sforza (1963), Morrill (1963), and Olsson (1965). On distance and orientation, see Tarver, Gurley, and Skees (1967).

received an equal number of out-migrants from i) to 1 for total concentration (i.e., all out-migrants from i went to the same region of destination); n the total number of possible regions of destination; and f_j the cumulated relative frequencies in decreasing order of relative frequency (i.e., f_1 is the percentage of migrants in the region of destination which received the highest number of migrants from i, among all out-migrants from i; f_2 is the percentage of migrants in the two regions of destination which received the two highest number of migrants from i; and f_n is thus necessarily equal to 100 percent). The same formula could of course be applied to the n flows of in-migration in region i as well as to the n flows of out-migration from i.

It should be noted, as is clear from Eq. (6.42), that the coefficient is a function of the number of regions of possible destination, and therefore of the degree of territorial subdivision used. This does not prevent comparison of the coefficient between the different regions of a same country (since n remains constant), but implies that international comparisons are highly hazardous.

The Gini coefficient of concentration does not, however, measure the degree of *spatial* concentration: it is only a measure of the degree of interregional dispersion, but space as such is not taken into account. In order to measure the degree of spatial dispersion, one could apply the so-called *coefficient of localization*[31] to migration flows. The procedure of computation is as follows:

1. Compute the percentage of migrants from i going to each region of destination j.

2. Compute the percentage of each region j in the total area of the country (from which the area of region i has previously been subtracted).

3. Subtract (2) from (1) for each region j.

4. Sum the differences between (2) and (1) over all regions j for which this difference is positive. The resulting figure varies between 0, for total spatial dispersion (each region j receiving a percentage of migrants from i, which is equal to its percentage in the total area of the country), to 1 for total spatial concentration. The results will obviously be more meaningful if the smallest possible spatial units are chosen.

These methods of measuring regional and spatial dispersion do not, however, provide an indication on the spatial orientation of migration. One way to measure regional orientation is to calculate a *"preference index"* (Bachi, 1961) for all possible regions of destination for a given region i of

---

[31]See Isard (1960, pp. 251–253); this is an application of the so-called "index of dissimilarity."

origin, in order to answer the question whether migrants from i prefer to move to region h or to region k (see example, Section 6.8.6).

The basic assumption on which the preference index is based, is that if out-migrants from i were indifferent as far as their region of destination is concerned, their choice of their region of destination would correspond to the choice of the average out-migrant of the country; in other words, one considers that regional indifference implies that the attraction power of a particular region of destination is equal for all regions of out-migration, for a given level of out-migration.

By dividing the number of in-migrants in region k through the total number of internal migrants of the country, one obtains what may be called the national (average) propensity to migrate to k, given that one is an out-migrant (from any region $i = 1, \ldots, n$). If one multiplies this national propensity to migrate to k by the total observed number of out-migrants from i, one obtains the number of out-migrants from i who would have migrated to k had these out-migrants from i behaved like the average migrant, i.e., had these out-migrants not shown any particular preference for region k (the preference that will be measured by this approach is thus a relative preference, because it is obtained by referring to the choice made by all internal out-migrants of the country).

The observed number of migrants from i to k will then be compared to this expected number $(\hat{M}_{ik})$ of migrants (expected in the case of indifference): the more their ratio is greater than 1, the more out-migrants from i prefer to migrate to k; the more their ratio is less than 1 the more out-migrants from i are repulsed by k. The formula for computing the preference index of i for k is thus

$$I_{ik} = \frac{M_{ik}}{\hat{M}_{ik}} = \frac{M_{ik}}{\sum_j M_{ij} (\sum_i M_{ik} / \sum_i \sum_j M_{ij})} = \frac{M_{ik} \sum_{\substack{i \neq k}} \sum_j M_{ij}}{\sum_j M_{ij} \sum_i M_{ik}} \tag{6.43}$$

Note that in computing the national propensity to migrate to k, the out-migrants from k have to be subtracted from the total number of internal out-migrants of the country, because out-migrants from k cannot express their preference for the region they are leaving.

By applying formula (6.43) to all possible regions of destination for out-migrants from i, we obtain the *regional preference scale* of these out-migrants. By definition, the sum (over all regions of origin) of the expected number of in-migrants in any given region k $(\sum_i \hat{M}_{ik})$ is equal to the total observed number of in-migrants in region k ($\sum_i M_{ik}$). Also by definition, the sum for any given region k of all positive differences between M_{ik} and $\hat{M}_{ik}$ (i.e., the total of all in-migrants who were not expected in region k but nevertheless preferred to migrate to k) is equal to the sum of all negative differences (i.e., the total of all in-migrants who were expected in region k but who did not migrate to k because they preferred another region).

When the sum (over all regions of origin) of these positive differences between observed and expected number of in-migrants in region k is divided by the total number of internal migrants of the country (out-migrants from k and in-migrants in k being excluded), one obtains the percentage of internal migrants whose arrival in k was not expected, but who nevertheless preferred k above any other region. This may be considered as a measure of the national preference for k, while the index of formula (6.43) provides only the preference for k as expressed by out-migrants from i.

We thus have the *national preference index* for region k:

$$I_k = \frac{\sum\limits_{h=1}^{n} (M_{hk} - \hat{M}_{hk})}{\sum\limits_i \sum\limits_j M_{ij} - \sum\limits_j M_{kj} - \sum\limits_i \hat{M}_{ik}} \qquad \text{for all } h \text{ such that } M_{hk} > \hat{M}_{hk} \qquad (6.44)$$

By applying formula (6.44) to all regions of the country, one obtains the regional preference scale as expressed by all internal migrants of the country, which may be considered as a measure of the regional (urban) hierarchy of this country.

Among the other approaches to regional hierarchy that have been proposed, a promising one seems to be the method based on *graph theory*.[32] Let us consider the $(n \times n)$ matrix of migration probabilities:

$$[p_{ij}] = \left[\frac{M_{ij}}{P_i}\right] \qquad \text{for all } i, j = 1, \ldots, n$$

In order to obtain the regional hierarchy as expressed by these interregional migration flows, one needs a *dominance criterion*, which could, for instance, be formulated as follows: region i dominates region j if $p_{ij} < p_{ji}$, i.e., if a resident from j is more likely to be attracted (through migration) by i than a person residing in i is to be attracted by j. (One could also add to this criterion the restriction that the relative difference between the two probabilities must be larger than some given level, in order to eliminate random

---

[32]See Rouget (1972); the reader not familiar with graph theory may skip this part and continue at Section 6.7.

phenomena.) A dominance relation obtained in this way for the set of all regions is necessarily nonreflexive and asymmetrical, and may be intransitive. If $p_{ij} = p_{ji}$ (or if the relative difference between both probabilities is inferior to some given level, for instance, 10%), the influences between the two regions are symmetrical. And finally, it is possible for certain regions to affect themselves, because of the interplay of internal relations.

For this type of relation, a 2-graph of influence may be constructed as follows: (1) the nodes of the graph are the n regions; (2) dominance of region i over region j is represented by two arcs pointing from i to j; (3) symmetrical influence between two regions i and j is represented by two arcs pointing in opposite directions between i and j; and (4) internal relations within a region are expressed by a ring around the corresponding node.

From this, we compute $_h\prod_k$ the iterated "power" of the hth order for node k (region k) of the 2-graph. This is done as follows, for any given region k

$$_1\prod_k = \sum_{j=1}^{n} a_{kj}$$

where a_{kj} is the number of arcs between k and j

$$a_{kj} = \begin{cases} 2 & \text{if } p_{kj} < p_{jk} \\ 1 & \text{if } p_{kj} = p_{jk} \quad \text{and for } k = j \\ 0 & \text{if } p_{kj} > p_{jk} \end{cases}$$

and $_2\prod_k = \sum_{j=1}^{n} (a_{kj}\ _1\prod_j)$. The iterated power of orders superior to h may be calculated in the same manner, but it is often sufficient to stop the iteration at the second power. The index of dominance may then be expressed as the percentage of the power of order h ($h = 2$ in this case) for region k, in the sum of the powers (of same order h) over all regions, i.e.,

$$\prod_k = \frac{_2\prod_k}{\sum_{\substack{i=1 \\ i=k}}^{n} {_2\prod_i}} \tag{6.45}$$

The same procedure may be applied for studying not only the degree of dominance (i.e., by summing over all regions of destination for a given region of origin), but also the degree of "being dominated" (i.e., by summing over all regions of origin for a given region of destination):

$$_1\overline{\prod}_k = \sum_{i=1}^{n} a_{ik}$$

$$_2\overline{\prod}_k = \sum_{i=1}^{n} (a_{ik} \,_1\overline{\prod}_k)$$

$$\overline{\prod}_k = \frac{_2\overline{\prod}_k}{\sum_{\substack{i=1 \\ i=k}}^{n} {_2\overline{\prod}_i}} \tag{6.46}$$

Note that, by definition, $a_{ik} + a_{ki} = 2$ for all pairs (i, k), and $\sum_i {_h\prod_i} = \sum_i {_h\overline{\prod}_i}$ for all orders h.

The larger the $\prod_k$, the more dominating is k, and the smaller the $\overline{\prod}_k$, the less it is dominated. It should, however, be emphasized that the most dominated regions are not necessarily also the least dominating. It is also conceivable that a region is simultaneously little dominating and little dominated, which could mean that it is independent with respect to the spatial system utilized.

Besides its simplicity, the method offers the advantage of simultaneously taking into account all interrelations (all "roads" in the terminology of graph theory) between regions. Moreover, the level of $_1\prod$ and $_1\overline{\prod}$ has a particularly important meaning in this method of measuring dominance and regional hierarchy; these $_1\prod$ actually represent weights, which are applied to the relation between regions: it is much more significant to dominate a region that itself is highly dominating, than to dominate a region that is little dominating; and similarly, a region has not to be very "proud" to be dominated by a highly dominated region.

The method, however, has some weakness. A certain degree of arbitrariness is introduced in the definition of "dominance": should the p_{ij} be expressed as a percentage of the region of origin's population or a percentage of the total number of migrants from the region of origin (i.e., as conditional probabilities)? Is the mere fact that $p_{ij} < p_{ji}$ a sufficient criterion for saying that i is dominating j? When, in order to eliminate some random phenomena, one adds the restriction that the relative difference between p_{ij} and p_{ji} has to be larger than some given level, how will this level of "significant" domination be determined?

Moreover, it should be emphasized that by using the migration probabilities p_{ij} one actually gives the same importance to each migration flow:

the quantitative importance (i.e., the number of migrants) of the flow is not considered. But, as already mentioned, this is corrected by weighting the flows according to the degree of dominance of the region one is dominating (or by which one is dominated). The method in fact implies that it is not so much the number of migrants involved that is important in defining a regional hierarchy, but rather the hierarchical quality of the dominated (or dominating) region.

6.7. EFFICIENCY OF MIGRATION

After analyzing the intensity and spatial orientation of migration flows, one may want to measure the demographic efficiency of these flows, that is, the relation between the intensity of the phenomenon and the resulting demographic impact.

In order to evaluate the impact of a phenomenon, one may estimate what the situation would have been if the phenomenon had not appeared, and compare, for instance, the observed rate of growth of the region's population with the rate of growth that would have been observed if net migration had been zero.[33] Also, by computing a rate of net migration with the final population as a base, one actually obtains a measure of the impact of migration. And when net migration is related to the total increase of population over the migration interval (i.e., the difference between final and initial population), one obtains the share of migration in the region's population growth. Because of the trend toward decreasing rates of natality in developed countries, this share is increasingly important. Moreover, because of the apparent trend toward equalization of regional rates of natality and mortality, within the same country, migration takes an increasing part in the process of regional redistribution of population.[34]

But these various simple ratios do measure only the impact of migration, they do not measure its *efficiency*. Indeed, a net migration figure, as utilized in these measures, may cover a wide range of migration phenomena: a small migration balance may be the result of large multiway migration flows that neutralize themselves, as well as an expression of people's spatial

---

[33]Note that this refers only to the direct impact, which is a minimum figure, since it does not take into account the *induced effects* of migration, namely, the natural increase due to migration.

[34]The share of migration in a region's population growth obviously also depends on the size of the region: all other things being equal, a small region is more likely to be affected by migration than a large one.

inertia. By relating the result of the phenomenon (that is, the migration balance) to the intensity of the phenomenon (that is, the number of migrations having produced this result), one obtains an estimate of migration efficiency.[35] The inverse of this ratio indicates the number of persons who have to move in order to obtain a regional redistribution of population of one unit: the larger the ratio, the smaller the number of moves required will be.

Migration efficiency may be estimated at three different levels:

1. *Interregional efficiency*, which is measured by

$$E_{ij} = (M_{ji} - M_{ij})/(M_{ji} + M_{ij}) \tag{6.47}$$

2. *Regional efficiency*, that is, the efficiency of migrations between a given region i and the rest of the country, which is measured by

$$E_i = \left(\sum_j M_{ji} - \sum_j M_{ij} \right) \Big/ \left(\sum_j M_{ji} + \sum_j M_{ij} \right) \tag{6.48}$$

3. *National efficiency*, that is, the efficiency of migrations between all regions of the country, which is measured by

$$E = \left[\sum_{\substack{i \\ \Delta > 0}} \left(\sum_j M_{ji} - \sum_j M_{ij} \right) \right] \Big/ \sum_i \sum_j M_{ij} \tag{6.49}$$

In the formula (6.49), only positive migration balances have to be summed at the numerator, because at the national level, the sum of all regional net migration figures equals zero for internal migration.

6.8. EXAMPLES

6.8.1. Direct Estimation of Migration

The Belgian census questionnaire submitted to all residents of Belgium on December 31, 1970, had a question on the previous municipality of residence, coupled with a question on the duration of stay at the present residence (less than one year, more than one year but less than two years, etc.). According to the results, 471,064 Belgian residents had changed their municipality of residence between January 1, 1970 and December 31, 1970, while the Belgian population register (which also covers the whole population residing on the Belgian territory) provides a migration figure of 538,927

[35]See Shryock (1959); an example is given in Section 6.8.6.

for the same period. Besides errors in notification and enumeration, how could this difference be explained?

The larger figure obtained through the population register is to be explained by different factors (Section 6.3): (1) multiple migrations by the same migrant during the period (this factor is probably not important here, since the period is short); (2) death in 1970 of some Belgian residents who had made during that same year 1970 an internal migration between Belgian municipalities; (3) international emigration in 1970 of some Belgian residents who had made during that same year 1970 an internal migration between municipalities.

6.8.2. The Place of Birth Method

Let us assume that, according to the 1960 census, 2000 persons were residing in an hypothetical region Z but were born in another region of the country, while 1000 persons who were born in region Z were enumerated as residents of another region. A census taken 10 years later shows that there are now 3000 persons residing in region Z who were not born in Z, while 2000 natives of Z now reside outside Z. The probability of dying (over the ten-year interval) for all out-migrants from Z (q_O) is 0.10, while the probability of dying for all in-migrants (q_I) is 0.20. How may we estimate region Z's net migration figure for the 1960–1970 period?

If we only compare place of residence to place of birth (Section 6.4.1), without taking into account mortality among migrants, we have

$$\hat{m} = (I_{1970} - O_{1970}) - (I_{1960} - O_{1960})$$

$$= (3000 - 2000) - (2000 - 1000)$$

$$= 0$$

As a first correction for mortality, we have to introduce deaths (during the period) among migrants who were already in region Z or who had already left region Z at the beginning of the period, i.e.,

$$\hat{m} = (I_{1970} - O_{1970}) - [(1 - q_I)I_{1960} - (1 - q_O)O_{1960}]$$

$$= (3000 - 2000) - [(0.8)2000 - (0.9)1000]$$

$$= 300$$

In other words, during the 1960–1970 period, 400 persons who had entered region Z before 1960 died in their region of in-migration, while 100 persons who had left region Z before 1960 died in their new region of residence. This leads to a new estimate of net migration of +300.

But migrants who entered or left region Z during the 1960–1970 period were also subject to the risk of dying. In the absence of any information on the timing of their arrival or departure from region Z, we may assume that they entered or left region Z at midperiod, so that we finally have to revive the cohort of surviving in-migrants and the cohort of surviving out-migrants over a five-year period. This is done by multiplying the figure of these cohorts by the inverse of unity minus half the ten-year probability of dying [see Eq. (6.4)]

$$\hat{m} = \frac{1}{1-(0.5)(0.2)}[3000-(0.8)2000]+\frac{1}{1-(0.5)(0.1)}[(0.9)1000-2000]$$

$$= 1556 - 1158$$

$$= 398$$

In other words, during the 1960–1970 period, there were 156 deaths among the in-migrants of the period and 58 deaths among the out-migrants of the period, so that net migration is now +398, while it is zero when no account is made of mortality among migrants.

6.8.3. The Vital Statistics and Survival Ratio Methods

In order to compare different methods for estimating net migration, let us consider the set of Belgian data in Tables 6.8 through 6.13. These data allow us to apply various direct and indirect methods (Sections 6.4.2 and 6.4.3) for estimating net international migration over the 1948–1961 period.

Tables 6.8 and 6.10 represent the necessary inputs for obtaining the age · structure of net international migration for those already born in 1948, thus having at least 14 years in 1961, while Tables 6.9, 6.11, and 6.12 enable us to calculate net migration for those born during the 1948–1961 period. Five methods were used: formulas (6.9) and (6.10) corresponding to the forward and reverse method, respectively; the average of both these methods; formula (6.13), which provides the true figure of net migration in the case of even distribution of immigration and emigration over the period; and finally, formula (6.13) adjusted for uneven distribution of the migration flows.

TABLE 6.8. Population by Age Group at the 1947 and 1961 Censuses[a]

Age group (completed years)	Enumerated population	
	December 31, 1947	December 31, 1961
0–6	834,420	1,059,309
7–13	797,452	989,390
14–20	901,009	841,394
21–27	969,781	808,280
28–34	710,635	904,906
35–41	911,269	939,951
42–48	912,132	680,156
49–55	773,326	846,834
56–62	630,076	799,531
63–69	518,657	612,850
70–76	—	408,467

[a] Source: *Recensement de la population au 31 décembre 1961*. Bruxelles: Institut National de Statistique, Tome V, Tableau 1.

Table 6.13 indeed allows us to estimate the average number of years spent by immigrants and emigrants (if multiple migration is excluded):

$$\frac{(89,924 \times 13.5) + (31,795 \times 12.5) + \cdots + (36,088 \times 0.5)}{89,924 + 31,795 + \cdots + 36,088} = 7.3 \text{ years}$$

for immigration, and for emigration we obtain a value of 6.7 years, which shows that international immigrants and emigrants spent on the average almost half a period in the country. Actually a value of 0.47 may be accepted

TABLE 6.9. Population by Age between 0 and 13 at the 1961 Census[a]

Age	Population	Age	Population
0	155,183	7	145,248
1	151,693	8	142,938
2	155,028	9	142,915
3	152,386	10	138,541
4	150,504	11	138,808
5	147,813	12	138,800
6	146,702	13	142,140

[a] Source: *Recensement de la population au 31 décembre 1961*. Bruxelles: Institut National de Statistique, Tome V, Tableau 1.

TABLE 6.10. Probability of Dying between January 1, 1948 and December 31, 1961 by Age Group[a]

Age group (age at beginning of the period, in years)	Probability
0–6	0.01482
7–13	0.01575
14–20	0.02352
21–27	0.02949
28–34	0.04192
35–41	0.07092
42–48	0.12513
49–55	0.21724
56–62	0.36553

[a]Source: Institut National de Statistique, Bruxelles; and Wissocq, B. *L'Evaluation des Soldes Migratoires par la Méthode de la Population Attendue.* B.A. thesis, Louvain, 1971, Appendix 2.

as a good approximation for both immigrants and emigrants, so that instead of using 0.5 in formula (6.13), we should use 0.47.

Results of each of these five methods are given in Table 6.14. As expected the difference between estimates is the smallest for the age groups

TABLE 6.11. Yearly Number of Births and Deaths in Belgium between 1948 and 1961[a]

Year	Births	Deaths
1948	150,416	108,016
1949	147,854	111,104
1950	145,672	108,236
1951	142,314	109,763
1952	146,064	104,178
1953	146,125	105,863
1954	148,538	105,033
1955	149,195	108,743
1956	150,210	108,761
1957	152,871	107,840
1958	155,048	106,051
1959	159,237	103,933
1960	154,784	113,938
1961	158,431	106,985
Total 1948–1961	2,105,759	1,508,444

[a]Source: *Annuaire Statistique de la Belgique*, Tome 83, Année 1962, p. 60.

TABLE 6.12. Probability of Dying Before December 31, 1961 for the
1948–1961 Birth-Cohorts[a]

Birth-cohort	Age at 1961 census (in completed years)	Probability of dying before December 31, 1961
1948	13	0.052114
1949	12	0.051535
1950	11	0.050989
1951	10	0.050414
1952	9	0.049839
1953	8	0.049234
1954	7	0.048558
1955	6	0.047796
1956	5	0.046938
1957	4	0.045917
1958	3	0.044712
1959	2	0.043252
1960	1	0.040799
1961	0	0.019585

[a] Source: Institut National de Statistique, Bruxelles; and Wissocq, B. *L'Evaluation des Soldes Migratoires par la Méthode de la Population Attendue.* B.A. thesis, Louvain, 1971, Appendix 2.

TABLE 6.13. International Migration Data,
1948–1961

Year	Immigration	Emigration
1948	89,924	45,486
1949	31,795	44,041
1950	21,922	36,509
1951	59,954	43,027
1952	52,150	38,845
1953	39,964	38,109
1954	34,604	34,085
1955	51,106	32,757
1956	52,593	36,696
1957	68,794	36,621
1958	47,124	40,297
1959	32,315	35,229
1960	42,248	32,189
1961	36,088	35,517
Total 1948–1961	666,581	529,408

[a] Source: *Annuaire Statistique de la Belgique*, Tome 83, Année 1962, p. 81.

TABLE 6.14. Age Structure of Net International Migration for Belgium, 1948–1961[a]

Age group (age on December 31, 1961)	Forward [formula (6.9)]	Reverse [formula (6.10)]	Average $\frac{(6.9)+(6.10)}{2}$	Formula (6.13)	Formula (6.13) adjusted
			Method used		
0–6	24,930	26,111	25,520	25,508	25,470
7–13	14,156	14,888	14,522	14,514	14,492
14–20	19,340	19,631	19,485	19,475	19,476
21–27	23,388	23,762	23,575	23,573	23,562
28–34	25,089	25,693	25,391	25,388	25,369
35–41	−1,231	−1,269	−1,250	−1,249	−1,248
42–48	−689	−720	−705	−704	−703
49–55	192	207	200	199	199
56–62	1,534	1,753	1,644	1,636	1,630
63–69	7,521	9,609	8,565	8,438	8,376
70–76	8,703	13,716	11,210	10,649	10,508
Total 0–76	122,933	133,381	128,157	127,427	127,131

[a] Source: Institut National de Statistique, Bruxelles; and Wissocq, B. *L'Evaluation des Soldes Migratoires par la Méthode de la Population Attendue.* B.A. thesis, Louvain, 1971, Appendix 2.

with a low probability of dying, and the average method provides estimates that are close to those obtained by assuming even temporal distribution of migration flows.

Another indirect method gives us the possibility of estimating the total (i.e., all ages) net migration figure: indeed, the data of Table 6.11 on births and deaths allow us to apply the vital statistics method (Section 6.4.2). By applying formula (6.6), one obtains

$$m = (9,189,741) - (8,512,195) - (2,105,759) + (1,508,444)$$

$$= 80,231$$

Finally, a seventh estimate of total net migration may be obtained directly by using the data on international migration flows as entered in the population register (Table 6.13):

$$m = 666,581 - 529,408$$

$$= 137,173$$

The difference between the latter figure and the 127,131 figure obtained by formula (6.13), adjusted for uneven distribution, is explained mainly by the fact that the population register figure concerns all ages, while formula (6.13) has not been applied to ages above 76 (in 1961), and by the consideration that many immigrants and probably even more emigrants do not register their entry or departure from the country.

The most puzzling result is the one obtained by the vital statistics method, which also concerns all ages, but which provides a net migration figure representing only 58% of the all-ages figure derived from the population register! One should expect that births and deaths are much more accurately recorded than migrations, but a distinction should be made between *de facto* births and deaths (all births and deaths that occurred on the national territory) and *de jure* births and deaths (those births and deaths that occurred to persons registered in the population register); the difference between *de facto* and *de jure* events is, however, relatively small and is for the largest part neutralized by the fact that deaths are subtracted from births, so that it seems difficult to explain the difference of 56,942 units (137,173 − 80,231) only by this legal distinction. There remains, of course, the problem of uncorrect enumeration in the 1947 and 1961 censuses, but this problem also arises when the other methods are applied.

6.8.4. Intensity of Migration: Rates and Expected Numbers

Let us consider Tables 6.15 through 6.17, derived from the 1971 Canadian census. The data of Tables 6.15 and 6.16 allow us to calculate the rate of migration (Section 6.5.1) between the 1599 municipalities of the

TABLE 6.15. Number of Male Migrants Surviving at Different Ages in 1971[a,b]

Age group (in years)	Number of migrants (males)
15–19	33,145
20–24	52,530
25–29	64,895
30–34	44,065

[a]Source: *1971 Census of Canada*, Vol. 1, No. 5, Table 13, pp. 14–17. Catalogue No. 92-745, Ottawa, November 1974.
[b]Persons of province of Quebec and whose municipality of residence in 1966 was different from the municipality of residence in 1971, but located in the same province.

TABLE 6.16. Population at Different Ages in 1966 and 1971 in the Province of Quebec

Age group (in years)	Enumerated male population	
	1966	1971
15–19	284,079	315,225
20–24	234,230	271,845
25–29	188,884	239,725
30–34	186,412	190,185

Source: *Statistics Canada*, Ottawa, 1971 Census, Catalogue No. 92-715, Vol. 1, part 2 (Bulletin 1.2–3), Table 7, p. 7-5.

TABLE 6.17. Number of Survivors (l_x) and Years Lived $(_5L_x)$ According to the 1970–1972 Life Table of the Province of Quebec by Age Group

Age group (in years)	l_x	$_5L_x$
15–19	96,943	482,957
20–24	96,240	478,797
25–29	95,279	474,557
30–34	94,544	470,642

province of Quebec for the 1966–1971 period, by age group. Since the rate of increase of population in the different age groups is less than 35%, we may obtain a good estimate of the population at risk by using the arithmetic mean of the initial and final population as base in the calculation of the migration rate. Since $_5L_x$ represents the number of years lived in the stationary population, we will have to divide by five the rate of migration over the five-year period 1966–1971 if we wish to obtain an estimate of the yearly rate of internal migration (see Table 6.18).

We are now in a position to compute the expected number of migrations, which will be made before reaching the age of 35 by the average resident of the province of Quebec (Table 6.19); this is obtained by applying the formula proposed by Wilber (see Section 6.5.3.2).

It appears from these results that, if the conditions of mortality and migration prevailing in the 1966–1971 period were to remain similar in the 20 years thereafter, we could expect that out of 100 male residents of the province of Quebec aged between 15 and 19 years 84 will have changed

TABLE 6.18. Rate of Internal Migration by Age Group for Males, Quebec 1966–1971

Age group (in years)	Base population	Yearly rate (%) $\frac{1}{5}$ (Table 6.15/base)
15–19	299,652	2.2122
20–24	253,038	4.1519
25–29	214,305	6.0563
30–34	188,299	4.6803

TABLE 6.19. Average Expected Number of Migrations

Age group (in years)	Total expected number of migrations in the age group (rate) $\cdot ({}_5L_x) = \hat{v}_x$	Total expected number of migrations made before age 35, $\hat{M}_x$	Average number of migrations, $\hat{\mu}_x / l_x$
15–19	10,684	81,331	0.84
20–24	19,879	70,647	0.73
25–29	28,741	50,768	0.53
30–34	22,027	22,027	0.23
Total	81,331		

their municipality of residence before reaching the age of 35, while if they are aged between 25 and 29, one out of two will have migrated before the age of 35. In order to interpret these relatively low figures, it should be emphasized that municipalities in the province of Quebec are rather large, and that only migrations between municipalities of the province were considered.

6.8.5. Intensity of Migration: Rank of Migration

In Table 6.20, the Canadian population is classified according to the number of intermunicipal migrations made between 1966 and 1971. These data allow us to calculate the probability of making during the period 1966–1971 a migration of rank n, given that one has already made a migration of rank $n-1$ during the same period, as in Section 6.5.3 (Table 6.21).

It thus appears that one-quarter of the Canadian population of five years and over had made at least one migration between municipalities

TABLE 6.20. Number of Intermunicipal Migrations Canada 1966–1971[a]

Age group (in years)	Sex	Population	Number of migrations					
			0	1	2	3	4	5 or more
5 and over	M	9,855,545	7,447,445	1,228,590	588,250	278,125	120,645	192,495
	F	9,861,660	7,450,435	1,280,975	597,675	274,815	113,180	144,585
	Total	19,717,205	14,897,880	2,509,565	1,185,920	552,940	233,820	337,075
20–24	M	940,770	602,370	129,995	76,840	46,275	25,725	59,560
	F	941,040	511,450	177,505	108,110	61,990	31,480	50,505
	Total	1,881,805	1,113,820	307,500	184,950	108,265	57,200	110,070
25–29	M	799,470	428,795	138,575	98,450	56,405	28,520	48,725
	F	780,025	432,395	148,250	96,520	51,870	23,440	27,550
	Total	1,579,495	861,190	286,825	194,970	108,270	51,960	76,270

[a]Source: *Statistics Canada, 1971 Census*, Vol. 1, Catalogue 92-745, Part 5, Bulletin 1.5–5, November 1974, Table 18, pp. 1–2.

TABLE 6.21. Probability of Making a Migration of Rank n

Age group (in years)	Sex	Rank of migration					
		0	1	2	3	4	5 or more
5 and over	M	0.76	0.24	0.49	0.50	0.53	0.62
	F	0.76	0.24	0.47	0.47	0.48	0.56
	Total	0.76	0.24	0.48	0.49	0.51	0.59
20–24	M	0.64	0.36	0.62	0.63	0.65	0.70
	F	0.54	0.46	0.59	0.57	0.57	0.62
	Total	0.59	0.41	0.60	0.60	0.61	0.66
25–29	M	0.54	0.46	0.63	0.58	0.58	0.63
	F	0.55	0.45	0.57	0.52	0.50	0.54
	Total	0.55	0.45	0.60	0.55	0.54	0.59

during the 1966–1971 period. But once a migration has been made, the probability is twice as large (0.48 vs. 0.24) to make a second migration, the probability of making a migration of rank n increasing when n increases: the more migrations one has already made, the more likely one is to migrate again during the same period. The population aged 25–29 has a "propensity" to make at least one migration, which is twice the propensity shown by the total population.

The probability of making a migration of a given rank is a little higher for males than for females, except at the age group 20–24, for which the probability to make a first migration is significantly larger for females (0.46 vs. 0.36); this is probably explained for the most part by nuptiality, women often moving to the residence of their husband.

6.8.6. Spatial Orientation and Efficiency

Table 6.22 presents the 1971 migration flows between and within the three linguistic regions of Belgium: the Dutch-speaking Flemish region (F), the French-speaking Walloon region (W), and the bilingual region of Brussels (B).

These data allow us to calculate migration rates, regional preference indexes, and efficiency rates. Since the migration interval is short (one year) it seems reasonable to consider that only the population residing in the region at the beginning of the interval was at risk of out-migrating, so that the population enumerated at the census on December 31, 1970 will be used

TABLE 6.22. Interregional Migration Flows, Belgium 1971[a]

From/To	F	W	B	Total number of out-migrations in 1971	Enumerated population on December 31, 1970
F	202,888 (65,481)[b]	7,146	12,809	19,955	5,478,555
W	7,111	169,981 (49,304)[b]	12,215	19,326	3,097,253
B	19,035	14,178	63,913	33,213	1,075,136
Total number of in-migrations in 1971	26,146	21,324	25,024	72,494	9,650,944

[a]Source: Institut National de Statistique, Bruxelles.
[b]The figure between parentheses, on the diagonal refer to the number of migrations between the *arrondisse-ments* (22 in the Flemish region, 20 in the Walloon region) of the region, while the other figures on the diagonal refer to the total number of migrations between all the municipalities of the region. The Brussels region is constituted of only one "arrondissement."

as a base population in computing rates of out-migration. We thus obtain Table 6.23.

It appears that out of 1000 residents of the Flemish region, 40 changed their municipality of residence during the year 1971, 25 of them having made a short-distance move (between municipalities of their arrondisse-ment of residence), 12 having made a medium-distance move (from one arrondissement to another in the same linguistic region), while only 3 left for

TABLE 6.23. Rates of Out-Migration by Linguistic Region, Belgium 1971 (in ‰)

From/To	Interregional migration				Intraregional migration			Total migration between municipalities
	F	W	B	Total	Between arrondisse-ments of the region	Between municipalities of same arrondissement	Total	
F	—	1.30	2.34	3.64	11.95	25.08	37.03	40.67
W	2.30	—	3.94	6.24	15.92	38.96	54.88	61.12
B	17.70	13.19	—	30.89	—	59.45	59.45	90.34

another linguistic region (2 of these going to Brussels). The residents of the Walloon region show a "propensity" to move, which is about 50% higher than the one expressed by the Flemish, and this is valid for every type of migration. The out-migration rates of the Brussels region are not comparable since it has a much smaller area than the other two regions; note, however, the high rate of short-distance migration (out of 100 inhabitants, 9 have changed their municipality of residence over the year, 6 of them for a short-distance move).

As a matter of exercise, we now calculate the index of *regional preference* (Section 6.6) for each of the 6 interregional migration flows. Applying formula (6.43), we obtain

$$I_{FW} = \frac{(7,146)(72,494 - 19,326)}{(19,955)(21,324)} = 0.89$$

with

$$M_{FW} - \hat{M}_{FW} = (7,146) - (19,955)\left(\frac{21,324}{72,494 - 19,326}\right)$$

$$= 7,146 - 8,003$$

$$= -857$$

$$I_{FB} = \frac{(12,809)(72,494 - 33,213)}{(19,955)(25,024)} = 1.01$$

with

$$M_{FB} - \hat{M}_{FB} = (12,809) - (19,955)\left(\frac{25,024}{72,494 - 33,213}\right)$$

$$= 12,809 - 12,712$$

$$= 97$$

$$I_{WF} = \frac{(7,111)(72,494 - 19,955)}{(19,326)(26,146)} = 0.74$$

with

$$M_{WF} - \hat{M}_{WF} = (7,111) - (19,326)\left(\frac{26,146}{72,494 - 19,955}\right)$$

$$= 7,111 - 9,618$$

$$= -2,507$$

$$I_{WB} = \frac{(12,215)(72,494 - 33,213)}{(19,326)(25,024)} = 0.99$$

with

$$M_{\text{WB}} - \hat{M}_{\text{WB}} = (12{,}215) - (19{,}326)\left(\frac{25{,}024}{72{,}494 - 33{,}123}\right)$$

$$= 12{,}215 - 12{,}312$$

$$= -97$$

$$I_{\text{BF}} = \frac{(19{,}035)(72{,}494 - 19{,}955)}{(33{,}213)(26{,}146)} = 1.15$$

with

$$M_{\text{BF}} - \hat{M}_{\text{BF}} = (19{,}035) - (33{,}213)\left(\frac{26{,}146}{72{,}494 - 19{,}955}\right)$$

$$= 19{,}035 - 16{,}528$$

$$= 2{,}507$$

$$I_{\text{BW}} = \frac{(14{,}178)(72{,}494 - 19{,}326)}{(33{,}213)(21{,}324)} = 1.06$$

with

$$M_{\text{BW}} - \hat{M}_{\text{BW}} = (14{,}178) - (33{,}213)\left(\frac{21{,}324}{72{,}494 - 19{,}326}\right)$$

$$= 14{,}178 - 13{,}321$$

$$= 857$$

The results show that the Flemish as well as the Walloons prefer to migrate to Brussels above the other linguistic region, while the residents of Brussels (who are for the largest part French speaking) prefer to migrate to the Flemish region. As required, the number of the unexpected in-migrants in each region (97 for Brussels, coming from Flanders; 2507 for Flanders, coming from Brussels; and 857 for Walloony, coming also from Brussels) is equal to the number of in-migrants who did not show up (97 were expected in Brussels, coming from Walloony, but they preferred another region; 2507 were expected to migrate from Walloony to Flanders, but they did not; and 857 were expected to go from Flanders to Walloony, but they went instead to another region).

The *national preference* index for each of the three regions may now be computed using the results just obtained; applying formula (6.44), we obtain

$$I_F = \frac{2,507}{72,494 - 19,955 - 26,146} = 0.095$$

$$I_W = \frac{857}{72,494 - 19,326 - 19,035} = 0.025$$

$$I_B = \frac{97}{72,494 - 33,213 - 25,024} = 0.007$$

The Flemish region appears to be by far the most preferred region, followed by the Walloon region and the Brussels region. It should be noted in this respect that the Flemish region was the principal gainer from the interregional migration flows (with $\frac{3}{4}$ of the total gains), while Brussels was the only one of the three linguistic regions to have a negative net migration.

Finally, we compute the various rates of *migration efficiency* (Section 6.7) (in %):

1. Interregional efficiency [formula (6.47)]:

$$E_{WF} = 0.25$$

$$E_{FB} = 19.55$$

$$E_{WB} = 7.44$$

2. Regional efficiency [formula (6.48)]:

$$E_F = 13.43$$

$$E_W = 4.92$$

$$E_B = -14.06$$

3. National efficiency [formula (6.49)]:

$$E = \frac{8,189}{72,494} = 11.30$$

It thus appears that migration flows regarding Brussels are the most efficient (14.06), particularly between Brussels and the Flemish region (19.55); for every 100 migrants moving between Brussels and the rest of the country, Brussels loses 14 inhabitants. Migration efficiency between the Flemish region and the rest of the country is slightly lower: for every 100 migrants moving in both directions between Flanders and the rest of Belgium,

Flanders gains 13 inhabitants. The overall efficiency for the whole of Belgium is just above 10%: for any 100 persons migrating (in any direction) between any of the three linguistic regions, there is a net regional redistribution of population of only 11 persons.

6.9. REFERENCES AND SUPPLEMENTARY BIBLIOGRAPHY

Bachi, R. Some methods for the study of geographical distributions of internal migration. Paper delivered at the International Population Conference, New York, 1961.

Bachi, R. Standard distance measures and related methods for spatial analysis. *Papers of the Regional Science Association* (Vol. X). Philadelphia: Regional Science Research Institute, 1963, pp. 83–132.

Biraben, J. N., & Duhourcau, F. La mesure de la population dans l'espace. *Population*, 1974, *29*(1), 113–136.

Cavalli Sforza, L. The distribution of migration distance. In J. Sutter (Ed.), *Human Displacements Measurement. Methodological Aspects.* Paris: Hachette, 1963, pp. 139–158.

Courgeau, D. Migrants et migrations. *Population*, 1973a, *28*(1), 95–129.

Courgeau, D. Migrations et découpages du territoire. *Population*, 1973b, *28*(3), 511–537.

Dionne, C. Estimation des soldes migratoires par la comparaison de deux recensements, *Recherches Economiques de Louvain*, 1970, *36*(4), 309–340.

Eldridge, H. T. A cohort approach to the analysis of migration differentials. *Demography*, 1964, *1*, 214–219.

Eldridge, H. T. Primary, secondary and return migration in the United States, 1950–1960, *Demography*, 1965, *2*, 444–455.

Haenszel, W. Concept, measurement and data in migration analysis. *Demography*, 1967, *4*(1), 253–261.

Hamilton, C. H. Practical and mathematical considerations in the formulation and selection of migration rates. *Demography*, 1965, *2*, 429–443.

Hamilton, C. H. Effect of census errors on the measurement of net migration. *Demography*, 1966, *3*(2), 393–415.

Hamilton, C. H. The vital statistics method of estimating net migration by age cohorts. *Demography*, 1967, *4*(2), 464–478.

Isard, W. *Methods of Regional Analysis.* Cambridge: MIT University Press, 1960.

Kulldorff, G. Migration probabilities. *Lund Studies in Geography* No. 14, 1955.

Long, L. H. New estimates of migration expectancy in the United States. *Journal of the American Statistical Association*, 1973, *68*, 37–48.

Morrill, R. L. The distribution of migration distances. *Papers of the Regional Science Association*, 1963, *XI*, 75–84.

Olsson, G. *Distance and Human Interaction. A Review and Bibliography.* Philadelphia: Regional Science Research Institute, 1965.

Pourcher, G. Un essai d'analyse par cohorte de la mobilité géographique et professionnelle, *Population*, 1965, *21*(2), 357–378.

Pressat, R. L'attraction dans les migrations intérieures. *Bulletin de l'Institut International de Statistique*, 1963, *40*(1), 450–456.

Rees, P. H., & Wilson, A. G. Accounts and models for spatial demographic analysis. *Environment and Planning*, 1973, *5*(1), 61–90 (Part I), 1974, *6*(1), 101–116 (Part II).

Rogers, A. The mathematics of multiregional demographic growth. *Environment and Planning*, 1973a, *5*(1), 3–29.

Rogers, A. The multiregional life table. *The Journal of Mathematical Sociology*, 1973b, *3*, 127–137.

Rogers, A. *Introduction to Multiregional Mathematical Demography*. New York: Wiley-Interscience, 1975.

Rouget, B. Graph theory and hierarchisation models. *Regional and Urban Economics*, 1972, *2*(3), 263–295.

Shryock, H. S. The efficiency of internal migration in the United States. *Proceedings of the International Population Conference*, Vienna, 1959, pp. 685–694.

Siegel, J. S., & Hamilton, C. H. Some considerations on the use of the residual method of estimating net migration. *Journal of the American Statistical Association*, 1962, *47*, 475–500.

Sly, D. F. Evaluating estimates of net migration and net migration rates based on survival ratios corrected in varying degrees. *Journal of the American Statistical Association*, 1972, *67*, 313–318.

Stone, L. O. Evaluating the relative accuracy and significance of net migration estimates. *Demography*, 1967, *4*(1), 310–330.

Tarver, J. D. Evaluation of census survival rates in estimating intercensal state net migration. *Journal of the American Statistical Association*, 1962, *47*, 841–862.

Tarver, J., Gurley, W. R., & Skees, P. Vector representation of migration streams among selected state economic areas during 1955 to 1960, *Demography*, 1967, *4*(1), 1–18.

Termote, M. Les modèles de migration: Une perspective d'ensemble, *Recherches Economiques de Louvain*, 1967, *53*(4), 413–444.

Termote, M. The Measurement of Commuting. In S. Goldstein and D. F. Sly (Eds.), *The Measurement of Urbanization and Projection of Urban Population*. Liège (Belgium): International Union for the Scientific Study of Population, 1975, pp. 211–224.

Thomlinson, R. A model for migration analysis. *Journal of the American Statistical Association*, 1961, *56*, 675–686.

Thomlinson, R. The determination of a base population for computing migration rates. *The Milbank Memorial Fund Quarterly*, 1962, *40*(3), 356–366.

Thornthwaite, C. W. *Internal Migration in the United States*, University of Pennsylvania Press, 1934.

Tugault, Y. Méthode d'analyse d'un tableau "origine-destination" des migrations. *Population*, 1970, *25*(1), 59–68.

United Nations. *Methods of measuring internal migration*, Population Studies No. 47, 1970.

Wilber, G. L. Migration expectancy in the United States. *Journal of the American Statistical Association*, 1963, *58*, 444–453.

Wunsch, G. Le calcul des soldes migratoires par la méthode de la "population attendue." Caractéristiques et évaluation des biais. *Population et Famille*, 1969, *18*, 49–61.

APPENDIX

TABLE A.1. Set of Coefficients for Ledermann's Model Life Tables (Both Sexes)

Age groups (in completed ages)	One-entry model life table (both sexes) based on $_5q_0$ (M/F) (%)			Two-entry model life table (both sexes) based on $_5q_0$ (M/F) (%) and $_{20}q_{45}$ (M/F) (%)			
	a_0	a_1	K	b_0	b_1	b_2	K
0–1	0.14570	0.85693	1.229	0.06676	0.84319	0.04377	1.231
1–4	−1.41745	1.43275	1.635	−1.47924	1.42199	0.03428	1.634
(0–4)	0.00000	1.00000	1.000	(0.00000)	(1.00000)	(0.00000)	(1.000)
5–9	−1.13976	1.08235	1.776	−1.66684	0.99057	0.29234	1.766
10–14	−0.90577	0.90356	1.778	−1.73940	0.75840	0.46237	1.754
15–19	−0.44621	0.78503	1.865	−1.67479	0.57110	0.68142	1.814
20–24	−0.27500	0.77120	1.885	−1.65396	0.53108	0.76482	1.822
25–29	−0.22437	0.76124	1.789	−1.92227	0.46558	0.94172	1.688
30–34	−0.14882	0.74292	1.674	−1.94621	0.42994	0.99690	1.552
35–39	+0.02037	0.69243	1.576	−1.98313	0.34356	1.11122	1.408
40–44	+0.29175	0.60466	1.507	−1.81175	0.23838	1.16669	1.299
45–49	+0.64463	0.48869	1.439	−1.55178	+0.10622	1.21824	1.165
50–54	+0.95183	0.40564	1.413	−1.30096	+0.01336	1.24950	1.074
55–59	1.21176	0.34991	1.405	−1.02641	−0.03982	1.24139	1.045
60–64	1.47928	0.29981	1.343	−0.43121	−0.03286	1.05964	1.071
65–69	1.74793	0.25201	1.288	+0.26217	−0.00670	0.82406	1.128
70–74	2.00630	0.21063	1.254	+0.84220	+0.00793	0.64565	1.157
75–79	2.29283	0.14834	1.245	1.50712	+0.01153	0.43578	1.206
80–84	2.55712	0.08771	1.238	2.15372	0.01747	0.22373	1.231
85–89[a]	—			—			

[a] $_5q_{85} = 337.80 + 0.69798\ _5q_{80}$.

TABLE A.2. Schedules of Divorce by Duration of Marriage

Durations in period difference	France	Great Britain	Sweden	West Germany
0	0	0	1	6
1	14	3	9	49
2	28	6	47	80
3	43	15	73	85
4	53	64	83	84
5	60	82	73	77
6	63	82	65	66
7	64	77	57	61
8	62	71	51	55
9	59	64	48	49
10	54	56	44	44
11	51	50	41	40
12	48	44	38	35
13	45	40	35	30
14	41	38	31	28
15	38	36	29	26
16	34	33	27	23
17	31	31	25	21
18	28	29	23	19
19	25	28	22	17
20	23	26	21	16
21	20	25	19	14
22	17	22	18	13
23	15	21	17	11
24	13	20	16	10
25	12	17	14	8
26	11	16	13	7
27	10	15	12	6
28	9	12	10	5
29	8	11	9	4
30	7	9	7	3
31	5	7	6	2
32	4	5	5	2
33	3	4	4	2
34	1	3	3	1
35	1	2	3	1
Total	1000	1000	1000	1000

TABLE A.3. Standard Set of Ratios of Probabilities of Survival of Total Population (Ever-Married or Not) to Population Single at Exact Ages

Exact age (years)	Males	Females
15	1.000	1.000
20	1.000	1.000
25	1.001	1.001
30	1.004	1.003
35	1.010	1.006
40	1.020	1.010
45	1.035	1.015
50	1.055	1.020

TABLE A.4. Standard Marital Fertility Schedule of Hutterite Women (1921–1930)

Age groups (in completed years)	Legitimate fertility "rates"
15–19	0.300
20–24	0.550
25–29	0.502
30–34	0.447
35–39	0.406
40–44	0.222
45–49	0.061

TABLE A.5. Standard Schedule of Births by Duration of Marriage

Duration (in period differences)	Schedule	Duration (in period differences)	Schedule
0	0.049	11	0.030
1	0.183	12	0.026
2	0.117	13	0.021
3	0.102	14	0.017
4	0.088	15	0.014
5	0.075	16	0.011
6	0.064	17	0.009
7	0.056	18	0.007
8	0.047	19	0.005
9	0.041	20	0.003
10	0.035	Total	1.000

TABLE A.6. Standard Fertility Schedules by Birth Interval (for Low-Fertility LF and High-Fertility HF Populations)

Duration (in period differences)	a_0,[a] (α_1) (A)	(B)	a_1, (α_2) LF	HF	a_2, (α_3) LF	HF	a_3, (α_4) LF	HF	a_4, (α_5) LF	HF	a_5, (α_6) LF	HF	a_6, (α_7) LF	HF	a_7, (α_8) LF	HF
0	25	14	2	2	2	2	2	2	3	2	3	3	3	3	4	4
1	35	44	22	26	16	20	16	19	16	20	17	20	17	20	19	20
2	15	17	33	33	33	33	33	35	33	36	36	36	37	36	37	36
3	9	9	16	17	19	20	20	21	20	22	20	22	21	23	20	23
4	5	6	9	8	11	9	11	9	11	8	10	8	10	8	10	8
5	4	4	6	5	7	6	6	5	6	4	6	4	5	4	5	4
6	3	2	4	4	4	4	4	4	4	3	3	3	3	3	2	3
7	2	2	3	2	3	2	3	2	3	2	2	1	2	1	1	1
8	1	1	2	1	2	2	2	1	2	1	1	1	1	1	1	1
9	1	1	2	1	2	1	2	1	1	1	1	1	1	1	1	1
10	—	—	1	1	1	1	1	1	1	1	1	1	—	—	—	—
Total 100	100	100	100	100	100	100	100	100	100	100	100	100	100	100	100	100

[a] (A) high incidence of premarital pregnancies (B) low incidence of premarital pregnancies.

INDEX

273